SLABBERT

SLABBERT
MAN ON A MISSION

ALBERT GRUNDLINGH

JONATHAN BALL PUBLISHERS
JOHANNESBURG • CAPE TOWN • LONDON

All rights reserved.
No part of this publication may be reproduced or transmitted,
in any form or by any means, without prior permission
from the publisher or copyright holder.

© Text Albert Grundlingh 2021
© Photographs, as credited individually
© Published edition 2021 Jonathan Ball Publishers

Published in South Africa in 2021 by
JONATHAN BALL PUBLISHERS
A division of Media24 (Pty) Ltd
PO Box 33977
Jeppestown
2043

ISBN 978-1-77619-037-9
ebook ISBN 978-1-77619-038-6

Every effort has been made to trace the copyright holders and to obtain their permission for the use of copyright material. The publishers apologise for any errors or omissions and would be grateful to be notified of any corrections that should be incorporated in future editions of this book.

www.jonathanball.co.za
www.twitter.com/JonathanBallPub
www.facebook.com/JonathanBallPublishers

Cover by Michiel Botha
Design and typesetting by Martine Barker
Set in Minion and Avenir

CONTENTS

Preface   vii

1 From pillar to post to professor   11

2 Becoming a politician   46

3 Parliamentary strides   63

4 Taking the lead   87

5 Turbulent times   104

6 Resignation   128

7 Into a brave new world   154

8 Transitions   186

9 'Van': Public image and private life   212

Conclusion   244

Acknowledgements   253
Notes   254
Sources   284
Index   296

PREFACE

Before attempting a biographical study, an author has to ask why he or she is prepared to devote a great deal of time and energy to recording and interpreting another individual's life. In this case, the answer is simply that the subject is so intriguing that it could not be resisted.

It is helpful to take a cue from Voltaire, who distanced himself from the cult of heroes but was convinced that 'through great souls we can gain access to the surprises of history, that is, those unexpected occurrences that are so essential to the broad picture when the "verosimile doesn't always occur"'.[1] Closer to home, one of South Africa's foremost historians, Charles van Onselen, has also grappled with the larger issues of biographical writing. Two questions intrigue him: '[T]o what extent does the subject act on history, and to what extent is history acting on the subject? It's where those questions intersect that you have authentic, deeply cognitive interactions. For me, the really magical moments in history come when you are dealing with the creative tensions that arise from ambiguity, contradiction or irony.'[2]

Anomalies of this kind certainly loom large in the life of Frederik van Zyl Slabbert. He came from an Afrikaans background, but unlike many of his peers at school did not have a stable home environment. In the 1960s he attended Stellenbosch University, which, as the alma mater of numerous cabinet ministers and premiers, was considered the breeding ground of National Party politicians. Although dubbed an Afrikaner golden boy with excellent prospects, at the height of apartheid he followed a different route into the predominantly English-speaking liberal Progressive Party to become a Member of Parliament (MP) in 1974. Highly regarded as an MP, in 1979 he

PREFACE

was 'crowned' leader of the reconstituted Progressive Federal Party (PFP), the official parliamentary opposition, and attempted to give direction to the party during a time of unprecedented political turbulence in South Africa. His role during this period, and the kinds of compromises he had to make, underlined the complex forces that buffeted the country unrelentingly and largely shaped the political landscape. But, in 1986, in a move that surprised many people, he resigned from Parliament, giving rise to a media frenzy. Slabbert's subsequent meeting, along with a number of Afrikaner notables (many of them regarded as left-leaning), with the banned African National Congress (ANC) in Dakar in 1987 kept him in the media spotlight. He seemed to attract more attention as a kind of 'rogue' politician than when he had been a regular in Parliament. Yet, after the seismic political changes of the 1990s, many of which he had ardently fought for, he was generally perceived, somewhat misleadingly, to have disappeared from the political scene.

The connection between politics and individual character traits is a vexed one. Hans Renders, the Dutch expert on the writing of biography, goes as far as to claim that 'the biographer has to make it clear that a person's private background has influenced his public achievements. If he fails to do that, he might as well not have written the biography.'[3] This injunction may be harder to observe than it first appears. However, in certain respects it has been argued that Slabbert's personal background and attributes fed into his politics. He was a man on a mission; politics happened to be the terrain he chose to express broader concerns. This was particularly so in explaining his proselytising zeal and charismatic appeal. Otherwise, one must be mindful that the dynamics of politics at times can override personal qualities.

The research for this book was aided by a number of relevant secondary sources, which included illuminating biographical essays by academics and others who knew him, as well as by informative academic theses on aspects of his party-political life. Besides these, the narrative is underpinned by Slabbert's own publications – he was quite a prolific author and commentator – and the valuable Slabbert Papers at Stellenbosch University, as well as some other collections there and elsewhere, a mountain of newspaper reports and a number of oral interviews. Unfortunately Slabbert did not keep a personal diary – as politicians are often inclined to do.

For the historian, sources are crucial, but one does not have to be a postmodernist to realise that they cannot provide all the answers. The innermost, elusive and often unspoken dimensions of a life can only rarely be fully captured. At times, the best one can hope for is to highlight certain trends. This is also the case with Slabbert, whose life in some respects was more enigmatic than that of many of his political and other contemporaries.

1
FROM PILLAR TO POST TO PROFESSOR

Childhood challenges

'I could not prevent my parents from engaging in an indiscriminate night of passion on the southern tip of Africa which resulted in my birth.'[1] Thus reflected Frederik van Zyl Slabbert in 1997 on his birth and that of his twin sister, Marcia, on 2 March 1940 in Pretoria. His parents were Petrus Johannes Slabbert from Pietersburg (today Polokwane) and Pretoria, and Barbara Thyssen, originally from Carolina in what was the Eastern Transvaal (today Mpumalanga). They were not married and, Frederik suspected, were likely inebriated when the twins were conceived after a party. What he regarded as the randomness of his birth fascinated him throughout his life as he tried to come to grips with the idea that he happened to be the product of such an arbitrary moment.[2]

His paternal grandfather, also Frederik van Zyl, insisted that Petrus marry Barbara. According to contemporary norms, it was the 'right thing' to do, and Slabbert's grandfather, an influential lawyer and farmer, as well as a three-term mayor of Pietersburg, would not have it any other way.[3] The marriage, however, was of short duration and rapidly disintegrated. On 26 February 1940, barely a week before the birth of his children, Petrus Slabbert, aged 22, enlisted in the Union Defence Force to participate in the Second World War.[4] His children were left in the care of their 19-year-old mother, who was occasionally given to drink.[5] Petrus was at odds with what he regarded as an unyielding and overbearing household, and soon after school 'he rushed into a blind rebellion and sowed his wild oats with a vengeance'.[6] Disappearing into the army seems to have been one of those acts; escaping paternal and domestic obligations by enlisting was a familiar pattern for many recruits.[7]

He served part of the war in East Africa. Warfare in this difficult terrain called for substantial numbers of technical, administrative and other support personnel, and relatively few men were deployed as frontline combatants. Slabbert was employed as a storeman for a while, and returned to South Africa in a similar capacity. His personnel record reflects that his conduct was generally regarded as satisfactory, yet there were also some hiccups. He was found guilty of appropriating military transport for his personal use, and of trying to cover it up by turning back the mileage. On another occasion, he was involved in a pub brawl with civilians in Gordon's Bay. He was above average in height (6 feet 2 inches, or 188 centimetres) – his son took after him – and probably quite a formidable opponent. For these transgressions, he was fined and demoted in rank.[8]

Unlike other soldiers who returned from the war traumatised by their frontline experiences and who battled to adjust to family life,[9] Petrus Slabbert suffered no such afflictions. He had in any case abandoned his family from very early on. He and Barbara divorced when the children were two years old and while he was still in the army.[10]

After demobilisation, he returned to Pretoria where he was employed in the civil service and worked in the Tender and Supplies Board. He had gone to war as a supporter of Jan Smuts and the United Party, but came back thoroughly disillusioned and switched his allegiance to the National Party.[11] It was not an uncommon political conversion among disgruntled ex-soldiers.[12] When Frederik was about five years old, his father turned up unexpectedly at their somewhat ramshackle house, 1006 Duncan Street in the Pretoria suburb of Brooklyn. He was a total stranger to the twins, and they shied away from his advances. Barbara and he then had an argument, which ended with her slapping him across the face. He stood up and left. The next time Frederik would see his father was when he was 16 years old. Barbara despised her former husband and made no bones about it either.[13]

The young Frederik nevertheless hero-worshipped his father in his pre-teen days, mainly because his grandmother depicted Petrus in larger-than-life terms. In his father's absence, it was impossible for him to evaluate his grandmother's praise. It was only later in life that he realised that she had inflated Petrus's qualities. Slabbert nevertheless tried to draw his father closer when he had his own children. But he found a man who 'had succumbed to the pressures of convention without really knowing why …'. Instead of the imposing figure that his grandmother had lovingly sketched, Slabbert found a man almost defeated by life. Although he was kind enough, he was 'lacking in self-confidence, apologetic to the point of irritation, overly sentimental and thriving on reminiscences of the past to cope with the pain and inadequacies of the present. A simple, inoffensive person.'[14] Slabbert's children also did not take to their grandfather.[15] Although Petrus might have appreciated his son's attempts to reconnect, it did not necessarily mean that he shared his political outlook. There is evidence to suggest that in the 1970s he approached the National Party MP for Kempton Park, GC du Plessis, to apologise for his son's political activities.[16]

Slabbert had a better, though complicated, relationship with his mother. He explained in 1985:

> I never doubted her love for us, and yet I somehow sensed that she could, or would, not tell me or my sister how to cope with life. This, looking back now, was the enigmatic part of her in my own emotional development. I knew my mother loved me but that I was essentially on my own when it came to facing up to whatever life presented … She was by far the

> most intelligent, exciting and original person in my young world, and in every conventional sense of the word she was a failure – as a mother, a wife, a worker, a neighbour, a socially responsible person. It did not lead me to dismiss convention, although I have always retained a strong scepticism of it. Early on, too, I developed a soft spot for the underdog, a tolerance for the outsider and the outcast.

While the negatives of the relationship were obvious, there were also positive spin-offs. From a young age, Slabbert recalled, 'it cultivated a sense of independence, a suspicion of blind authority and of automatic adult "wisdom".[17] It was a quality that his daughter, Tania, later articulated as his having an 'old soul'.[18] He never seemed to harbour any hostility towards his mother, and poignantly remembered her death (from alcoholism) and funeral in 1974.[19]

There was some irony in the fact that while Barbara had qualified as a social worker, and had some affinity for her profession, she had failed to fulfil the parenting role expected of her. The children were allowed to roam free, running in and out of storm-water drains in the neighbourhood and linking up with older children intent on mischief and more. At the nearby Pretoria East Primary School, which they first attended, it quickly became apparent to their teacher and the headmaster that the twins had been rather neglected. The school contacted their grandfather, who insisted that the mother should come to Pietersburg with the children. They travelled in a Hudson Terraplane car and the young Slabbert marvelled that they arrived safely despite their mother's erratic driving. Grandfather Frederik was blunt: Barbara must give up her children so they could have a proper upbringing. She was deeply hurt, but financially not in a position to resist. Later, Slabbert vividly recalled the sombre separation between mother and children. At a nearby farm they sat on her lap in the lounge while she softly wept against their backs. On the gramophone played the mournful songs of the popular Afrikaans crooner Chris Blignaut: 'Daar's 'n saal wat hang daar aan die muur' and 'Troudag-klokkies lui vir jou en my' ('There is a saddle hanging against the wall' and 'Wedding bells for me and you').[20]

Their mother returned to Pretoria the following day. Shortly afterwards, it was decided that they should go to live with their uncle and aunt, Fred and Martha Stakes, both medical doctors, in Johannesburg. Here they resided at number 96, 7th Street, Linden, and attended Jan Celliers Primary School. It was an elite Afrikaans school and some of the young Slabbert's classmates were the children of prominent National Party politicians. Slabbert remembered that when the National Party won the election in 1948, the teachers burst into tears of joy. Their uncle and aunt, being English-speaking and dyed-in-the-wool United Party supporters, were less ecstatic. At home they sought to introduce a measure of bilingualism and insisted that the children speak English at table. It was no wonder that at Jan Celliers, Frederik and his sister were looked down on as not being from an 'Afrikaner home'. The Slabbert twins' stay in Linden ended when they became too much of a handful for the exasperated Stakeses. In 1951 the children were moved back to live with their grandfather in Pietersburg, and they went to Marabastad Farm School, which was close to the grandfather's farm. Despite living close to the school, they were placed in the hostel.[21]

Slabbert's grandfather, like his relations in Johannesburg, was a solid United Party supporter. In fact, he had stood as the United Party candidate for Pietersburg in the general election of 1943. He was a man of some local stature, having served three terms as mayor, and in 1933 he had been elected president of the Transvaal Municipal Association.[22] He gave a good account of himself in the 1943 election campaign: the National Party candidate, the well-known old campaigner Tom Naudé, obtained 2 899 votes and Slabbert 2 643 – a margin of only 256. He stayed active in United Party politics until the early 1950s.[23]

It is a moot point whether his grandfather's political involvement influenced the young Slabbert substantially; the most that can be said is that he grew up in a household where oppositional politics must have featured generally. Slabbert junior only rarely referred to his grandfather's politics, but he was not averse to quoting him on other issues. In 1974, his first year in Parliament, upon being harangued for daring to speak on agricultural matters, he admitted that he was not a farmer but that did not mean that he was ignorant. 'My grandfather,' he commented, 'always used to say that one does not have to lay an egg to know whether it is rotten or not.'[24]

Slabbert and his sister arrived at Marabastad Farm School at the tail end of the era of rural white poverty in South Africa, but there were still a fair number of poor white children at the school. One of them, Koos Nel, was so poor that he came to school dressed in sackcloth. On one occasion he irritated the teacher, who pulled young Koos out of his desk. The boy fell down, and it was instantly clear that he was stark naked underneath the sackcloth. The teacher started kicking him, and the young Slabbert instinctively jumped out of his desk, shouting, 'No sir!' Koos thanked him during the break, but for his efforts both Slabbert and Koos were given a thorough hiding. The incident is revealing, as the young Slabbert did not hesitate to choose the side of the wronged.[25]

A marked feature of life at Marabastad Farm School was the gratuitous violence among the rumbustious boys. At the time, such behaviour was often regarded as a normal outlet for excess energy. Fisticuffs on the playground were common, and Slabbert once had to prove his mettle against a boy who carried the title of the strongest boy in the school. Slabbert participated reluctantly but won the fight. As a follow-up, Slabbert was beaten up by the older boys.

Teachers, as we have noted, did not hesitate to cane the boys. When Slabbert told his friends in the hostel about a black friend he had on the farm, the teacher overheard the conversation and accused him in crude racist language of being overly friendly with black people. This was sufficient reason for a severe caning to be administered.

Reflecting back on this, Slabbert later claimed that the incident so distressed him that 'Marabastad Primary School was the beginning of my political consciousness'.[26]

Slabbert and his sister enjoyed life on the farm at weekends and during holidays, especially the delicious meals prepared by his grandmother. Her activities in the kitchen, however, were curtailed after she broke her hip in a car crash and could no longer move around freely. The twins once again had to move to a new school, this time Pietersburg Primary School, where they were placed in the hostel.[27]

Pietersburg, at the time Slabbert was growing up, was developing into a modern country town. High-rise buildings started to appear, along with traffic lights at increasingly busy intersections: in the 1950s, cars jostled uneasily with donkey carts for parking space, while cattle being herded to the abattoir occasionally obstructed the road.[28] During Slabbert's youth, the town almost symbolically displayed the kind of ambiguity and transitional character that in the fullness of time became a hallmark of Slabbert's life.

From Pietersburg Primary, Frederik and Marcia moved to Pietersburg High School, which at the time was dual medium (Afrikaans and English). In the late 1950s it was an expanding institution of over 800 pupils and occupied an impressive new building.[29] The twins were academically strong. Years later, Frederik recalled that he found Latin difficult but that it was an excellent subject for sharpening one's intellectual abilities.[30] He also had an affinity for light-hearted foolery with words, and at the age of 16 had a piece of doggerel verse published in the high school annual.[31] The Slabberts were popular among their peers, and it was no real surprise that in their final year (1958) they were chosen as head boy and head girl.[32]

What added to their appeal was that both excelled at sport. Marcia was captain of the netball team and maintained a lifelong interest in sport, continuing to play golf until well into her seventies.[33] Frederik was keen on rugby, which at the time was the pre-eminent Afrikaner game and closely linked to forceful Afrikaner nationalism. Competition between Afrikaans and English schools on the rugby field was especially fierce. He later saw this as 'our way of coping with a perceived sense of social and cultural inferiority as well as of achieving excellence'. The game was also charged with personal significance. 'The recognition it brought me at school,' he said, 'gave me confidence and a sense of acceptance that for a time was more important than the enjoyment I derived from taking part. Being first-team captain and considered a very good loose forward obliterated any discomfort about not having had a normal family life or having parents who might be regarded as socially awkward.'[34]

Other factors helped to offset the complications of his tangled family life. The pupils at Pietersburg High came predominantly from homes of a similar social status, so that Frederik, given his grandfather's standing in the community, was relatively easily accepted by his peer group. His personal attributes must also have helped. A contemporary at school described him as 'a most likeable chap', with a concern for others.[35] While all of this was important in his teenage years, his personal circumstances could not be wholly suppressed. Despite the concerns of his grandparents, Frederik still had a need to belong to an ordinary family. A school friend recalled that when he invited Frederik to spent a weekend at the family farm outside Pietersburg, the latter revelled in the family atmosphere and was most grateful for the opportunity.[36] It was almost as if he was looking for a family.

An important feature of Slabbert's childhood was the kind of relationships he had with black people. While one should be careful not to read a person's later life in terms of youthful experiences, Slabbert himself believed that some of the experiences he had as a youth had an abiding influence and bearing on his critical disposition at university and after. One of these was the relationship he had as a young child with the family's domestic worker, known simply as Florina. One night, the two small children were left on their own by their mother. Frightened by a Pretoria storm, and with the flowers outside their window casting menacing shadows on the wall, they waited petrified but in vain for their mother to return. Terrified and lonely, Frederik suggested to Marcia that they go to Florina, whose bed was in the garage. Once there, he later recalled, 'and we had snuggled in behind her ample frame it was like bedding down in a bomb shelter of security. Florina's comfort and love predisposed me kindly and instinctively towards black mammas for the rest of my life.'[37] It was these kinds of encounters that caused Manie van der Spuy, a friend of Slabbert's and a former psychology lecturer at the University of Cape Town (UCT), to reflect on 'whether his experiences with this black substitute mother who clearly salvaged much of his early emotional development had any effect on the shaping of his later political sentiments. I would think it might have had a profound effect, even if only unconsciously.'[38]

Besides Florina, Slabbert had a close relationship with William Dini, a playmate on his grandfather's farm. While many white boys of that generation who grew up on farms often recall that they used to have black friends, and later in life these friendships waned and eventually evaporated completely, in Slabbert's case he saw more in this friendship than was customary. Although William Dini also disappeared from Slabbert's life, in retrospect he identified certain salient characteristics that in general helped to shape his friendships: 'I recognised him [William Dini] as one of those irrepressible, spontaneous, inquiring spirits that have always attracted me.'[39]

Slabbert's positive experience in this regard contributed to a much more sensitive disposition towards black people than was the norm among his peers. He remembered with disgust how some of his friends attacked a black man who had missed the regular 9 pm curfew in Pietersburg, when all black people were supposed to leave the white part of town. His friends regarded this as 'fun', but the 16-year-old Slabbert was literally nauseated as he tried to stop them. After the incident, he embarked, with some success, on a campaign to put an end to such senseless behaviour.[40]

He also seems to have developed early an aversion to what he later called 'ideological, value-laden content to concepts of nationality, ethnicity or race'. This was in contrast to the outlook of the largely rural Afrikaner community in which he was raised, where the validity of such a point of departure was accepted without much reflection. He was furthermore made aware of this kind of thinking on a school visit to the Cango Caves, outside Oudtshoorn in the southern Cape. He recalled their entry into the main hall of the caves. 'I will never forget,' he wrote, 'the lights being dimmed, organ music filling the darkness, and a deep voice announcing, "Civilisation came to South Africa with the landing of Jan van Riebeeck on 6 April 1652."' Although only 16, he claimed to have thought: 'How completely and utterly absurd.'[41] There is no reason to suggest that Slabbert's recollection of this incident might have been influenced by his later understanding of South Africa's past, but it certainly was a quite unusual observation for a young white schoolboy in South Africa in the mid-1950s.

Another formative and important experience during Slabbert's youth was his strong religious commitment as a Christian, also at the age of 16, during a camp of the Student Christian Association at Winkelspruit, Natal. Such outings were held regularly for Afrikaner youth. In his autobiographical writings, he argues that his newfound religious zeal had much to do with the fact that he came from a broken home, coupled with uncertainty and a longing for the approval and admiration of fellow believers. Whatever the deeper motivation, he was certainly sincerely devout and dedicated. He spent much time reading the Bible, praying for and preaching to the sick at missionary hospitals, and doing excessive penitence for his presumed sins, to the extent that he even apologised to the somewhat surprised townspeople from whom he had stolen some fruit two years earlier.[42]

He recalled that at the time he was an 'A-grade' zealot, and a friend described him as being 'God intoxicated'.[43] His religious convictions fluctuated over time and gradually waned, but the underlying values never disappeared altogether. While his original religious involvement began as a psychological need for acceptance, it sparked an enduring intellectual and spiritual inquiry and a quest for what can be considered the 'truth', as well as a concern for ethical considerations.[44] At the time he left school, though, he was driven by an unalloyed religious outlook and convinced that his chosen path would be that of a dominee (minister of religion) in the Dutch Reformed Church. He only fleetingly thought about studying medicine. Upon being counselled by well-known church leaders, such as Beyers Naudé (before he left the Dutch Reformed Church) and Professor Ben Marais, Slabbert was even more convinced that he should become a man of the cloth. This stemmed from his personal convictions, but the position of dominee in Afrikaner communities at the time also bestowed considerable prestige.[45] Although this was a secondary perk, there is no evidence that Slabbert viewed it as an incentive; he probably regarded it merely as a by-product of the profession.

Slabbert matriculated in 1958. He had had an eventful youth, more so than many of his contemporaries. It had been marked by several discontinuities, and by a need to constantly readjust to new circumstances – a quality that would stand him in good stead later in his career when, and on an epic scale, the need for change in South Africa became a rallying cry. Despite the interruptions in his young life, he claimed not to have been unhappy, as he was cared for at home and enjoyed life at school. He had also had Marcia at his side through all their youthful travails. Reflecting upon their fractured childhood, Slabbert later stated:

> The most important memory of our childhood was that emotionally we had to battle on our own. The bond between Marcia and me was strengthened through this and it remained so for the rest of our lives. Our grandmother could not really look after us as she was incapacitated. My grandfather was a busy lawyer in town. Where my mother

and father were was a puzzle. Aunt Martha and Fred Stakes were only too grateful to be rid of 'the twins'. From early childhood Marcia and I realised that we were dependent upon each other for support and succour. It created a relationship which survived many problems and divergent experiences throughout our lives, and it grew stronger over time.[46]

Marcia felt much the same, though given the general lack of gender sensitivity at the time, she was somewhat aggrieved that her grandfather at times favoured her brother over her.[47]

Student life

After school, Slabbert started his university studies with a view to becoming a dominee. Entrance qualifications at the time demanded a first-class matric pass (an average of over 60 per cent), and, depending on the kind of degree the prospective student had in mind, a third language (German, Latin or French) besides Afrikaans and English, and/or mathematics. Slabbert had the required average in the following subjects: Afrikaans higher grade, English lower grade, Latin, science, mathematics and biology.[48]

For his first year, Slabbert went to the University of the Witwatersrand (Wits) in 1959. He was able to board with family members in Johannesburg, which helped to reduce the costs. At the time, he recalled, he was probably a 'latent Nat' and joined the Afrikaanse Studiekring (Afrikaans Study Circle), but was sufficiently wary not to join the Ruiterwag (roughly translated as Mounted Guard), a junior form of the Broederbond, when approached to do so.[49] He applied for, and obtained, a bursary from the Helpmekaar Vereniging (Help Each Other Movement), an organisation that had been established in 1916, after the Boer rebellion of 1914, to assist impoverished rebels. The organisation's prudent management of its funds meant that it was able to provide financial aid for many a needy Afrikaner student over the years.⁵⁰ Apart from the bursary, Slabbert worked during university holidays as a sanitation officer to help pay for his studies.

Two incidents in particular made an impression on him at Wits. One was when Robert Sobukwe, the leader of the Pan Africanist Congress (PAC) and a lecturer in African languages, addressed a crowd of predominantly black people on the campus. As one of the few whites at the meeting, Slabbert admitted that he felt a bit like Piet Retief in Dingane's kraal (a reference to the well-known incident in 1838 when the Voortrekker leader and his men were killed when they went unarmed into the Zulu king's kraal). What unsettled Slabbert further was that that the crowd insisted that they were ready to govern South Africa at that point. He regarded this as an 'exotic' idea. The other incident was when he was rattled by the arguments of Professor Eddie Roux, an outspoken botany lecturer who had organised the Rationalist Thinkers Forum, which questioned the existence of God. To Slabbert this was blasphemous in the extreme.⁵¹

After a year at Wits he moved to Stellenbosch University, where the Dutch Reformed Church's theological seminary was located. He had to complete a BA degree before he could be admitted to the seminary. One of the reasons for the move to Stellenbosch was in order to take classical Hebrew, which was not formally offered at Wits and was a prerequisite for admission to the seminary. As a filler subject, he also continued with sociology, which he had started at Wits. Little did he know that sociology was destined to become a career choice. His overall undergraduate record was respectable but not outstanding. In 1960 he obtained the following grades at Stellenbosch: Greek II, 6; Afrikaans-Nederlands, II, 6; Sociology II, 5; Hebrew I, 7. In the following year, he graduated with Afrikaans-Nederlands, 5; Sociology, 7; and Hebrew II, 7.⁵²

Stellenbosch at the time was considered a premier Afrikaner institution. Thousands of young white men and women, overwhelmingly Afrikaans-speaking, descended on the town to attend the university.

They came mainly from the Cape Province but also from further afield, as Stellenbosch had successfully manufactured a reputation as the Athens of the south – a place of academic excellence with a unique student life amid scenic natural surroundings. In terms of intellectual life, Stellenbosch was to Afrikaners what the Oxbridge universities were to the national life of Britain, or the Ivy League universities to America.

The university was also closely connected to the ruling National Party. Slabbert later graphically described Stellenbosch as 'the uncomplicated and charmingly oak-lined avenue of mobility to the upper slopes of "volksdiens" [service to the nation]. The university was a force to be reckoned with in the affairs of state. It had connections and had to be taken *very* seriously.'[53] By and large, there was also considerable support for apartheid. Even those individuals who might have had their doubts, one academic explained, 'neither expressed "voice" publicly or within the system, but simply "exited", opting instead for the quiet life in a stream of Afrikaner conformity.'[54]

Slabbert did not fit the usual profile of a Stellenbosch student. Whereas many students came from solid middle-class family backgrounds, with parents who believed in the sanctity of marriage, even if contrived at times, Slabbert's home life, as we have seen, was much more complicated and marked by discontinuities due to his absent and divorced parents. Moreover, in a broader sense, Slabbert's close connections with black people from an early age predisposed him to be suspicious of apartheid policy formulations that spoke of black people in the abstract, in rarefied terms rather than as people of flesh and blood.[55] It meant that when he landed at Stellenbosch, he brought with him a conception of black people that was largely absent from the mindset of many pro-apartheid university staff, students and townspeople. Black people might well have featured as objects of missionary endeavour, a major thrust of the theology faculty, but as a result of influx control measures there were few black people in town, and neighbouring Kayamandi was still a relatively small township. Ironically, the intellectual development of apartheid thinking at the university took place without real engagement with black people.

Slabbert lived at Wilgenhof, the oldest male student residence at Stellenbosch. Life in residence carried a particular imprint of tradition and *esprit de corps* that could become all-consuming. The university rector in the 1960s, Professor HB Thom, regarded residence culture as an integral part of the university experience. He argued that one could perhaps 'distinguish between academic life and resident life, but they cannot be separated'. According to Thom, they were 'two sides of the same thing'.[56]

Wilgenhof had in this respect developed a reputation that was almost second to none. The existence of an exceptional sense of camaraderie or 'residence spirit' was facilitated by the relatively small number of students who lived there, and by the fact that all the rooms opened onto a common quadrangle, which encouraged easy mingling and made for intense student discussions and debates. It was later even claimed that this discursive culture contributed to the fact that a number of Wilgenhof old boys made their name in politics, including Slabbert.[57]

Slabbert himself commented upon his initial experiences at Wilgenhof, likening it to a 'total institution' that ruled one's entire life and required absolute loyalty. 'Any concern with the outside world,' he later said, 'is lobotomised away by the immediacy of residence life.'[58] During their first two weeks at Wilgenhof, students were subjected to the 'most intense orientation/initiation/abuse imaginable, both physically and mentally'.[59] Slabbert experienced this at first hand. When he arrived in Stellenbosch, he took a taxi from the station to the residence, as he did not know the town at all. Upon arrival at Wilgenhof, and just as he was about to pay for the taxi, some of the senior students exaggeratedly pretended to welcome him, paid the taxi fare and even carried his baggage from the car into the residence. But once the taxi had departed, they pounced.

Within 45 seconds, he said, his clothes were stripped from his body and he stood there only in his underwear. They also trampled on his sunglasses and tore his scarf, shouting, 'You mustn't think that this a fashion show, you know! Here you behave yourself! Here you must know your place!'[60]

Yet, for all its harshness, there was supposed to be an underlying logic that was not immediately apparent but was part of a bigger picture. The initiation he experienced, Slabbert claimed, was designed to alert the newcomer not to act in an unreflective manner. He elaborated on the supposed rationale behind the rituals: 'Every time you unthinkingly carried out an order, you had to shout "parrot" repeatedly.' At the same time it was drummed into him that 'the place', as the institution was called, required almost unconditional loyalty. Paradoxically, this 'strengthened independence'.[61] Ultimately, the aim, instilled somewhat roughly and contradictorily, was to incorporate the residence's perceived values, including a critical outlook.

Discussions and debates in the residence allowed for a fair degree of latitude, provided that a point of view could be substantiated. Thom in general regarded this dimension of residence culture as a wonderful bonus, 'as without realising it, one experienced a true schooling for life'.[62] He was not far off the mark. Slabbert later recalled that he benefited greatly from the variety of discussion groups at the university.[63] For many of his generation, the cut and thrust of these groups was a 'major formative experience'.[64] Besides this, 'the place' also had a sense of concern for others. What stood out for Slabbert was the way in which one was accepted as a person. In a particular case, he remembered how an impoverished student was helped to complete his studies through a fund established by his housemates.[65]

It was at Wilgenhof that Slabbert made acquaintances that were to last a lifetime, in particular Jannie Gagiano, later to become a lecturer in political science at the university. Gagiano was one of those irreverent characters that Slabbert was easily attracted to, not least because Slabbert found in him a worthwhile foil for testing his own ideas. Although they were often at cross-purposes, there was mutual respect. A lifelong friendship was born at Wilgenhof. Slabbert also became *primarius* (head student) of Wilgenhof in only his second year, which for a relative junior was most unusual at that time.[66] He had to step into the breach in June 1963 when the incumbent head student was expelled for irregular conduct. Slabbert was to serve for four months.[67]

Slabbert seems to have found in Wilgenhof a place where he could test his intellectual mettle by engaging in robust debate. It was also a close-knit community that held him in esteem and recognised his leadership qualities. Fellow students, keen on wide-ranging and lively debates, often filled his room.[68] For someone from a dislocated background, the acceptance of his peers in a new 'home' could only have been a morale booster. Although Wilgenhof provided an enabling environment, it should be borne in mind that Slabbert came to the residence as a relatively hardened youth, having already spent much time in school hostels. That experience likely facilitated his entry into the rough-and-tumble world of Wilgenhof. It also prepared him, somewhat later, to become a resident warden for other male residences on the Stellenbosch campus. In this role, Slabbert, though he well understood student pranks and the like, could also insist on decorous behaviour when required. On one occasion, during a formal dinner at Simonsberg residence, he threatened to walk out when the students persisted on banging on the tables with broken wine bottles.[69]

Another domain central to Slabbert's early student life was rugby. Although he had come to Stellenbosch to learn Hebrew, he was also attracted to the university because of its long-standing and countrywide reputation as a 'Springbok factory'. Initially Slabbert had a consuming passion for the game.[70] He had played for Transvaal Under-19 while at Wits, and at Stellenbosch he was chosen for the university first team and the Southern Universities XV, and played two games for Western

Province (one as reserve) when the regular number eight loose forward was injured. He trained indefatigably and, outside the official sessions, would practise for long periods on his own by throwing a rugby ball against the zinc pavilion of Coetzenburg rugby field, to sharpen his handling skills.[71]

Rugby at Stellenbosch, as the legendary Dr Danie Craven observed, was a name 'to conjure' with, a magical word, and a rugby player was admired by all and sundry.[72] Slabbert was a beneficiary of this environment, which bestowed exceptional accolades on its stars. Such admiration must have added to a sense of achievement, particularly if it came from seasoned rugby supporters. In this sense Stellenbosch helped to build upon and enhance Slabbert's natural sporting abilities in a popular game. Yet his exposure to the way in which rugby players were excessively fêted also alerted him to the way the game was a kind of 'social narcotic to anything else going on in our society'.[73] The impact was thus contradictory. Slabbert gradually became less rugby-obsessed as the game started to impinge on the time available for study.

The Stellenbosch to which Slabbert came in the 1960s was one in which Afrikaner nationalism dominated. HB Thom was a committed Nationalist and tried to steer the university firmly along the chosen path. Yet, for all this, he was equally aware that the world beyond the university was changing. While the ANC and PAC were banned, South Africa had become a republic, and the economy was booming, underneath the apparent surface calm the dynamics of Afrikaner society were evolving as a result of increasing affluence and the need to stave off increasing criticism of apartheid. In 1966, referring to increased consumerism and a growing lack of interest in traditional Afrikaner cultural life, Thom warned that 'the danger signals are flashing'.[74] The notion of what it meant to be an Afrikaner was to become increasingly contested in the decade to come.

One of Slabbert's early intellectual concerns at Stellenbosch, however, was not Afrikaner ethnicity per se, but how to reconcile

Christian principles with the emergent ideological order in South Africa. In 1962, aged 22, he wrote what must count as his first published reflections on how to resolve certain contradictions in South African society. Firmly rooted in theological thinking, he was concerned that the 'principles of ideology are being sanctioned by religion and that the state is enveloped in a haze of untouchability'. The head of state, according to him, was invested with 'papal status and the ministers fulfilled the priestly function to oversee right and righteousness as dictated by the ideology'. This placed a special onus on believers 'not to read the Word of God according to what may appear as right, but rather according to what is right in the eyes of God'.[75]

This kind of thinking must have distinguished Slabbert from many of his peers at the time. Overall, the university was under the spell of the apparent logic of Verwoerdian apartheid, and to argue against it called for considerable debating skills and analytical abilities. It would, however, pay dividends later in his career, as Slabbert, in addressing sceptical political audiences, had already honed his skills on campus during the 1960s.[76]

At the time, though, there were other concerns weighing on the young Slabbert. Eighteen months into his seminary studies, he was becoming increasingly disenchanted with what he had thought was his chosen career. There was an unnerving incident in Langa township, outside Cape Town, when an attempt to do missionary work was cut short and he and his party, including an elderly and almost frail professor, were chased away by the inhabitants. That was the last time he did missionary work; his doubts had increased. While the experience was unsettling, his dissatisfaction was born not so much out of disillusionment with a failed missionary endeavour, but rather from a more fundamentally cerebral and intellectual decision that religion as it was presented by the church no longer made any sense. In particular, a clash with a professor of theology, who insisted that apartheid was God's will, left him aghast. The inner turmoil involved in Slabbert's turning away from theological studies should not be underestimated. He agonised over the decision; after all, one was 'called' to higher service and he had reached a point where, as he put it, he was now 'uncalled'. Jannie Gagiano further contributed to his scepticism, but more basic and less rarefied issues, such as the church's prescriptions regarding premarital sex, also irked him.[77] In career terms, while abandoning his theological studies closed down future prospects, it did, however, allow him to pursue his intellectual bent more freely.

Slabbert now turned to sociology, which he had been studying out of interest alongside theology, and passed his honours year with distinction. He followed this up with an MA with distinction in 1963 and a PhD in 1967. Later in life, in 1999, he recalled that the new direction he had embarked upon was the 'beginning of an unrestrained assault on my mind which to this day has not ended'.[78]

Slabbert's switch from theology to sociology was also significant in other respects. Jannie Gagiano believes that what Slabbert did, substantively, was to substitute one form of reverence for another: '[H]e [Slabbert] shifted from his Christian faith to a faith … in theories as a way of reflecting on his own faith-based commitments and starting to disassemble them …'[79] There is also another dimension related to Slabbert's change of heart (or mind). He might well have left religion, but did religious zeal leave him altogether? He gave up saving souls, but he might well have started on another journey that ultimately ended up in political proselytising. Of course it is in the nature of politics to conduct oneself along such lines, but in Slabbert's case his original wellspring had a religious, messianic base. Slabbert himself recalled that in many discussion groups he participated in at Stellenbosch, his arguments often veered towards the need to convert and convince.[80]

Ironically, in terms of career trajectory, Slabbert can in certain respects be compared to none other than Hendrik Verwoerd, who was so closely associated with apartheid. Both were relative outsiders to the Afrikaner elite – Verwoerd as a Dutch-born immigrant and Slabbert coming from a dysfunctional family and a deprived background. Both started off studying theology and later switched to sociology – a discipline that has been called a 'haven for academics whose church has failed them'. (Intriguingly, the Stellenbosch sociology department of the early 1970s that Slabbert joined was stocked with a significant number of refugees from theology.) Both excelled as notable figures on the Stellenbosch campus. Moreover, both at different times were driven by a sense of mission to resolve the racial situation in South Africa, each in his own way.[81] The similarity ends, though, with not only the political chasm between the two, but also a generational void and a marked difference in personality. While Verwoerd had a studied aloofness about him, Slabbert was infinitely more gregarious and no dry-as-dust academic.

One can argue that as a sociologist he regarded it as an essential part of his education to experience life in the raw. Or perhaps it was not even intellectual impulses that prompted him and Jannie Gagiano to occasionally visit Cape Town to sample the nightlife and mingle with the underworld, 'generally romanticising the marginal people of society'. He recalled that 'more than one sunrise found us on a train to Stellenbosch or sitting at the docks of Table Bay reflecting on the uniqueness of life'. Their deliberations were, he ruefully conceded, also 'compounded by our futile pursuit of promiscuous sexual relief and a throbbing hangover'.[82]

Career moves

While studying towards his doctorate, Slabbert was employed as a temporary junior lecturer in the sociology department at Stellenbosch. Once he had obtained his degree, he could start looking further afield for employment. This came in the form of a position at Rhodes University in Grahamstown (today Makhanda). Slabbert's application was well supported by Dian Joubert, a senior lecturer and one of Slabbert's mentors. Apart from commenting favourably on Slabbert's academic abilities, Joubert described him as a 'very able lecturer [who] brings to his classes a happy combination of authoritative knowledge, effective transmission and humour'. He was, moreover, 'well-liked as a speaker at meetings and symposia on and off the campus'. Joubert, however, saved his highest accolades for Slabbert's ability to transcend the obvious and to deploy a sense of the sociological imagination:

> Many, if not most of our Sociology majors leave the university with a knowledge of social facts, but with an inability to ask and answer the pertinent, really sociological questions. With Dr Slabbert this ability follows from his well above average intelligence, sound common sense, social sensitivity, personal experience of a variety of social settings and his dedicated study of the methodology of the social sciences. All of this has made him a 'natural' sociologist – which cannot be said of all our South African colleagues.[83]

Slabbert's application was successful and he skipped one rank to be appointed as senior lecturer. The move to Grahamstown was a new adventure for him. He looked forward to the experience and remarked that there were actually few things holding him back from leaving Stellenbosch.[84]

He started at Rhodes in 1969. By this time he was already a family man, having married Mana Jordaan, a fellow Stellenbosch student, in 1965; their first child, Tania, arrived in 1967 (for a more detailed discussion of Slabbert's family life, see Chapter 9). He decided to buy a house, which he claimed was necessary as it was difficult to obtain suitable rented accommodation.[85] He was given a warm welcome in Grahamstown, was invited to several discussion groups and asked to join the Round Table, and was impressed by the easy relationship between town and gown. Sporting-wise, he also contributed by coaching the First XV.[86]

Politically, the climate at Rhodes differed from that at Stellenbosch, but Slabbert found the academic arguments essentially the same, and the students not that dissimilar. He noted, somewhat cryptically, that they only wore different coloured blazers.[87] Generally, he appreciated being exposed to a good cross section of the various disciplines in the staff common room. It kept him on his toes, and he had to be careful, he remarked, as to how he deployed his 'sociological jargon' because political scientists and philosophers were quick to pounce.[88] Slabbert was particularly impressed with Daantjie Oosthuizen, an ex-Stellenbosch philosopher who came to Rhodes in 1957. Although Oosthuizen died in April that year, shortly after Slabbert's arrival, he could associate himself with Oosthuizen's outlook that 'intellectual life is about the non-stop subversion of orthodoxy and dogmatism, whether in politics, academia or civil life'.[89]

The head of the sociology department was Professor James Irving, who had been there since 1946. Slabbert described him as having an 'old-world charm' and as one of the few 'gentlemen scholars' left. He had a wide reading knowledge of social science literature, but Slabbert regarded him as not particularly interested in 'delivering the goods' in terms of academic publications. Administratively, Slabbert described Irving as an 'outstanding failure': the library facilities were poor and the offices sparsely furnished.[90] Formal curricula bore little resemblance to what happened in class, and classes were presented unsystematically.

After an initially positive view of Rhodes, Slabbert's enthusiasm gradually waned. He claimed to have been allocated too heavy a teaching load, the department carried too much deadwood, and he did not have enough time to do research. In his view, the department had no status in the university and Irving's successor would have to rebuild it from scratch.[91]

It is also at this time that he fleetingly considered leaving academe altogether. He met a personnel manager from Lever Brothers, in Durban, during a presentation in Grahamstown and the two instantly hit it off. Slabbert was flown to Durban for an interview and offered a position as assistant manager on a salary of R6 500 – more or less the equivalent of a professor's salary at the time. He considered the offer, as he wanted more money – Dian Joubert regarded him as more materialistic than most other sociologists.[92] In the end, however, he decided against it. His situation was not so dire that he felt compelled, as he put it, 'to darken the doorsteps of capitalist citadels with my shadow. Difficult as it may be to believe, I have become (God have mercy) a committed sociologist.'[93]

Although nothing came of it, his brief flirtation with Lever Brothers showed that Slabbert, at the age of 29, and with only seven months' full-time employment as an academic, was, despite his claim to being a dedicated sociologist, not shy of exploring other options. For the time being, though, he saw his future in academe. Yet he had sufficient confidence in his own abilities and talents to envisage a future beyond that of a mere lecturer. As a matter of fact, he mentioned that at Rhodes he was aware that in certain circles he was being discreetly punted for higher honours. Moreover, while at Stellenbosch, he claimed he was told that if he watched his step (*mooi loop*), he would one day become rector of the institution.[94] That, of course, was not to happen, but in 1979, after five years in politics, he decided that if he was not elected leader of the Progressive Federal Party that year, he would allow his name to be put forward as a candidate for vice chancellor of the University of Cape Town.[95] In the event, his selection as party leader put paid to this possibility. It was only in 2008 that his earlier youthful idealism to become a luminary in university education materialised in a different form when he was chosen for the ceremonial role of chancellor of Stellenbosch University.

In the meantime, though, in 1969 he was to reconsider his position at Rhodes. In a letter to SP Cilliers, the head of the sociology department at Stellenbosch, he hinted that, following the Lever Brothers episode, he was missing the department at Stellenbosch.[96] Slabbert had a long-standing relationship with Cilliers, who had not only acted as supervisor for his doctoral thesis but also influenced him in other respects. Slabbert regarded the relationship with Cilliers as one of the important turning points in his life, and was particularly grateful that Cilliers impressed upon him the importance of not allowing intellectual engagement to rule out the wisdom of common sense.[97]

Cilliers followed up on Slabbert's hint by phoning him to inquire about possibilities. Slabbert was not at home at the time, but phoned Cilliers back after returning from a party where he had consumed some wine. Under the circumstances, Stellenbosch beckoned even more strongly. He arranged to meet Cilliers at Port Elizabeth airport to thrash out the matter. By the time he drove back to Grahamstown, he had decided to relocate to Stellenbosch.[98]

Before Slabbert left Stellenbosch for Grahamstown in early 1969 he had been, according to Joubert, keen on the possibility of a professorship at Rhodes,[99] but after his stay there he found the environment increasingly restrictive. Although he was prepared to stay on if he had to, he was not all that keen on the prospect.

The Stellenbosch offer of a senior lectureship, coupled with being warden of a men's residence, came at the right time. In explaining his decision, Slabbert quoted Neil Smelser, the sociologist of collective movements: '[I]t was the result of a combination of conduciveness, strain, belief, precipitants and mobilisation,' but added that that still says 'boggerol'. Ultimately, apart from what he considered an increasing lack of intellectual stimulation, he could not, despite some vague possibilities, see himself making rapid headway at Rhodes given the nature of the hierarchy at the university. Once he had taken the decision, he also admitted to an 'unlocalised yearning for Stellenbosch'.[100]

Though keen to return to Stellenbosch, Slabbert was also wary of what he might be expected to teach there. He preferred to stay clear of the service courses that the department offered to students in agriculture, nursing and physical education.[101] In his view these were rather demeaning, and he referred to them as the 'sociology of planting carrots, carrying bedpans and recreation'.[102] His interests were, it seems, more rarefied and directed towards meta-theory.

But Stellenbosch did not quite seem the same place, and he claimed in retrospect that establishment attitudes towards him had changed. This might have been as a result of a petition he spearheaded, arguing for a better political dispensation for coloureds.[103] Jannie Gagiano also informed him that he (Gagiano) had been approached by the security police to provide information on certain lecturers, including Slabbert. The two laughed it off, but Slabbert realised that he was no longer 'viewed simply as an errant son, but as a potential enemy of the state – incredible dictum!'[104]

The security police's interest in Slabbert perhaps says more about the police than it does about Slabbert. One would be hard-pressed to describe his appointment at Stellenbosch at the time as academically or politically radical. A scholar like T Dunbar Moodie, who also showed an interest in working in the local sociology department, was promised a position by Cilliers but rejected by the university hierarchy on the grounds that he was a 'a communist and anti-apartheid'.[105] Similarly Slabbert's friend Manie van der Spuy, the psychologist, who had no trouble obtaining positions abroad, was turned down for a 'puny junior lectureship' at Stellenbosch as he was considered politically suspect.[106] Slabbert was not quite tarred with the same brush.

Nor can Slabbert's sponsor, Cilliers, be regarded as radical. Although he was strongly in favour of full civil rights for coloureds, he supported the overall apartheid framework of separate homelands for black people.[107] Cilliers was also in some respects an organisation man and was instrumental in establishing the Association for Sociology in Southern Africa (ASSA), in opposition to the conservative South African Sociology Association (SASOV), which had a colour bar in its constitution. Although the ASSA later gained a reputation as a radical organisation, its founding history does not necessarily reflect that. Figures like Cilliers had easy access to high-ranking government officials, and Cilliers had actually approached General

Hendrik van den Bergh of the security police before the first ASSA conference in Lourenço Marques (today Maputo) to inform him of developments.[108] In an overall context, the world of South African sociology that Slabbert entered at this time was not particularly radical. At Stellenbosch, under the aegis of Cilliers, who was only slightly left-leaning, Slabbert would have been safely ensconced.

But Slabbert was also his own person. After barely two years at Stellenbosch, he moved to the University of Cape Town. He applied for a chair at UCT, but it was given to Jan Loubser, also a product of Stellenbosch. Loubser, who was a committed critic of apartheid and had earlier emigrated to Canada, returned when he was offered the UCT position. Politically, Slabbert could well have been attracted to Loubser, and it would appear that Loubser also made some tentative promises that if Slabbert moved to UCT as a senior lecturer, promotion might soon follow.[109] The promotion did not materialise, despite the fact that he became acting head of department when Loubser decided to return to Canada. Slabbert became a popular figure on campus: his classes were oversubscribed, as they had been at Stellenbosch, and he was approachable and known to be conscientious in dealing with academic obligations.[110] Yet his ambitions remained unfulfilled.

It was at this point that a chair at the University of the Witwatersrand beckoned. Slabbert moved to Johannesburg in the second half of 1973 as a full professor and head of the sociology department at the academically youthful age of just 33. Moreover, he had produced no explicitly academic publications, though one was in press.[111] Of course, in the academic world since then, where until recently publications tended to override much else, a candidate like Slabbert would not even be shortlisted for such an appointment. At that time, however, there was not the same emphasis on publications, and indeed, the number of candidates with doctoral degrees in sociology and university experience was rather limited.[112]

Slabbert received strong backing from the influential Cilliers. In his recommendation, Cilliers described Slabbert as an 'outstanding sociologist with a very keen analytical mind and a thorough grounding in both methodology and substantive theory'. He praised him for being one of those rare academics 'who can bring his analytical and theoretical skills to bear on the study of concrete situations'. Cilliers furthermore stressed Slabbert's lecturing and interpersonal skills, concluding that if his recommendation 'may perhaps sound too good to be true, it is because I have very seldom been so wholly enthusiastic about a student and a colleague as I find myself about Dr Slabbert'.[113] This assessment of Slabbert's qualities was later echoed by Jannie Gagiano: 'He is very articulate. He can argue well, he can write well, he can assemble an argument very well. He can analyse well.'[114] Over and above this, he also had a kind of personal magnetism; a film-star appearance combined with self-deprecating wit made for an attractive package.

There were, however, other qualities that shaped him as a person. His apparently casual demeanour could be misleading. 'In everything he does, he wants to see an outcome. He wants to be significant. He has to have a sense of agency,' Gagiano commented.[115] The prognosis for an easy fit between these qualities and academe was not good. The bureaucratic subculture of the academic world, known for moving at a measured and often snail-like pace, was not the ideal environment for accommodating dynamic individuals with a sense of immediate urgency.

It is therefore perhaps not all that surprising, given Slabbert's driven personality, that he would encounter some obstacles. At Wits he found a fractured department, and it soon became apparent that he would have his work cut out to correct matters.[116] It was a frustrating prospect. He subsequently explained why his academic career had assumed a somewhat peripatetic character:

> Each time I moved, it was in the hope that I could find a better opportunity to become a competent academic. Wits was the fourth place where this hope had been frustrated.

> I inherited a bureaucratic and administrative mess; there were virtually no research funds and a senior colleague was riddled with complexes and problems. I enjoyed lecturing but did not have enough time to do research and read and had visions of becoming, at the age of thirty-three, a second-rate academic housekeeper for the rest of my life.[117]

Slabbert was not exaggerating the problems at Wits. His successor, Dunbar Moodie, recalled that there 'were deep divisions – outright conflict in fact – within the department'.[118] The academic world is known for internecine warfare of this kind and it is never easy to mediate. It can, however, also be seen as something that comes with the territory. Moreover, at the time Slabbert was appointed new heads of department had considerably more jurisdiction in shaping their environment than is the case today.[119] Slabbert, though, was not in it for the long haul. A former colleague recalled that at Wits 'he had become bored by sociology'.[120] It was precisely at this time that the Progressive Federal Party started to woo him. This effectively ended his formal academic career. In the literature on the nature of academic alienation, the question of lack of influence often arises. Even when social status and remuneration were favourable, for some intellectuals prestige 'must offer more than bread, it must allow access to a court of glory'.[121] In Slabbert's case, he clearly yearned for more, perhaps not fully realising what that would entail.

Cilliers was somewhat disappointed with Slabbert's decision to quit academe. He felt that had Slabbert stayed on at Stellenbosch, he would not have experienced the same disenchantment. Cilliers based this on the view that so-called *verligte* (enlightened) members of the staff at Stellenbosch had played vital roles as public intellectuals in influencing politicians, which added another dimension to academic life, ensuring vitality.[122] Whether Slabbert would have agreed is a moot point.

In terms of academic developments, it is also worth noting the subsequent trajectory of the Wits sociology department. From 1975 it went into a growth phrase, with new leadership and a thorough overhaul of its offerings and theoretical points of departure, including a substantial dose of Marxian analysis.[123] Slabbert might have welcomed the new dynamism, but it is doubtful if he would have been a supporter of Marxism. Be that as it may, he left the department on the cusp of new, much more radical departures in his discipline. Had he remained in academe these developments might have had a rejuvenating effect on his sombre outlook at the time.

Twists and turns of theory

Intellectually, as has already been hinted, Slabbert's life was shaped by a specific set of contemporary concerns that had traction in certain circles during his stay at Stellenbosch. Apart from Jannie Gagiano and some others, this revolved around individuals such as André du Toit and Johan Degenaar in the political philosophy department, who introduced Slabbert to the classic works of existentialist and critical philosophy.[124] Degenaar and Du Toit were acknowledged as outstanding academics, though their political views were often regarded by the establishment as suspect.

Degenaar was the leading figure in involving promising young academics in a discussion group that turned out to have an abiding influence on many of them.[125] As a prominent exponent of Socratic didactics, Degenaar had a small but academically potent cult following, and he was respected for expounding notions of non-fundamentalist political pluralism along the lines of an established tradition in certain quarters in Stellenbosch of the open discussion (*oop gesprek*).[126] In this company Slabbert found kindred spirits. From his theological grounding he migrated to a variety of philosophical positions. In general, his interest moved from the subjective and concrete to the objective and abstract, increasingly searching for laws and regularity, which in turn led him into social theory and the philosophy of science.[127]

His MA thesis had reflected none of these interests. It dealt with the more practical and mundane issue of the vocational choices of students. Topics such as these, with an empirical basis, were standard fare in sociology departments at the time.[128] Yet in perusing his thesis one is struck by the fact that Slabbert was particularly concerned about whether class was a crucial determinant in career preferences.[129] It is speculative but tempting to see this concern as an indication of his own position; his less than affluent background and uncertainty about his career prospects at the time might well have played a role in the way the study was conceived.

His doctoral thesis foregrounded an interest in meta-theory. His promoter, Cilliers, had visited Harvard, Cornell and Duke universities on a study visit in 1954–1955, and had returned from America a firm disciple of Talcott Parsons' structural functionalism, a paradigm with considerable appeal at the time.[130] Structural functionalism revolved in part around a consensus of values generated by certain institutions as preconditions for optimum societal functioning. In his doctoral thesis, Slabbert set out to evaluate the theory from a methodological point of view. His concern was to assess the 'validity of some of the claims by its proponents and to decide the merits of the standards employed by those who reject it'. The outcome, he suggested, would also have wider implications for sociology as a discipline.[131]

An examiner, whose report on the thesis is available, was very positive about the quality of work. He found it rigorously argued and felt that the candidate was able to rise above the material and develop his own perspectives. The thesis, moreover, was seen as making a substantial contribution to knowledge by emphasising the need for methodological sophistication in dealing with and evaluating sociological theories.[132]

In later years, Slabbert commented, tongue in cheek, that the thesis 'was so esoteric that I am still the only person who can get excited about it'. It was not all in vain, though. As he had to develop a position outside Parsons' own framework in order to evaluate it, he claimed that the exercise sharpened his analytical skills and alerted him generally to the problem of tautological arguments, insofar as that which actually has to be explained reverts back in a circular fashion to the theory or paradigm itself.[133] This awareness, Slabbert claimed, permeated his subsequent academic outlook, and he developed an inbuilt suspicion of grand theories of social change. He explained:

> The dogmatic confidence, the academic pig-headedness of some Marxist and functionalist scholars, and particularly those students who were desperately searching for a secular eschatology, were no different from some of the devout souls at Stellenbosch who resolutely tried to take me on a mental route march through to the Kingdom of God. Emotionally I felt 'a plague on the arrogance of both your creeds!'[134]

Slabbert was academically quite brave to have attempted a study of structural functionalism, as Parsons' prose presented a challenge. Wilmot James, a sociology student at the time, recalled that Parsons 'wrote in a manner that brought injustice to the clarity of which the English language is capable. To read Parsons was an effort and a task. Many persisted because they thought that opacity was the way of genius and therefore worthy of understanding.'[135] Because he had to plough through Parsons to make it intelligible to himself, Slabbert was able to convey the essence of the theory in a comprehensible manner to students and, moreover, to apply it to South Africa. In this respect, in terms of values generated and social stability, four institutions were regarded as crucial: a solid family life, a growing economy, a fair legal system and the maintenance of social order by the state. Although this may appear as self-evident, at the high point of apartheid-induced centrifugal forces these notions had something of a radical ring to them.[136]

The possibility of applying Parsons to the South African scenario and developing a critique along lines that showed up the system's dysfunctionality must have held a certain appeal for Slabbert. Gagiano believes that for a while Slabbert was quite comfortable in the Parsonian zone.[137] Parsons, as other commentators observed, also had a moral dimension to his systems analysis.[138] This might equally well have spoken to Slabbert so soon after he had forsaken theology. Slabbert, however, was not an uncritical adherent of Parsons; it was more a matter of being intrigued by his analysis, and at the same time keeping a critical distance without rejecting it outright.[139] Slabbert corresponded with Parsons, and when the latter visited South Africa, at a time when Slabbert was already in Parliament, the two did meet. It turned out to be a bit of an anticlimax; the elderly Parsons at that point was more interested in the cultivation of strawberries than systems theory.[140]

The appeal of structural functionalism started to decline as South Africa moved into the turbulent 1970s and 1980s. The paradigm's key concepts of order, balance and consensus came to be viewed as inconsistent with a society increasingly riven by conflict. In South Africa the benefits of modernisation implicit in structural functionalism seemed not to have had the desired effect of easing social tensions, but on the contrary had enhanced the ability to implement apartheid and contributed to strife. In the social sciences this led to a decisive turn away from structural functionalism towards more radical conflict theorists and variants of Marxism.[141]

As noted above, Slabbert had an aversion to closed systems of thought, and for this reason he was also sceptical of Marxism. Academically, though, mainly because he was an MP by this time, he did not contribute to the decade-long debate that raged throughout the social sciences. He had had his own encounter with real-life communists much earlier, however. While in Oxford during an official study visit in 1965, he slipped away from the formal party, explored Oxford on his own, and happened to end up at a meeting of the British Communist Party. After the meeting, Slabbert met some of the members informally. They had a vigorous debate, and, after consuming a fair amount of cognac, and despite initial disagreements, seemed to find some common ground.[142]

His intellectual acuity opened doors, but his restless nature and unfulfilled ambition did not allow him to grow to full academic maturity. While his scholarly instincts stayed with him during his political career, as an academic he did not leave behind a substantial body of significant writings. That he had the ability to do so is indisputable; that he did not had to do with competing attractions, personal preferences and wider aspirations. The allure of academe started to fade as new fields of practical derring-do beckoned. The word now had to become flesh.

In retrospect, Slabbert did not enter the university world as an empty vessel, waiting to be filled by academic knowledge. Given his problematic domestic background, his early religious devotion and his experience with black people, he had already developed his own views of the world, which he could use as a yardstick for gauging new sets of knowledge. The essential elements for the construction of a critical disposition were in place, though the way this would play out could not readily be predicted.

Stellenbosch University, despite the conservatism of the time, meant much for him. It allowed him to ground his kind of proselytising instincts in a rational manner; it provided him with opportunities to debate apartheid's shortcomings in a rigorous way, which stood him in good stead later on; it gave him the chance to measure his own academic acumen against that of others; and, given where he came from, it helped to build confidence to the extent that at the age of 28 he was told that 'if he watched his step' he might even become rector. In all of this he had good and supportive lecturers and friends. He also claimed to have experienced more than enough academic freedom to express himself fully.[143]

The university furthermore imparted the possibility of a sense of critical thinking and academic detachment. In later years, a fellow sociologist articulated what he regarded as the core of Slabbert's scholarly outlook: 'Living with ambiguity, seeking out the grey areas of uncertainty, was for Van the hallmark of an intellectual.'[144] This might have been a liability in the netherworld of politics, but it can also equip one to wield razor-sharp analysis, as Slabbert often did. While Slabbert was not made by Stellenbosch in the way that some of his peers were predestined to join the National Party, Stellenbosch did, in contradistinction, in an almost reverse form, help to shape him.

2
BECOMING A POLITICIAN

Precursors

Although Slabbert's decision to enter politics obviously rested with him as an individual, there were some earlier developments that, it can be argued, primed him, or at least predisposed him, to consider such an eventuality. Some of these had taken place on an informal level at Stellenbosch, while others had a wider basis.

During the 1960s and 1970s, select university staff members regularly organised various informal discussion groups, which became long-standing and regular features of off-campus academic life. These discussions were marked by considerable intellectual ferment, and critical engagement was encouraged through open debate. The politics of the day and its wider ramifications were closely scrutinised. The local Catholic priory also participated, and some of the brothers contributed to the intellectual mix. Guests from outside were often surprised by the progressive nature of these discussions and the way in which certain Afrikaner participants positioned themselves on the left.[1]

Slabbert was prominent in these discussions, and they provided him with selective but challenging company in which to cut his political teeth. He was quick to point out discrepancies and duplicity. At one off-campus meeting, an academic who was also a Broederbonder argued that even if one had reservations about apartheid, one should still pretend to be loyal to the National Party with a view to promoting reform by stealth. Slabbert's response was simple: 'But then you are taking everyone for a ride.'[2]

Another precursor to his formal political career was a grouping called Synthesis, which operated in Johannesburg, Durban and Cape Town. Participation was by invitation. It hovered on the fringes of formal politics, involved a number of top-level individuals, and cut across racial lines. The group was started by a Flemish-Belgian physician, Dr Louis van Oudenhove, who was keen for South Africans to learn more about population groups other than their own. Synthesis drew in people such as Japie Basson of the United Party, Colin Eglin of the Progressive Party, the Zulu leader Mangosuthu Buthelezi, educationalist Dr Richard van der Ross, who was involved with the coloured Labour Party, and MT Moerane, the editor of *The World*. Slabbert joined this exalted company as early as 1970 and acted as secretary-treasurer. Synthesis not only served as an important networking group but also allowed face-to-face interaction between people who in the ironclad racial demarcations of apartheid South Africa would hardly have had the opportunity to discuss matters of common interest. For Slabbert, who later in his career put great store by the positive chemistry that meetings under favourable circumstances between opposing groups could generate, Synthesis was an early exposure to the potential of such occasions. It was, however, an initiative that raised the ire of Prime Minister John Vorster, who sought to cast the group in a sinister light as a secret and pernicious influence.[3]

Slabbert's involvement with discussion groups had an unexpected spin-off. At Stellenbosch one of the groups was addressed by the National Party's Dr Piet Koornhof, deputy minister of what at the time was called 'Bantu affairs'. Koornhof reassured his audience that the government's homeland policy was having the desired effect and that urban black people were satisfied with the arrangements. Ever the academics, Slabbert and Jannie Gagiano thought that such an assertion needed to be tested. Coincidentally, Slabbert had to be in Johannesburg for Marcia's wedding, and thought he could visit Soweto at the same time with view to testing Koornhof's claim.

Through the good offices of MT Moerane, arrangements were made for him and Gagiano to meet some prominent Soweto locals. Their strategy was to convey Koornhof's ideas and policies, pretending that they supported these, and then to note the result. They were not prepared for the outcome. Slabbert later recalled: 'We experienced abuse, threats, hysterical anger and inarticulate frustration. It washed over us, wave after wave.'[4] The fury was such that one of the locals feared that the two Afrikaners might actually be killed.[5] It was only after they had explained what their real purpose was in coming to Soweto, and that they were not actually Nationalists, nor pro-apartheid, that the mood subsided. They were then made to feel welcome, and there was even a sense of appreciation that young Afrikaners from Stellenbosch were prepared to undertake such a venture.

The meeting had a profound effect on Slabbert. Initially he felt a mixture of negative emotions, yet in retrospect he regarded it as a 'very, very important occasion'.[6] This kind of engagement underscored Slabbert's scepticism that government policies were in accord with the wishes of the majority, and that to claim it was so was misleading in the extreme. It was a realisation that he would carry with him well into the future. The legendary Percy Qoboza, who took over from Moerane as editor of *The World* in 1974, was also involved in the arrangements that day. In 1979, when Slabbert was chosen as leader of the parliamentary opposition, Qoboza reflected: '[W]hile Soweto cannot entirely take credit for the shaping of Van Zyl Slabbert, it contributed in no small way in making Van a sensitive man ..., the night ... was something of a baptism by fire for the young Afrikaner intellectual. His soul was cleansed ... You are going to hear a lot about this guy. You can surely take that as a prediction.'[7]

Besides such almost Damascus-road experiences, there was also a more analytical side to the gradual sharpening of Slabbert's political awareness. Part of this related to wider developments in Afrikaner society. During the 1960s South Africa experienced an unsurpassed economic growth rate of six per cent, and Afrikaners were the main beneficiaries of this windfall. The middle class expanded rapidly and, fuelled by a new consumer culture, shifts in Afrikaner world-views became readily apparent. There occurred a gradual loosening of the ties to *volk* and Afrikaner culture, and politically the possibility of a more differentiated, open society appeared slightly less remote than before.[8]

In the first half of the 1970s, Slabbert picked up on these developments in an academic article that first appeared, in shortened form, in the press. He argued that the ruling National Party now had to deal with increased internal tensions in mediating between expanding elite groupings and traditional working-class formations. With the opening of new opportunities in business and commerce, young Afrikaners were increasingly asserting themselves outside traditional occupations such as teaching and the ministry. Being less dependent ideologically on time-honoured political and cultural scaffolding prompted a greater sense of indifference, though Slabbert cautioned that apathy should not be equated with major political change. Nevertheless, he predicted that material progress and concomitant adjustments in world-views would vie to a greater extent than before with old-style allegiances. 'The majority of young Afrikaners,' he argued, 'are preparing for a petty-bourgeois existence where they will become the Babbitts of Bellville, Benoni and Bloemfontein.'[9] With these developments, the possibility also existed that with the right strategic approach, their political allegiances could also be shifted. Slabbert's broad observations were supported by empirical opinion surveys, which in 1971 indicated that almost 20 per cent of the Afrikaner elite were open to other political messages than those of the National Party.[10]

At the same time, there emerged from within Afrikaner ranks what was called a *verligte* (enlightened) grouping, which positioned itself in opposition to those considered arch-conservative Afrikaners, labelled as *verkramp* (reactionary). The *verlig-verkramp* struggle generated considerable heat, but overall *verligtes* fell short of embracing the kind of liberalism touted by the Progressive Party, led by Colin Eglin. In broad terms, *verligtes* still believed that gradual and effective change could best be initiated from within party structures rather than from outside.

It was these Afrikaners that the Progressive Party started to target as potential dissidents in the early 1970s. The party realised that in trying to make headway, it should try and shed its image as an almost exclusively English-speaking faction, amounting to little more than a pressure group often viewed as anti-Afrikaner in its outlook. In order to broaden the party's electoral base, it was essential to draw Afrikaners into the fold. Eglin launched a bold programme to rejuvenate the party, and a deliberate attempt was made to woo select Afrikaner groupings. An Afrikaans-language party journal, *Deurbraak*, was launched to encourage debate and open up lines of communication with Afrikaners. A concerted effort was also made to organise symposia in which members of the party could interact with prominent *verligtes* and subject the party's policy to scrutiny with a view to possible adjustments that would attract more voters. At one such symposium Slabbert attended in Pretoria in 1972, he was particularly attentive and pensive.[11]

Although Slabbert was concerned about practical ways to address the major political issues in South Africa, he had some reservations about the efficacy of a strategy partly reliant on *verligte* Afrikaner support. He argued at the time that the 'important point is that different Afrikaner *verligtes* respond to different and sometimes contradictory tensions'. He illustrated this by citing a minister of religion who might encourage frugality and compassion while a businessman was more concerned with profits. Both might make *verligte* political noises but their objectives and points of departure differed. This impeded the potential for the growth of a *verligte* movement as 'different Afrikaners are simply *verlig* about different kinds of things'.[12] Ultimately, however, the increase in the number of individual *verligtes*, despite the fact they had yet to cohere, did hold out a promise for the future.

By this stage, Slabbert was an increasingly sought-after speaker on political matters, especially on university campuses. He remained detached in his analysis, trying to detail how different political parties sought to deal with South Africa's central dilemma of power-sharing. During a speech in Stellenbosch he succinctly outlined the quandary of the National Party in trying to protect white interests while at the same time having to make concessions to black people in order to implement the ambitious homeland project. The opposition United Party was casting around to find a practical policy, and in its absence justified the party's existence mainly by pointing out and capitalising on government errors. The Progressive Party, through its policy of a qualified franchise, offered a select group of black people a better dispensation but would leave ordinary blacks, who actually needed the vote the most, out in the cold. This speech was widely welcomed for its dispassionate analysis.

At the University of Cape Town, he spoke more extensively on a broader range of topics, including relations in the workplace and the cultural dimensions of possible impending changes in South Africa.[13] He was equally interested in the machinations of power that benefited white privilege.[14] It was clear that during this time Slabbert was probing more actively than before the dynamics of various manifestations of the political and social order in South Africa. He had moved away from esoteric academic theorising, but was still intent on injecting a scholarly and clinical element into his understanding of the nature of South African issues.

The decision

This spike of interest happened to coincide with wider developments in parliamentary politics. Not only was the Progressive Party trying to reinvent itself, but certain factions within the middle-of-the-road United Party also realised the need to be more reform-minded in order to counter the National Party more effectively. With an eye on the 1974 general election, the so-called Young Turks of the United Party, including Horace van Rensburg, Japie Basson and Dick Enthoven, approached Slabbert and his Stellenbosch colleague Nic Olivier to stand in two relatively safe Johannesburg seats. Slabbert was not very enthusiastic about the offer, as he had qualms about the United Party's controversial participation in a government commission investigating what were regarded as 'suspect' organisations and individuals, which had led to the arbitrary persecution of some of Slabbert's friends.

Despite their reservations, Slabbert and Olivier flew to Johannesburg to meet with Van Rensburg and Enthoven, as well as other United Party luminaries. They met at Van Rensburg's house, and the convivial evening, with plenty of carousing, masked the serious political discussions that took place. Nic Olivier eventually agreed to stand as a candidate and Slabbert also shifted his position by moving from a resolute 'no' to a possible 'maybe'. Van Rensburg asked both to sign membership forms; Olivier duly did so, but Slabbert, who was having second thoughts, slipped the form into his pocket. To their chagrin, Van Rensburg and his wife later searched in vain for his membership card.[15]

Colin Eglin, who yet had to be fully apprised of developments, was aghast when it dawned on him that Slabbert might cast in his lot with the United Party. He managed to track him down in Johannesburg and the two met in the airport parking garage. Eglin was relieved to hear that Slabbert was still open to other propositions. Slabbert now found himself in a predicament. He had encouraged Nic Olivier to take the United Party route, yet he was not prepared to join him in that journey. At the same time, he had Eglin cajoling him to stand as the Progressive Party candidate in Rondebosch, Cape Town. He had limited time to make up his mind. A few minutes before the deadline of 11 December 1973, he phoned Eglin to tell him: 'I am your candidate for Rondebosch. I prefer a challenge to a safe seat.'[16]

There was something almost burlesque about Slabbert's launch into politics: flying to Johannesburg to meet representatives of the moderate United Party, in which overall he had little faith, then careening to a boisterous yet important gathering where he was almost persuaded to change his mind, and then being hunted down by an anxious Colin Eglin, who ultimately convinced him to stand for the Progressives in Rondebosch. It was not a cool, calculated entry into the robust world of South African politics, and it was also somewhat ironic that it should have been the United Party that first forced the issue. But, then again, Slabbert's path in life was seldom neatly mapped out.

Slabbert did not necessarily enter politics because he was interested in white party politics per se. He had a wider view of South Africa's intractable problem of equitable power-sharing and social equality. Coupled with this was what he described as the dilemma between 'political awareness, morality and political action'.[17] This was at the root of endless academic debate and moral posturing without actually contributing much to meaningful change. While he still valued the cut and thrust of academic debate and the way such clashes could crystallise issues, he also felt that more was needed and that he was ready to explore other ways of doing that. Having attended many discussion groups and academic seminars, Slabbert came to the down-to-earth conclusion that if one felt compelled to oppose the government, 'one had to go out on the pavement and oppose; one could not oppose in one's sitting room because no one would know about it'.[18] He was preoccupied with how 'not only to analyse or to declare my commitment to certain values, but to find some practical way of pursuing the latter so that they made sense in terms of the former'.[19]

That Slabbert had chosen the Progressive Party as a suitable vehicle for reaching such a goal was not completely unproblematic. Virtually throughout its existence the Progressive Party was viewed as the party of big capital, mainly because of its connection with Harry

BECOMING A POLITICIAN

Oppenheimer, supremo of the Anglo American Corporation, who at various times helped to fund the party. Big capital interests held that the possibility of rising tensions had to be blunted before discrepancies in the system became the basis for uncontrollable political confrontation. One route was the establishment of a solid black middle class. The National Party and the United Party were considered either too hidebound or moribund, or both, to effectively address the situation, which for all intents and purposes left only the Progressive Party as a viable alternative. It would be misleading simply to read the Progressive Party's policies as a reflection of the needs of capital, but the linkages can equally not be blithely dismissed. In the minds of black protest movements, there existed a strong suspicion that the wish of capital to create a strong middle class, which would leave the proletariat out in the cold, would ultimately run counter to the overall political desire of black people.[20]

Slabbert was well aware of the strengths of anti-capitalist analysis. Indeed, even shortly before joining the Progressive Party, he had his reservations about the party as representative of big capital and argued that it was only in idiosyncratic South Africa that the party could be regarded as left-wing; anywhere else it would have been seen as right-wing.[21] At Wits University, where Slabbert was based in the early 1970s, anti-capitalist academic analyses had become more strident, and it was probably here that Slabbert picked up the first whiffs of more radical dissent. Once part of the Progressives, though, he was more circumspect and preferred to project the party's followers as coming from a variety of backgrounds, without fully explaining the larger interests of the party.[22] He was also given to making light of the association between the wealthy and the party: 'My Afrikaans friends ask me why I'm Prog, while my Prog friends ask me why I'm poor!'[23]

In 1973 the party itself had come to a crossroads. It had to take into account that in the general elections of 1961, 1966 and 1970 it had fielded a total of 68 candidates in 40 different constituencies but had only managed to win a single seat. Its track record could barely be worse. The redoubtable Helen Suzman had been the party's sole parliamentary representative for 12 years and she increasingly felt the strains of such a burden. If the party could do no better than to keep returning only one MP, she argued, serious consideration should be given to the possibility of disbanding the party, winding up its affairs and leaving individuals free for extra-parliamentary work. This was a view shared by Colin Eglin as party chairman, and apparently also by Harry Oppenheimer. The 1974 election was therefore going to be a crucial contest. There were, however, some other trends that appeared more favourable for the party. Relative calm prevailed in the country, which meant that the usual 'black peril' scare tactics of the National Party would have less traction. Prime Minister Vorster had embarked on a so-called detente policy towards the rest of Africa, which opened up the opportunity to prod him to also be more proactive at home. And, as noted already, there was an increasingly free-floating Afrikaner *verligte* vote, while the United Party seemed to be rather less united than its name implied. Finally, the economy was fairly stable despite a rise in the inflation rate.[24]

While Slabbert would certainly have been aware of these trends, it still remained a risk to sacrifice a secure top academic position – he referred to academe as a particularly pleasant form of 'sheltered employment'[25] – for the topsy-turvy world of politics. Even though he would only have to give up the Wits position once elected, and not as soon as he had been nominated, politics remained a risky venture in the long run. Nevertheless, given the circumstances under which he accepted the nomination, it is highly unlikely that he would have done a calculated cost-benefit analysis of the situation. He later explained: 'A combination of factors interlocked to propel me towards a decision based on reasonable assumptions which turned out to be false.'[26] At the age of 33, then, the young Slabbert was about to enter the political arena.

'A star candidate':
The 1974 Rondebosch parliamentary election

For the 1974 election, the Progressive Party had a carefully worked-out strategy to concentrate their energies in certain key constituencies where they had a reasonable chance of winning, and to handpick quality candidates for these seats. Colin Eglin came in for some criticism for making an offer to Slabbert before full consultation with the Rondebosch constituency committee, and he had to persuade some members that Slabbert subscribed to the basic principles of the party and that his lack of experience would not be a huge impediment.[27]

Eglin had chosen Rondebosch as a target seat despite the fact that in the previous election the Progressive Party had not fielded a candidate there, as the sitting MP was Sir De Villiers Graaff, the leader of the United Party. However, as the demarcation commission had altered the boundaries of the constituency, the United Party thought it wiser to move Graaff to the safer neighbouring constituency of Groote Schuur.[28] Although Progressive Party workers had steadily beavered away in the constituency well before the election, and the new boundaries favoured the party, Slabbert would still have his work cut out to turn a marginal seat into a winning one. It was not as safe a seat as that which the United Party would have offered him on the Rand. Slabbert claimed not to have minded this, and in terms reminiscent of his competitive sporting career he welcomed the challenge. He had serious reservations about whether he would win, and was also aware that his candidature was in part a decoy strategy to stretch the United Party by drawing workers away from the Sea Point constituency in the hope of improving Eglin's candidacy there. Nevertheless, whatever the outcome, he regarded it as an 'interesting experience'.[29]

Slabbert's opponent in Rondebosch was Brian Bamford of the United Party, who was a sitting Member of the Provincial Council. Internal wrangling in the United Party meant that Bamford's campaign got off to a slow start. Bamford, however, had the blue blood and other qualities that the voters of Rondebosch would immediately have recognised. As one letter to a local newspaper explained, Bamford had 'the proverbial golden spoon in his mouth (English, Bishops, Oxford) in a notoriously English suburb which, politically, is also sadly Rip-van-Winkle'. Slabbert by contrast had none of Bamford's attributes and would be seen as an 'Afrikaner from the Transvaal'.[30] But Slabbert was not intimidated by Bamford, despite the latter's greater experience, seniority and local appeal. Before the campaign began he casually invited Bamford to meet him in 'relaxed circumstances to reflect on the necessity and usefulness of it all'.[31] The meeting only took place after the election, when the two shared a bottle of whisky.

Slabbert's dedication to the task at hand could not be faulted. He still had to honour his lecturing commitments at Wits, and for the first few weeks of the campaign he flew 3 000 kilometres each week between Johannesburg and Cape Town. From Monday to Wednesday he would be lecturing in Johannesburg, and then from Thursday to Saturday electioneering in Cape Town, before the return flight to Johannesburg on Sunday. He subjected himself to this punishing schedule in the hope of ensuring that his campaign had personal exposure and high visibility.[32] It was not only the logistics that were demanding; he also had to move between two worlds – the 'aloof, private and slightly bohemian world of academia and the involved, public and very conventional world of politics'.[33]

Slabbert later recalled that 'he worked himself to a standstill', and neglected his wife and family, all to 'feed the fire in the belly'. The last weeks of the campaign were particularly frenzied: 'I had been talking, shaking hands, writing statements, addressing house meetings, fielding voters from the pavement, meeting opinion leaders, placating prima donnas, lunching journalists and editors almost non-stop for six, seven weeks.'[34] Besides regular public meetings, Slabbert also spoke at between 80 and 90 house meetings, with 50 to 120 people attending each one.[35] It was nothing less than full immersion. The ceaseless activity took its toll, and the few moments he had for reflection caused him occasionally to doubt the wisdom of the course he had embarked upon. 'Every night,' he said:

> I would end up alone either in a flat or a guest room somewhere in the constituency. I suppose fatigue precluded an objective awareness of what was happening to me. Everything in me resisted the kind of life I was heading for. The loss of anonymity, the false confidence of public speaking, the boring conventionality, the intellectual dullness of pub-talk politics, the obligatory ritual of public life. I was off my mind to let myself get trapped into it. Yet, the next morning, I was into the day's appointments and demands as if it were all that mattered.[36]

Despite his reservations, it can also be argued that Slabbert found the campaign trail exhilarating. It appealed to all his senses: the challenge of conveying political logic to voters; the emotional satisfaction from interacting with a range of people, which energised him; and the competitive element in electioneering, where the outcome is not necessarily assured. He might privately have complained about the demands and the routines that all this entailed, but almost unwittingly these became, for the time being, part of his lifeblood – an almost fatal attraction.

As the Progressives' star candidate, he was hailed as the individual who had set the campaign alight.[37] Even a seasoned campaigner like Sir De Villiers Graaff had to admit, in complimentary yet understandably reserved terms, that Slabbert was 'a bright young fellow'.[38] More fulsome praise came from the veteran journalist Gerald Shaw, writing in the *Cape Times*:

> In years of watching politicians at work, I have never seen a novice candidate as gifted as this one ... We will be hearing

from him again, whether or not he wins at Rondebosch. This is a young Afrikaner of unusual intellectual brilliance. But his intelligence is severely practical. He never puts a political foot wrong and answers trick questions like a seasoned campaigner. On a platform he comes across as a man of honesty, resolution and strength of character. In all, he is the most remarkable newcomer in politics for some considerable time. And he has a sense of humour.[39]

Slabbert was not oblivious to the kind of appeal he exuded. He realised that his background rendered him unusual for the context in which he was operating. Being an Afrikaans-speaker, a foe of the government and a product of Stellenbosch University were not normal credentials for aspirant politicians in quintessentially English Rondebosch. He had, he said, an almost 'mystical appeal to English-speaking voters in those days. I was eulogised as some seven-day charismatic wonder that could swing the dog by its tail.' At some house meetings he was introduced as the new Jan Smuts, invoking the revered South African statesman of a previous generation, and 'grey-haired ladies were weepy and misty-eyed' as the nostalgia of yesteryear kicked in. Such adulation embarrassed him, but, as he said, 'there was nothing to be done about it'.[40]

His magnetism extended further than elderly ladies. He was also fêted on the 'Women's Page' of the *Cape Times* (at a time when such separate editorial arrangements were still regarded as acceptable), where women of all ages could appreciate the qualities of the Progressive candidate for Rondebosch. In almost swooning terms, a female journalist heartily welcomed the fact that he was adding glamour to a political scene that usually epitomised extreme dullness. He was depicted as huge and handsome and exuding a 'genuine South African type of charm'. When he addressed a crowd 'his face becomes vital and full of enthusiasm. It is very catching. Quite smashing in fact.'[41] Slabbert had become the poster boy for modern electioneering in South Africa, which went beyond the nuts and bolts of politics and policy choices.

Not everybody, though, was as impressed by what they regarded as misleading glitz and glamour. For some, it was just too Hollywood. Slabbert had no political record, it was said; his party was relatively weak; and if he were to be elected it would take him a considerable while to learn the ropes of Parliament and apply his knowledge of South Africa to the realities of parliamentary politics. What was required was a more realistic appraisal of the candidate and less film-star adoration. Respectable newspapers, it was argued, should not sink to the level of screen tabloids such as *Stage and Cinema*.[42]

While Slabbert's personal charisma certainly had an impact, this was matched by the quality of his political exposition. In terms of policy, four issues featured strongly in the 1974 general election: the nature of race relations; South Africa's standing in the international community; the question of internal security; and economic matters. These overarching concerns regularly emerged during the overall campaign, but for the purposes of local electioneering the Progressives in Rondebosch directed their attacks on the shortcomings of the National Party and the United Party. The National Party was misleading on issues such as power-sharing, while the Progressives claimed to have genuine power-sharing in mind, which would work to the benefit of all South Africans. The United Party was portrayed as an ineffective opposition, while the Progressives presented themselves as the champions of forceful opposition to the National Party.[43]

Slabbert's first public meeting took place at Rondebosch Town Hall on 13 February 1974, before a crowd of about 400. Word soon got round that there was an exciting new candidate in the normally sedate constituency, and as the campaign progressed he attracted larger numbers. On 28 February he addressed an enthusiastic crowd of 900 people in the Claremont Civic Centre. Lacing his address with witticisms, he attacked the National Party's policy of building homeland power blocks, saying that this would really entail whites' retaining ultimate power while parcelling out the homelands as small blocks. As for the United Party, all they were capable of in terms of reform was to 'pour new wine into old vats and sell it as vintage Cabernet'.[44]

In addition to running a celebrity candidate, a further modern electioneering ploy was to bring more high-profile individuals on board to share Slabbert's platform. Thus, latching on to Slabbert's former prowess at sport, cricketing great Eddie Barlow and Springbok rising star Morné du Plessis were roped in to add lustre to Slabbert's image as part of a new generation of progressive South Africans. With the Newlands rugby and cricket grounds conveniently situated in Rondebosch, this ensured a mix of local ambience, sporting luminaries and preferred politics in the minds of local voters.[45]

The campaign had an intimate quality and a community feel to it, while gently ruffling some feathers at the same time. It was fun, Slabbert later recalled, to 'disrupt the establishment, to confuse bridge parties, knitting circles, book clubs and cake sales with new options'.[46] Underlying this, though, was a serious organisational network that ran like clockwork.

Besides establishing Slabbert's presence in Rondebosch, party strategists furthermore considered that it would benefit their overall campaign to parade him further afield. Thus, Slabbert appeared on his old stamping ground of Stellenbosch. With the Town Hall filled to the rafters with about 1 200 people, many of them students, the meeting was the biggest in the Boland region, and those in the know claimed that the last time it had been so packed was in 1948, when Jan Smuts had spoken there. Slabbert delivered his usual hard-hitting analysis, focusing on shortcomings in National Party policy, and also emphasised how coloured people in the Boland were being short-changed by the policies of the ruling party. Despite some intermittent heckling from students, Slabbert's speech was well received, with a standing ovation from a large part of the audience.[47]

BECOMING A POLITICIAN

Polling day was 24 April 1974. Voting proceeded smoothly, with a 78.83 per cent turnout. The results were, however, only available in the small hours. At 3.15 on a Thursday morning it was announced: B Bamford (United Party) 4 930 votes; FvZ Slabbert (Progressive Party) 6 498 votes. Slabbert had won by a clear majority of 1 568 votes.[48]

He and Mana were outside the Wynberg magistrates' court when the results were announced. It was a time of merriment and madness. Standing on the top of a Volkswagen Kombi, they were surrounded by 'screaming, cheering and crying people'. He responded equally enthusiastically, but at the same time he asked himself: 'Sweet suffering grace, what am I going to do now?'[49] Others also thought that despite the euphoria he was a bit at sea. He had no 'cooking clue' as to how to proceed, his sister Marcia later recalled.[50] But for sustenance he could draw on the fact that the Progs, now with seven MPs, had improved their general showing in the election, even if it was from a low base.

3
PARLIAMENTARY STRIDES

Becoming House trained

Slabbert used the term 'House trained' to describe his initial exposure to Parliament.[1] It carried an almost irreverent tone, a reference to domestic animals that have to be trained to behave. He now also had to be tamed and domesticated to fit into the required mould.

Outside the House of Assembly, despite the fact that the apartheid edifice seemed as firm as ever, there were signs that a decade or more of unprecedented calm might be ending. In 1973, strike action by black workers in Durban challenged the prevailing labour regulations in what became a recurring cycle throughout the country. On the diplomatic front, Prime Minister Vorster continued to try to establish closer relations with African countries such as Gabon and Côte d'Ivoire. The converse of this initiative was the need to strengthen the military to defend what were regarded as South Africa's interests in South West Africa (Namibia). In 1974, the collapse of the Portuguese colonial empire, in the wake of the Carnation Revolution in Lisbon (25 April), and the subsequent independence of Mozambique and Angola, fuelled the need for increased military capacity. At the same time, apartheid planning came under increasing pressure as the demographic survey of 1969 had revealed the unsettling fact that the growth of the black population far exceeded the numbers originally envisaged to be accommodated in the homelands. It was against this backdrop, with indications that change was possibly in the air, that Slabbert embarked on his political career.

His induction into the South African parliamentary world,

however, was preceded by an unusual detour for a white South African at the time. He accompanied Colin Eglin on an official visit to Zambia, Kenya and Nigeria. Apart from regarding Slabbert as 'a highly compatible travel companion', Eglin felt he was 'a new factor in our politics which could convey to our African hosts a refreshing interpretation of developments in South Africa'.[2]

Slabbert was still reeling from the changes in his life. He recalled that within a few months, he moved from being an academic teaching and writing papers in Johannesburg to being received by African dignitaries. 'There was no self-evident career path between the two,' he mused, 'and certainly no motivational consistency on my part which made any sense of it. In many ways I was in transition and I felt a heightened awareness brought on by the unfamiliarity of new experiences.'[3]

In Lagos, Nigeria, the hustle and bustle, the crowded streets, the heat and humidity, and the large number of informal settlements came as a culture shock to visitors used to neatly ordered and regimented white South Africa. Slabbert spent hours walking through the alleyways, among the stalls and shacks. As a sociologist, he was quick to note how communities functioned and how individual networks and basic entrepreneurial skills helped individuals to survive from day to day. This was in stark contrast to South Africa, he observed, where the state, through influx control measures and forced removals, tried in vain to address issues of urbanisation and in the process destroyed community initiatives. It was a theme he would return to time and again. Based on his experience in Lagos, he warned: 'What a hangover we were preparing for ourselves.'[4]

Back in South Africa the visit elicited a mixed response. With one or two exceptions, the English-language press generally commented favourably. In the National Party camp, John Vorster, who was trying to establish his own contacts with African leaders, was dismissive. The minister of foreign affairs, Hilgard Muller, was mildly supportive, as the visit seemed to have generated goodwill. In contrast, an enraged PW Botha, then minister of defence, accused the emissaries of being unpatriotic and consorting with 'gangs and murderers'.[5]

The Afrikaans press fell into line behind Vorster and Botha. Slabbert, as an Afrikaner, was targeted in particular. *Die Burger* had a field day, crucifying him in a mock interview and then only allowing him to respond after it had been published. Although by no means a stranger to devious press tactics, he was most annoyed by what he called 'blatantly prejudiced and amateurish journalism'. If the emotions unleashed by such irresponsible reporting had to impact on his family, he warned, he would hold the newspaper responsible.[6] What emerged from this was that the young Slabbert, clearly perceived to be a potential political threat, would not be easily intimidated by the gnarled and cynical veterans of the Nationalist press. In this respect, he was up against the redoubtable Piet Cillié, editor of *Die Burger*. Cillié had developed a negative reputation in the eyes of some Stellenbosch academics because he always implied: 'I am just as clever as you are, perhaps even more so, but I have influence and you not, because I do not allow [myself] the luxury of criticising as if I have no ties with [Afrikanerdom].'[7]

Before his African safari, Slabbert received a rapid introduction to the party-political machinery. This entailed, among other obligations, becoming the main speaker at political rallies. The surprising victory of Alex Boraine, former president of the Methodist Church, in a by-election in Pinelands in June 1974 was achieved at least in part in the afterglow of Slabbert's earlier triumph in nearby Rondebosch. Boraine's campaign was fully supported by Slabbert, and Boraine would become a close confidant.[8] Although language-wise they came from different backgrounds, both shared relatively deprived family circumstances and, as youngsters, had felt called to teach in Sunday schools in dusty townships.[9]

The year 1974 was dubbed the start of the 'progressive renaissance' in South African parliamentary history, as there was a definite swing to the left away from the established National Party and United Party.

With seven capable MPs in its ranks, the Progressive Party for once appeared to have more potential than merely being of nuisance value.

Eglin prioritised three issues for the rejuvenated party: uncompromising adherence to the party's basic values, which included stressing the importance of the rule of law, individual dignity and civil liberties and justice; emphasising the need for effective communication with party members, focusing on pressing everyday issues instead of flighty political theories; and, above all, the need for the Progressives to assert themselves forcefully in the parliamentary arena. The party also had to take advantage of the shifting regional political terrain as anticolonial developments in neighbouring Angola, Mozambique and Rhodesia increasingly underscored the need for change in South Africa. At the same time, internal party dynamics had to be heeded, as the growth of the party and the influx of new members meant that the vested interests of the 'Old Progs' – older, true-blue, English-speaking – and the demands of younger and often brasher members had to be accommodated.[10]

Slabbert was particularly drawn into deliberations regarding the much sought-after Afrikaner vote. With the party's increased parliamentary representation it was hoped that *verligte* Afrikaners would consider it more seriously as an alternative. It was also gratifying that the party was having an invigorating effect on white English-speakers. Slabbert went so far as to talk about an 'awakening of political consciousness' in this group and how they were 'deeply concerned and involved in South Africa and its future'.[11] This was an important shift, as an earlier observation by UCT academic David Welsh had characterised white English-speaking 'sub-culture as one of easy-going tolerance, and a *laissez-faire* attitude to the society around them. They mistrust enthusiasm and ideology.'[12] The situation started to change, particularly after the independence of Mozambique from Portugal in 1975, as English-speakers became more aware of the changing colonial world around them. What they were concerned about, among other things, was that politics might start to impinge on business to a greater extent than before. This called for a more careful appraisal of the South African circumstances, which fed into a greater interest in effective party politics. Although the Progs might have benefited from changing political sensibilities, such sentiments did not necessarily translate into greater financial contributions to the party. Slabbert found this to his chagrin, as the extensive plans he had devised for a research secretariat floundered for lack of funding.[13]

As a newcomer, Slabbert does not appear to have been overawed by his induction to the august parliamentary chamber. On the contrary, right from the start he made light of time-honoured parliamentary rituals and even cast aspersions on MPs, whom he mocked as being more interested in their housing subsidies and pensions than in their constituencies. When these remarks, made informally at a social function, appeared in the press, he felt obliged to apologise in Parliament.[14]

Slabbert's maiden parliamentary speech, on 21 August 1974, was suitably serious. Not surprisingly, it had a measured, academic ring to it, as he began by saying he would draw upon his former career as a sociologist to analyse objectively what he regarded as the central paradox of white politics in South Africa. This, he argued, was the fact that although MPs were elected democratically by the white voters to whom they were accountable, their responsibilities extended far beyond the usual mandate, as Parliament was also functionally involved in black politics even though black people of course had no say in Parliament. It was 'against this paradox' and the associated dilemmas, he concluded, that he would take a 'bold stand'.[15]

Beyond emphasising what he regarded as the key issue, he proceeded in academic mode to suggest that the institution of Parliament as a whole should subjected to rigorous analysis. He considered it a privilege to be part of an institution that was directly involved in the historical conflict in South Africa. He was intent upon finding clarity as to how this institution functioned and how it discharged its obligations.[16] It was almost as if he was presenting a proposal for an academic project. The point of departure was that Parliament's efficacy and unquestioned authority as an institution could not merely be assumed and had to be assessed clinically.

His first speech transcended the usual party-political issues in that it provided a meta-perspective on Parliament. It made a considerable impression on sections of the press gallery, and one journalist, Scott Haig, later singled it out as a speech that all newcomers to Parliament should try to emulate.[17] Such praise might well have been too fulsome, but it is nevertheless clear that right from the start the quality of Slabbert's parliamentary oratory and his broader vision were recognised.

Others were more sceptical as the parliamentary session proceeded. One strand of criticism was that his speeches were too rarefied and cerebral, unsuited for the hurly-burly of South African politics. He preferred to read from notes, moving systematically from one point to the next with little digression.[18] Although Slabbert might have elevated the general level of parliamentary debate, it was not necessarily appreciated as such. His presentations contrasted too much with the fire-and-brimstone speeches that were a hallmark of parliamentary debate at the time. John Vorster, a noted parliamentary debater, summed it up: 'Parliament is not the place where you must bring your lectures; you must bring your flesh-and-blood political speeches if you want to succeed.'[19]

Slabbert himself was aware that he had to tweak his speeches in order to communicate with the wider public, who were kept informed by the parliamentary reporters, yet at the same time to try to be constructive in engaging the government on a rational basis. Over time, he became more adept at striking a balance.[20] While he shed elements of his academic style in the House, it does not mean that he also dispensed with an academic way of thinking. 'Slabbert was essentially an academic who remained an academic throughout his political career,' one commentator observed.[21] But he was hardly a naive dreamer with his head in the clouds. He had a solid understanding of what was required of him and a healthy disrespect for academics who became so obsessed with their own ideas that the outside world passed them by. He was especially disdainful of academics who became 'intellectual junkies of the "change industry", mouthing the shibboleths which guaranteed acceptance in academic circles where moral outbidding substituted for analysis'. In line with this, he also warned in no uncertain terms against academics who overreached themselves: 'There is no greater danger to a society than an academic who regards himself as a political expert, and whose confidence in his analytical framework outstrips his ability to come to terms with the socio-economic realities in which he lives.'[22]

During the first parliamentary session, Slabbert homed in on the issue of informal settlements and the government's policy of influx control, which placed restrictions on the movement of black people by means of pass laws and regulations applicable to urban settlements. The legislative maze that structured influx control was embedded in the idea of black homelands, established along ethnic lines and supposed to accommodate the black population on a permanent basis. By and large, black people in the cities were only regarded as temporary sojourners in the predominantly white urban areas. Slabbert labelled this as 'an act of political administration which stands without precedent in the modern world'. The practical situation of urban black people received little or no attention. Pointedly, he focused on the contradiction: 'Constitutionally they may be regarded as not being there at all, but it is a simple matter of fact that they are there and will be there forever.'[23]

In order to gain first-hand experience, Slabbert and Alex Boraine paid a visit to the Crossroads informal settlement close to Cape Town. There they came across a hard-working black man who was at his wits' end. He had to cope with a large family and an incapacitated wife, and to add to his woes the authorities threatened to send his family, who were unable to fend for themselves, back to the

Transkei. While visiting the man, Slabbert was arrested for being in the area without a permit. When he refused to comply, he was issued a summons. He appeared in court and was found guilty, but was let off with a caution and discharged. Slabbert subsequently tried in vain to contact the relevant minister, which strongly brought home the general bureaucratic indifference to the plight of desperate people. 'The appalling ignorance and indifference displayed in Parliament on the whole issue of squatting incensed me,' he later recalled. But he also learned 'that my sense of individual outrage was of absolutely no consequence in politics. I had to control my anger and probe for the weak spots and perhaps, if lucky, I could make some contribution in solving a problem.'[24]

It is noticeable that a fair number of Slabbert's interventions had to do with the way in which apartheid legislation directly impacted on ordinary people. Besides influx control, the Population Registration Act of 1950, which legally classified people along racial lines, was another flashpoint. On more than one occasion he was approached by so-called mixed-race couples and families whose lives had been deeply and direly affected by the Act. He regularly interceded with the relevant authorities to have classifications overturned, occasionally with more success than was the case with the migrants at Crossroads. Often it depended on the judgement of the deputy minister entrusted with making such decisions; apart from his personal outlook, the deputy minister also had to take into account the potential political fallout of his actions. Slabbert found, though, that if he could establish an amicable relationship with the deputy minister, it sometimes helped to smooth the way.[25]

He also sought to contribute to areas in which he had some experience. As a former sportsperson, he thought that a critique of the government's sports policy could be meaningful and constructive. During the 1970s the international anti-apartheid sporting boycott was rapidly gaining momentum. In an effort to stave off potentially threatening developments, the government devised a complicated formula, distinguishing between different sports, competition levels and sporting bodies before exceptions to the overarching apartheid rules and arrangements could be allowed.[26] The policy, Slabbert observed, 'had so many legs that it sounds like a centipede out of step with itself'.[27] He proposed a much simpler system, comprising selection on merit at national level, sufficient sporting facilities for black people and allowing sports clubs to be autonomous without interference from politicians. The government subsequently adapted the sports policy in piecemeal fashion, not necessarily because of critiques from the likes of Slabbert but, more pressingly, because of the country's increasing sporting isolation during the 1980s.

As a bright novice in the opposition ranks, he could not have been surprised when seasoned National Party veterans subjected him to a baptism of fire. PW Botha in particular was in attack mode and regarded the Progs as a negative influence to be marginalised. He set his sights on certain Prog MPs, and warned Slabbert to be careful, as he was also after his blood. Slabbert was unshaken, and retorted that Botha 'had a political bloodlust that will make even Count Dracula look like bushveld mosquito that has lost its way'.[28] Although he generally tried to steer away from personal insults, he was not above occasionally dipping into his arsenal when exasperated. Thus, after listening to a rambling diatribe by a National Party MP against black people moving from the eastern Cape to the western Cape, Slabbert could no longer contain himself. He sniped at the speaker, telling him that if his brain were to be filled with dynamite and detonated, the blast would not be strong enough even to lift his glasses from his nose.[29] For this remark he had to apologise.

Another favourite tactic from the government benches – somewhat disingenuous but repeated often – was the accusation that he and the opposition were unpatriotic towards South Africa. Slabbert saw this for what it was, namely, that there was 'no greater sign of political bankruptcy in a power group than when it tries to smother criticism or opposition to its policy under the pseudo-banner of a patriotic debate'. He made it clear that he was not 'going to take any notice of pious moral lessons on patriotism from the other side of the House who sanctimoniously make as if all the troubles in this country are the other people's responsibilities and other people's fault, but never their own'. For him the 'first test of patriotism is that one places the interests of one's country and its peoples above those of party-political gain, personal gain or even personal bloodlust'.[30]

In evaluating Slabbert's first term in Parliament, it is interesting to note the opinion of John Vorster. The prime minister, who refused to greet Slabbert in the parliamentary hallways, was sceptical about his performance.[31] He thought that the press inflated Slabbert's image and that it was premature to tout him as a future prime minister. Vorster also claimed that as Slabbert was a backbencher in a small party, he had limited time to debate issues and his wider ambitions would be steadily stifled.[32] To be sure, Slabbert did at times find parliamentary life unrewarding. In 1977 he wrote to a friend that he was not looking forward to returning to Parliament to 'stir the fetid old pot'.[33]

Yet he worked exceptionally hard in Parliament. The limited number of Prog members meant that each one had to cover several bases. 'We were all very busy,' Alex Boraine recalled, 'and preferred it that way.'[34] An assessment of their workload during the 1974 session shows that the seven MPs made an average of 34 speeches and asked 72 questions.[35] Slabbert was the Progressive spokesperson on several portfolios: defence, social welfare and pensions, community development, sport, agriculture, water affairs, forestry and national education. The party's limited number of representatives meant that they were not allocated much parliamentary time, but Slabbert certainly had more than enough issues to keep him occupied, besides his role within the party as such. Despite Vorster's disdain for Slabbert as a fellow parliamentarian, the overriding impression is that, as far as his first session was concerned, Slabbert emerged with credit. Nor did he find the experience so distasteful that he had reservations about the career path he had chosen. Later on, he would develop misgivings about Parliament. In this respect, Vorster was correct in his assessment, though Slabbert's disillusionment was not necessarily the result of stunted ambitions.

It is also worth assessing Slabbert's parliamentary endeavours in a wider context, beyond the nuts and bolts of Parliament. Slightly more intangible but ultimately of greater importance is the way in which Slabbert, along with some his colleagues, introduced a new tenor of discussion in the House. One of the characteristics of Parliament before 1974 was the ideological divide between an elitist, predominantly English, liberal opposition, disdainful of Afrikaner susceptibilities, and the ruling National Party, with its large Afrikaner and mainly conservative following. Slabbert introduced the possibility of reshaping the debate, foregrounding the need to fundamentally rethink South Africa's future political prospects in an effort to resolve potential conflict between black and white and alleviate oppressive social conditions.

This was in contrast to the dated and sterile clashes between white opponents held hostage by thought patterns with diminishing relevance. During his first session in Parliament he made it clear that 'we are burdened to a large extent here with traditional differences in our politics … We cannot afford this artificial political division where people are squabbling among themselves instead of discussing the real questions of South Africa, across the floor of this House.'[36] Some commentators have argued that 'Slabbert broke the conceptual logjam in white party politics. Indeed … one of Slabbert's greatest (and probably undervalued) contributions to South African political history is that he subliminally changed the terms in which members of the ruling party thought about the country's politics.'[37] Others would go even further and claim that, in the long run, Slabbert 'more than any other person deserves credit for destroying the faith the NP (National Party) leaders in Parliament had in the credibility and morality of the apartheid policy'.[38] These assertions need to be placed in perspective, without necessarily detracting from the catalysing role played by Slabbert. Especially after 1976, for example, increasing internal black hostility and mounting foreign pressure, which concentrated the minds of the rulers, should be factored in. But it was indeed Slabbert, almost from within the fold of Afrikanerdom, who added a different kind of yeast to the parliamentary brew.

Soon after Slabbert's induction into Parliament, a major political realignment took place among the opposition parties. The once-powerful United Party under Sir De Villiers Graaff started to buckle under the weight of its own contradictions. Graaff's political schooling had taken place in a South Africa where issues such as republicanism and English-Afrikaner relationships were paramount; these were now supplanted by what appeared to be even more intractable black-white questions. He valiantly struggled to keep the disparate factions in his party together. At the same time, the party had an increasingly jaded image. 'Its style,' as Slabbert pointed out, 'was geared towards the blandness of agricultural shows in the *platteland* and charitable fêtes and cake sales in the "proper" urban suburbs.'[39]

At the heart of the matter was the fact that the United Party had no coherent policy regarding black people. This caused considerable friction within its ranks, and attempts to remedy the situation proved futile. The party saw several breakaways before it disintegrated completely. Harry Schwarz, a firebrand on the left of the party, hived off with some other Young Turks to form the Reform Party, which joined the Progressives in 1975. Desperate attempts to resuscitate the ailing United Party included the adoption of a different name, the New Republic Party, in June 1977. It was, however, dealt a final blow when the seasoned Japie Basson's more liberal faction also decided to join the Progressive Party, which then changed its name to the Progressive Federal Party (PFP).

Slabbert did not play a key role in the actual negotiations. However, as a general facilitator and a relative newcomer without any of the scars of earlier bruising battles in opposition ranks, his contribution was considerable in helping to resolve antagonisms. Eglin employed him in this capacity because of his communication skills, but more importantly because he felt that Slabbert was cut from the same ideological cloth as earlier Progressives such as Helen Suzman, which ensured that the party's message would not be diluted.[40]

With these developments, the PFP could explore fresh opportunities. Slabbert, though, was adamant that they should be united behind a common goal and that the amalgamation should not merely be a convenient political arrangement. He explained:

> For me, the important thing is that what is this opposition about? It's not just a question of getting together all opposition parties. What is the thrust you hope to develop? ... We need to draw as much support from the electorate, demonstrating quite clearly that there are Whites in South Africa who are prepared to negotiate coexistence on all levels, and to take into consideration all the implications. If we can't get consensus on this, then the concept of a broad-based Opposition becomes meaningless.[41]

This was a strong call at an appropriate time. White South Africa had just been shocked by the ferocity and extent of the black youth uprising in Soweto in June 1976, which spread to other parts of the country. The overall political landscape would never be quite the same again. Sections of the white electorate came to realise that the government's policy no longer provided unconditional safeguards. This prompted a need to rethink the nature of white politics, and the PFP as a refashioned political entity was geared towards that goal.

The 1977 general election saw the PFP return to Parliament with 17 members, an increase of ten. This shift was also evident in Slabbert's own Rondebosch constituency, where his majority increased from 1 568 votes in 1974 to 3 873 in 1977.[42] He had made his mark as a solid and formidable political player. No wonder he was dubbed the 'Mohammed Ali of the PFP'.[43]

While Slabbert had made a distinct impression as a promising parliamentarian, he was at the same time given cause to reflect on the nature of opposition politics. More than ever the realisation dawned on him that 'you needed iron in the soul not to lose faith in what you believed or lose sight of your objectives'. What was required was 'to keep plugging away patiently without the prospects of immediate reward and always be prepared for failure and disappointment'. One had to hope that eventually 'the cracks will show and when they do it is better to search for more light than to perpetuate the darkness'.[44] In the process, it was also necessary to construct a workable political model equipped to deal with the demands of a diverse society.

Visionary thinking

Early on in his career, Slabbert realised that it was all well and good to puncture government policy but it was decidedly more difficult to construct alternative frameworks. His main concern was the creation of an overarching equitable system. As a social strategist who preferred to operate on a meta level, as opposed to dealing with routine matters pertaining to technical bargaining, he was one for imagining 'new social landscapes'.[45] Thinking in systemic sociological terms, the possibility of a new political imaginary with different structures held a certain appeal for him. He was, however, not blind to the realities. 'It is the natural inclination of the academic,' he explained, 'to qualify, reformulate and complicate choices ... and this is right and proper. But this is a luxury denied the politician. To the extent that a liberal wishes to be a politician, he or she is going to have to make an overt political choice.'[46] These choices were increasingly pared down during Slabbert's parliamentary career. It was, however, precisely such an eventuality that Slabbert thought the PFP should try to avert.

Slabbert found the level of discourse in Parliament disappointing.

Political parties were first and foremost intent on protecting their turf, and in this way 'nonsense, hyperbole and good old-fashioned bullshit become an essential part of the ritual of Parliament'.[47] This shortcoming underscored the need, he thought, for more constructive engagement. What was required was to move away from sterile debates towards potentially more fruitful discussions about future constitutional processes.

Right from the start of his parliamentary career he made it clear that the central issue in South African politics was that of power-sharing.[48] He had the ear of people like Colin Eglin, who appointed him to head the party's constitutional commission in order to formulate a new policy. Slabbert's brief was to incorporate 'old principles' but at the same time to take 'new social, economic and political developments into account'.[49] He relished the opportunity and found it an invigorating time, as he could draw on all of his academic expertise as well as that of former university colleagues and acquaintances. Moreover, a three-month fellowship at Rhodes University allowed him time to work uninterruptedly, away from the daily grind of practical politics.[50]

The commission's report was ready in October 1978, and represented a bold departure from existing South African arrangements. It suggested that a new constitution should be the product of a process of negotiation involving all the relevant role-players. This could take any length of time and was ideally envisaged as a consensus-driven process. The main features of a proposed new constitution were the preference for a federal state, with a universal franchise, a Bill of Rights, entrenched individual rights and proportional representation, the sharing of executive power between majority and minority parties, a minority veto and a constitutional court as the final arbiter in disputes.[51]

All of these dimensions could be debated, but the question of a minority veto in particular was potentially contentious. Slabbert explained the dynamics of this by arguing that the threat of veto and deadlock would usually act as a spur to promote further negotiation and compromise. If one group tried to block legislation permanently, it would run counter to the entrenched Bill of Rights and the issue could then be resolved on another level.[52]

Later on, and especially during the turbulent 1980s when political fault lines hardened considerably, Slabbert backtracked on the idea of a minority veto and power-sharing in the cabinet. Another issue, and a long-standing pillar of Prog policy, was that of the qualified franchise, a legacy of nineteenth-century Cape liberalism that set certain educational and financial criteria before the franchise could be obtained. Slabbert had long been uncomfortable with this arrangement because of its inherently discriminatory nature, and because the conditions to propel people, and particularly black people, to obtain the vote were anything but propitious.[53] Although in political terms the qualified franchise was meant to reassure white voters that they would not be swamped, it was impossible to justify in a wider context.[54] The time had come to dump the qualified franchise as an antiquated notion. Indeed, it is surprising that it took so long to be jettisoned. The Liberal Party, which had disbanded in 1968, had embraced the universal franchise as early as 1960.[55]

The completed report was presented to Eglin, who expressed his satisfaction. The next step was for him and Slabbert to embark on a campaign to promote the adoption of the report as party policy. Slabbert regarded this as the 'real cutting edge of the difference between academic and political life'. He was fully aware that 'a set of constitutional proposals can charm you intellectually by the manner in which they are consistent with their initial assumptions'. In this respect he found 'our set of proposals charming'. However, the real test resided 'in the art of politics to … convert constitutional assumptions into political trends'.[56]

With this in mind, Slabbert and Eglin toured the major cities and towns to put the proposals before party members and invited audiences. The plan was then presented for ratification before the national federal congress in Durban. Two issues in particular drew fire. The one was the question of who should participate in negotiations and whether political prisoners and exiles should be included. After a heated debate, it was decided that these groupings should be included, provided they abjured violence at the time of the convention. The other issue revolved around a minority veto, which Slabbert, as noted above, qualified to such an extent that it appeared as a workable mechanism. He must have felt some satisfaction when the national congress adopted the proposals.[57]

Newspaper reports on the proposals varied predictably, with the white English-language press generally hailing the scheme as an important intervention and the Afrikaans press attacking it as dangerously deluded. PW Botha, who had replaced Vorster as prime minister in September 1978, rejected the idea of a national convention outright, arguing that South Africa had already had a national convention (in 1908–1910) and was a sovereign country in its own right, with Parliament the only body that had the power and authority to decide on future constitutional developments. If Parliament's supremacy were to be eroded, it could only lead to instability.[58] Slabbert had also identified Parliament as a major player, but for a different set of reasons, namely, that Parliament was the actual cause of disaffection, as it fully controlled the limited life chances of black people.[59]

In the black press the proposals were criticised for pandering too much to white interests.[60] Slabbert found discussions on the proposals with black opinion-makers awkward. In a private seminar, he was somewhat taken aback that some black politicians could blithely reject the proposals as racist without actually having seriously studied them or teased out the possibilities. He was, however, not blind to the dynamics at work. To these black people, he explained, 'we represented the "mink and manure" liberals who were either trying to "have our cake and eat it" or had to demonstrate our integrity by capitulating our intellects and morals to indulge their sense of political deprivation or our own presumed sense of racial guilt'.[61] Such a forthright dissection is revealing. Slabbert, despite his liberal outlook, was clearly not taken in by identity politics and facile comments, regardless of who paraded them. Although he was sympathetic to the plight of frustrated black politicians, he was also not prepared to allow them to play manipulative games. He was equally wary of sanctimonious moral one-upmanship masquerading as politics.

Besides Slabbert's political work on constitutional issues, in the back of his mind he also thought about the possibility of keeping an academic career alive. Realising that he did not have enough academic publications, he spoke to David Welsh of the politics department at UCT, who invited him to co-author a book about South Africa's future political prospects.[62] The book appeared in 1979, shortly after Slabbert had finished his work on the party's policy, under the title *South Africa's Options: Strategies for Sharing Power*. It was a detailed analysis of constitutional possibilities, informed by a critical discussion of comparative examples. The emphasis was on the basic realities that whites, as a result of a shrinking demographic base, growing black opposition and foreign pressure, were rapidly facing diminishing options. The choice lay between a drift towards a siege-type military dictatorship and a realisation that all-party negotiations were required to hammer out a new constitution along liberal-democratic lines.

The book was subjected to considerable scrutiny. Slabbert's chapters were criticised for insufficient theory, despite the fact that he was otherwise recognised as a sophisticated intellectual thinker.[63] His main aim, however, was to write as a practising politician and not to foreground the theoretical scaffolding. Another line of criticism was that the authors were too narrowly focused on white elite leadership and not enough on how the politics of the masses, as well as economic considerations, could influence developments.[64]

Among other sceptics, doubts remained. Ultimately, no copper-bottomed guarantees could be provided for whites. Moreover, given the general pitfalls of multiracial democracies elsewhere based on universal franchise, much would be at stake during the process of negotiation.[65] In addition, it was argued that, in their urgency to resolve the South African impasse, Slabbert and Welsh had placed too much emphasis on a liberal-democratic model as a panacea, without taking into account the necessary preconditions for such a model to function effectively. Drawing upon comparative examples, such preconditions would include large-scale industrialisation across the country, a plethora of sophisticated voluntary organisations, social affinities despite divisions, high levels of literacy, relative parity of income and a general sense of national identity as a people. Without these elements in place, an equitable system of democracy, though not impossible, would be much more difficult to attain. In this respect, academic critics cautioned: 'A liberal democracy does not depend on good intentions but on social complexity and socio-economic developments in society.'[66]

To be fair, the final two chapters of *Options* consider other possible frameworks and note some concerns.[67] Later on, in 1988, Slabbert also voiced his reservations about liberal constitutional arrangements. It did not serve much purpose, he pointed out, 'to transplant some European constitution onto the South African situation and argue away the empirical contradictions with questionable "if only" clauses'. He emphasised that 'constitutional preferences have to be related to real political forces and only then can one begin to anticipate the elements of a likely or probable democratic constitution for South Africa'.[68]

Regardless of the debates about the ideal type of constitution for a country as diverse as South Africa, these were important interventions in terms of Slabbert's political trajectory. As far as white parliamentary history is concerned, his work represented the first coherent attempt since Union in 1910 to alter fundamentally existing constitutional arrangements pertaining to the country as a whole. It went far beyond the changes that the National Party had effected with the homeland system. What is more, although it is all but forgotten today, the proposals, which in the 1980s gradually morphed into the PFP policy of power-sharing, resembled parts of the post-apartheid constitution that took shape during the early 1990s. A colleague, Robin Carlisle, later highlighted this as Slabbert's key contribution to politics.[69] Early on, then, his political acumen pierced the mist of future South African developments. As far as details are concerned, it also outstripped the exiled ANC's constitutional planning, which at this stage remained largely mired in the rhetoric of the Freedom Charter.[70]

Slabbert's prominent role in the formulation and promotion of the constitutional proposals, as well as his skill in getting various sections of the party to accept them, raised his profile considerably. The white English-language press made much of his performance, and his exposure to party officials across the country elevated him from an ordinary backbencher to a policy-maker in the rough and tumble of opposition politics. Despite all of this, Slabbert still had misgivings about the prospects of a political career. He had not yet played his full hand, though his hand was to be forced perhaps sooner than he had anticipated.

Becoming leader of the opposition

Slabbert's pre-parliamentary career had seen him take on a number of leadership positions, from head boy at school and *primarius* at Wilgenhof residence to chair of the sociology department at Wits. It was almost a given that once in Parliament he would also be elected to party leadership positions. Yet this was not immediately the case. Although approached to take on the positions of Cape provincial leader of the party, chair of the federal executive and national chair, he turned all these overtures down.[71]

The reason for such reticence was that Slabbert was not very hierarchically minded and did not wish to be forced into a situation in which he had to carry all the burdens of leadership and be slotted into a specific, designated role. Endless committee meetings and routine organisational aspects of the party held little appeal, though he realised the importance of administrative efficiency. For him it was a personal preference to play an active role in politics per se, as opposed to being distracted by the need to oil the party machinery. He saw the party primarily as a way into politics rather than an entity that was entitled to call unreservedly upon his devout membership.[72] This kind of pragmatism made him wary of assuming a leadership position until he was convinced it could be made to dovetail with his political goals.

Slabbert's separation of these roles could easily lay him open to charges of selfishness. But, then again, he was aware of his own strengths and shortcomings and how he could best contribute to the party's aims. His reluctance to become involved in official party structures should not necessarily be read as disdain for party proceedings. Alex Boraine remarked that he excelled in party caucus debates: '[H]e was in his element, and although many good contributions were made by other members, it was almost as if we were waiting for him to give the final word and direction – and he never disappointed his colleagues. His style was fairly laid-back and relaxed, but on occasion he could be very tough, and he never suffered fools gladly.'[73]

Although the PFP had emerged from the 1977 election in fine fettle, it experienced some growing pains, partly as a result of the merger with various sections of the now-defunct United Party. The situation called for adroit leadership, which Eglin, as a participant in bruising internecine battles with former members of the United Party in the past, did not always provide. Slabbert picked up on undercurrents in the party, even from old Progs who had always supported Eglin, but he did not think that the dissatisfaction with Eglin would last long.[74] The tensions did not die down, and Slabbert came under increasing pressure to make himself available as a leader. In terms of public relations, Slabbert outshone Eglin: he was the young, charismatic and eloquent newcomer, as opposed to the older, phlegmatic and at times gruff Eglin, of whom it was said that he had the 'bedside manner of an angry crocodile'.[75] The two men, though quite different in demeanour, had considerable respect for one another. Slabbert was not prepared to oppose Eglin.

At the time, he was in fact giving serious attention to leaving Parliament by allowing his name to be put forward as a possible candidate for the vacant vice chancellorship at the University of Cape Town. His chances of success were less than 50 per cent, but it is clear that at this stage he was still keeping his career options open. The result of the nomination, though, was that party members who preferred the prospect of Slabbert as leader rallied to keep him in politics and promote his position.[76] Of course, it is possible that Slabbert could have used the UCT principalship to exert leverage within the party, but there is no evidence for this. What did happen was that the campaign to make him leader gained momentum, and increasingly Slabbert could no longer shy away from full commitment.

Matters came to a head when Eglin mishandled a controversial issue in Parliament. He was accused (wrongly) by the Nationalists, and especially by a theatrical Pik Botha, the minister of foreign affairs, of conveying sensitive information to Donald McHenry, the United States ambassador to the United Nations. Eglin was pilloried as being unpatriotic, and was generally vilified in Parliament. The matter was a red herring to draw attention away from the looming Information Scandal, which involved massive irregular and unauthorised state spending to promote South Africa's image abroad. Instead of the PFP's capitalising on the government's discomfort, the opposite happened, and Eglin's inept attempt to explain his contact with McHenry allowed the National Party to take the initiative. Eglin's bumbling defence counted heavily against him as a leader. The event also negatively influenced the PFP's showing in two by-elections. It seemed as if the writing was on the wall for Eglin. At a federal executive meeting on 27 July 1979 he lost a vote of confidence by 25 votes to 19. This left the door open for Slabbert, but considerable backroom manoeuvring took place before he was elected unanimously as leader on 3 September 1979.[77] He was the youngest official leader of the opposition in the history of the South African Parliament.

Slabbert claimed that he accepted the position with reluctance.[78] This may well have been the case, as he was not yet fully convinced of politics as a career, as indicated by his interest in the UCT position. The leadership of the party, however, offered the opportunity to play a more meaningful role from the front. He was used to taking the lead, and it was a challenge he could not resist, though he was aware that it would be a daunting task. The first sentence of his acceptance speech, delivered in Afrikaans, solemnly intoned: 'I hope that I shall have the strength to do this work properly and I hope that I shall not disappoint you.'[79]

The relationship between Slabbert and Eglin, despite some initial strain, soon got back on track to one, as Slabbert described it, 'of bluntness devoid of pettiness'.[80] Before Slabbert's nomination, they had met at Eglin's house to thrash matters out. Joyce, Eglin's wife, had reservations about entertaining Slabbert but later changed her mind. She played the role of the good hostess and then left the two men to talk. The following morning she commented to her husband: 'Judging by the number of empty wine bottles in the kitchen, you and Van Zyl must have had quite a session last night.'[81]

There was some newspaper speculation as to whether Slabbert, coming from an academic background, would be resilient enough as leader to 'take the spit and sawdust' of the political ring. Those close to him had no doubt that he would give a good account of himself. He knew power, they said, and how it was deployed. It would be a mistake to judge him by his usual cordial and affable behaviour.[82] A political journalist who had watched Slabbert closely in Parliament was more than impressed: 'He could get into the rough and tumble of party politicking as only the best could. The awesome sight of an overwhelming Nationalist majority in Parliament seemed to inspire rather than frighten him.'[83] The veteran Prog MP Helen Suzman had another concern – whether he had enough staying power.[84] At this point it was a question that only the future could answer, and the answer would not be easy. Slabbert now had to steel himself for formidable challenges. As the newly elected leader of the opposition, he was about to enter one of the most turbulent decades in South African history.

4
TAKING THE LEAD

Initial issues and impact

In his acceptance speech as leader, Slabbert made clear the differences between the PFP and the government. He raised four issues that could serve as a litmus test for judging the intent and relevance of the government's evolving constitutional policy, aimed at arriving at a new, more equitable dispensation: whether it would be only white people who would be allowed to decide on a future political dispensation; whether black people would be regarded as full citizens of South Africa; whether the law would be used to force people to belong to specific racial groups; and whether detention without trial was necessary for the maintenance of law and order.[1]

The speech was welcomed by the English-language press, which regarded it as a succinct analysis of the basic constitutional questions facing South Africa.[2] Although the Afrikaans press did not respond directly to the issues Slabbert raised, his leadership as a talented politician was nevertheless welcomed. His task would be, it was suggested, to prompt the government to do 'the right thing at the right moment' and to oppose revolutionary tendencies outside Parliament.[3] There was also a sense that Slabbert, who was regarded as a fellow Afrikaner, could be expected to make a positive contribution to South African politics because, as opposed to his predecessors in the PFP, he 'carried a true instinctive Afrikaner feeling as far as our race predicament is concerned'.[4] Though Slabbert would have welcomed the goodwill, he would not have shared the assumption of a common and innate Afrikaner understanding of racial issues.

Slabbert found the initial period of leadership a lonely experience, but the demands of the new position and the quickening and exacting tempo of his daily life did not leave much room for self-reflection and he settled down soon enough.[5] He had assumed the position of leader of the opposition after only five years in Parliament. Not yet being fully moulded or weighed down by years of service, he was, as a colleague observed, quick to impose his own style on the PFP. The frills of leadership did not appeal to him, nor was he given to flattery or overgenerous praise of others – he expected them to do what they did as par for the course – and he shied away from fawning supporters. For many it was 'leadership with a difference'.[6]

He excelled not only as a thinker but also as someone who was keen to implement plans. Yet for all this, there was also a downside. He could occasionally be dismissive of colleagues, and his dominance was such that some talented members drifted away. Moreover, outside of elections, he had a limited interest in the nuts and bolts of party organisation, which meant that the party's electoral machinery deteriorated over time.[7]

Slabbert did not have much of a respite from the usual undercurrents prevalent in any political party. In his case it involved smoothing the ruffled feathers of individuals such as Harry Schwarz, who was on the conservative wing of the PFP. More seriously, he also had to act against the seasoned veteran Japie Basson, a man of considerable standing in Parliament. Against the wishes of the PFP caucus that the party should not be associated with the government's projected President's Council – an advisory body consisting of government-nominated white, coloured and Indian members – Basson had declared himself willing to serve on the council. This was Slabbert's first real test as far as party discipline was concerned. Although he did not relish the idea of acting against a politician as respected as Basson, he felt he had no alternative, as Basson's statement openly contradicted party policy. Slabbert duly suspended him from caucus, and Basson, who had changed party allegiances before, now joined the National Party. To Slabbert's chagrin, Basson then proceeded to tag the PFP as a 'boycott party', always ready to sabotage government initiatives. It was an appellation that stuck, and Slabbert thought that it tarnished the PFP's image among the electorate.[8]

As a newly elected leader, though, he set off on a comprehensive 'meet the people' campaign, explaining PFP policy and acquainting himself with regional party officials. Over the course of a three-week tour, he held more than 20 well-attended public meetings. Slabbert's speeches, it was reported from the eastern Cape, 'were unerringly on target and on the right level, with a rich mixture of humour and sympathy'.[9]

While Slabbert was well received, it remained to be seen whether generally the new leader would have a meaningful impact at the polling booth. The first test came early. Four by-elections took place before the end of 1979, in Edenvale, Eshowe, Durbanville and Worcester. The last three were not really within the reach of the PFP to win and were more cases of showing the flag. The Nationalists won these comfortably, albeit with reduced majorities.

Edenvale was different. Here the PFP triumphed handsomely over the National Party and the New Republic Party to win by a margin of 1 162 votes. Significantly, it was the National Party's first by-election loss since 1948. Change seemed to be in the air. The Edenvale result cemented Slabbert's position as leader, boosted party morale and helped to project him as a thoughtful politician with an honest intent to address key South African issues.[10] 'I pulled no punches about our policy and Edenvale showed we can take seats away from the National Party,' Slabbert commented.[11] Although he emerged as the star of the show, due credit should also be given to the PFP's electoral machine, which at this point was firing on all cylinders. Slabbert benefited much from the work of Neil Ross, the party's election organiser, also known as 'Ross the Boss', for his meticulous planning and attention to detail in implementing campaign strategy. Slabbert paid him the compliment of being the best political organiser in South Africa.[12]

Slabbert's next challenge was his response as leader of the opposition in the no-confidence debate of 1980 – traditionally an acid test for a new leader of the opposition. He gave the speech on 4 February 1980 and began by addressing PW Botha directly, acknowledging the latter's long parliamentary experience and his heavy burden as prime minister. Slabbert then embroidered on a number of issues, focusing especially on the government's reluctance to start negotiations for a new constitution that would include all South Africans, its tardiness in abolishing discriminatory apartheid measures, and its inadequate planning for projected population growth.[13] Although those on the opposition benches must have experienced many false dawns down the years, for once it appeared that there was a new and invigorating presence, as yet uncontaminated by successive failures. The English-language press, as was by now the norm, reported favourably and at times even fulsomely. The Afrikaans press was predictably more circumspect but thought he had passed the test, as he did not talk down to Afrikaners and preferred to analyse politics rationally.[14]

In 1981 Slabbert faced his stiffest test as Botha called an early general election. Ideally, he might have wanted more time to establish himself firmly as opposition leader, but it was not to be. Slabbert believed that Botha's decision stemmed from an awareness that the emerging right-wing threat to the National Party needed to be nipped in the bud, and that economic conditions were such that although the government could still afford salary increases for civil servants, rapidly rising expenditure – not least on defence – would cast a shadow over the longer term.[15]

The PFP chose to concentrate on three areas during the election: the government's administrative incompetence to plan outside apartheid structures; the rising inflation rate; and the lack of constitutional planning for the country as a whole.[16] A key constitutional issue, which Slabbert repeatedly raised, was that as long as stringent racial classifications – as decreed by an all-white Parliament – prevailed and determined politics, meaningful constitutional deliberations would be stymied. The government constantly tried to formulate solutions for people, he explained, claiming to provide security, but 'the only way a constitution can guarantee security is if it reflects the wishes of people who actually participated and committed themselves to the framing of it'.[17] 'Real security,' he commented cryptically, 'does not lie only in the range of your guns but in the unity of all our people.'[18] Such unity was, however, only a distant chimera, and the PFP realised the importance of emphasising more immediate material concerns that impinged on voters. To a greater extent than before, 'bread and butter' issues featured in the party's campaign as the PFP sought to demonstrate that under the National Party the country had become steadily poorer. The party's national research director, Nic Olivier (who had moved from the United Party to the PFP), later claimed that the emphasis on financial matters had benefited the campaign.[19]

Although Slabbert was unopposed in his Rondebosch constituency, it only meant that he was freed up to work tirelessly on the campaign trail. Apart from regular television appearances, where his photogenic qualities regularly trumped those of the belligerent and ageing Botha, Slabbert travelled more than 28 000 kilometres and addressed 69 public meetings, often addressing more voters than Botha had attracted at the same venues.[20] It was a gruelling campaign that took its toll. 'On a personal level,' Slabbert recalled, 'I worked until fatigue was a sore in the pit of my stomach.'[21] He regularly addressed three or four meetings a day, and only occasionally allowed himself the luxury of relaxing with a glass of wine and some good music in the homes of close friends. Clearly, in terms of work ethic and commitment to the cause, Slabbert could hardly be faulted.

The 1981 election was a high-risk exercise for the PFP. They had rejected the President's Council as an inadequate negotiating tool, as it excluded black people.[22] If the voting public had reservations about this step, it could easily have backfired. The results, though, seem to have vindicated the gamble. The PFP made the most substantial gains of all parties and pushed its representation up from 17 to 26 seats, including six seats won from the ruling party. The party also achieved a morale-boosting victory over a National Party cabinet minister – Dawie de Villiers in Gardens, the first cabinet minister to be defeated since 1948.[23] Overall the results reflected, in some respects, a change in the political landscape.

Slabbert was pleased with the outcome. 'Whatever the reasons people voted for the PFP in 1981,' he said, '(and these may be numerous, fickle and even unrelated to those I [had] hoped for) I felt satisfied that I had not pulled any punches or misled them about the difficulties that ... lay ahead.'[24] While Slabbert's assessment was sober and modest, the English-language press was much more lavish in its praise. He was invariably described as a man of 'great ability, conspicuous integrity and sound political judgement', with the potential to assert nationwide influence in the near future.[25] The Afrikaans press cautioned against seeing Slabbert as a 'Moses who would be leading his people to the promised land'.[26] Slabbert, who was well aware of the pitfalls of an emergent personality cult, for once might have agreed with an otherwise antagonistic press.

We should guard against an overly robust interpretation of the fact that, as a result of the 'Slabbert factor', the PFP had made substantial inroads into the Afrikaner vote. An effusive English-language press might have liked to imply as much, but the reality was rather more complicated. Much of the gains made by the PFP had to do with the implosion of the New Republic Party (the reincarnation of what was left of the old United Party), whose members defected mainly to the PFP and to a lesser extent the National Party.[27] The PFP, it has been claimed, never attracted more than five per cent of Afrikaners.[28] This helps to put Slabbert's position into perspective, and calls into question the notion that he, as an Afrikaner, would necessarily attract other Afrikaners. What was more likely was that Afrikaners may well have attended PFP meetings in greater numbers than before, but stopped short of actually voting for the PFP. They preferred to stay within the fold of the National Party, advocating change from within.[29] Many Afrikaners also remained sceptical of the PFP's constitutional proposals, which had a series of built-in checks and balances to prevent unfettered majority rule. These were regarded as fig leaves to cover up ultimate and untrammelled black rule.[30]

On a personal level, Slabbert had a most unnerving experience when his study caught fire the night after the election results were announced. His children, Tania and Riko, had slept in the study the previous night; fortunately they were back in their own bedrooms when the fire broke out. The flames were so intense that his whole library was destroyed. Despite strong suspicion of arson, police investigations failed to track down anyone responsible. Slabbert suspected that the PFP's improved showing in the election accounted for the attack. He had also received threatening phone calls and had his car tyres slashed. Moreover, he had to deal with rumours circulating in the parliamentary corridors that the security police suspected Riko of starting the fire.[31] His library was restocked, and although he was grateful for the generous public response, he regretted the loss of the many irreplaceable items and his own notes.

In the political arena, there were new forces at work after 1981. In the wake of the government's reform moves in the field of labour relations, following the Wiehahn Report, and promises of cautious constitutional changes, the National Party split in 1982, with the right wing hiving off to form the Conservative Party, under the leadership of Dr Andries Treurnicht. The new party took with it 25 per cent of the National Party's branch structure in the Transvaal and 16 MPs defected. Slabbert saw in this development the possibility of a new balance of power, with the government increasingly dependent on the PFP for support. This would allow the PFP to move beyond merely being the official opposition and to actually exert some influence on the direction of events and the exercise of state power.[32] At this point it was a feature of Slabbert's political outlook that he was constantly looking for opportunities to promote the party's chances of moving closer to power.[33] His view was that the party could benefit from such a development without sacrificing its basic points of departure. What he had in mind at the time was for the party to be 'tough in principle but flexible in strategy'.[34]

Slabbert's willingness to consider such an option was not favourably received by all concerned. Older Prog MPs in particular, as a result of many bruising encounters with the National Party, had developed a deep aversion to any form of cooperation with the government.[35] Apart from personal predilections, there were different emphases on the nature of the party's underlying liberal ideology. Though he obviously subscribed to general liberal values, Slabbert did not, in political terms, necessarily strategise according to the precepts of the older generation of liberals. Their views were based on the assumption that the franchise – in one form or another – represented the ultimate and simplest solution to the political impasse. Slabbert was uncomfortable with the weight assigned to the franchise, and saw it as just one element, albeit an important one, in a more complex scenario of various checks and balances. He regarded himself as a conflict theorist, in search of a variety of constitutional mechanisms to unlock the South African puzzle and limit the possible abuse of power.[36]

One of these mechanisms, drawn in part from the work of the German academic Theodor Hanf on the nature of divided societies, was consociationalism, or, more simply, agreed power-sharing. Hanf, who had a close academic relationship with Slabbert, argued that such arrangements were essential pre-emptive measures to ward off a situation in which reason only flowed from 'blood-fresh memories', and where people learnt not *from* history but *through* history'.[37] In this sense, Slabbert's approach to politics went beyond the assumption that change simply implies that one set of principles must triumph over another. His position might have shifted later, but in the early 1980s this was an avenue he preferred to explore. He took seriously the fears and apprehensions of many whites regarding change, realising that these constituted a political reality that had to be allowed for in constitutional terms. Nor did he necessarily regard the PFP as an outright liberal party, as was often the case as far as the public was concerned. Although the party had some elements of South African political liberalism, he said, 'the history of the party was too diverse and complicated to depict it as a pure liberal party'.[38] With only mild exaggeration he also summed up the PFP as a 'bohemian party. It was an extraordinary collection of individuals. There were academics, professionals, yuppies …'[39] It was precisely the hybrid nature of the party that allowed for various political models other than exclusively pure liberal ones to be considered. In 1983, however, the government's proposal for a tricameral parliament was to present Slabbert with a huge quandary.

Outflanked? The 1983 referendum

The Botha government had its own programme of reform and the envisaged pace at which it should proceed. Botha firmly believed that racial and ethnic groups should form the basic structures upon which the political and social system should be based, and that these building blocks had to be arranged in such a manner that precluded democratic competition between the different races. Moreover, he was also convinced that orderly change could only emanate from Afrikaner leadership. As Afrikaners had the most to lose by relinquishing control over the state, their trust should be maintained with every step of reform.[40]

The President's Council did much of the groundwork for constitutional change within this format, and in July 1982 its guidelines for change were accepted by the National Party. In May 1983 a Bill was brought before Parliament, and in August it was debated at length, before Botha announced that a referendum for white voters would be held on 2 November 1983. The proposed new constitution was historic in the sense that it represented a break from the Westminster system, with its simple majoritarianism in one chamber. The main characteristics of the proposed tricameral parliament were that there were to be separate chambers for whites, coloureds and Indians, with white representation being greater than the combined total of the other two groups. An executive president was to be elected by the leading parties of all three houses, but, given the numerical preponderance of whites, it was more likely than not that a white president would be elected. Black people were to be left out of the equation, as they were, it was argued, accommodated in the homeland system.[41] Within government circles it was believed that, despite some shortcomings, these developments were a decisive step forward. South Africa had reached a point, it was said, where it should be bold enough to carve out a new future for itself. The pressure from within and outside the country demanded a new but responsible departure.[42]

Slabbert outlined in Parliament that the government proposals failed to meet the PFP's minimum requirements for a realistic constitutional transition. He emphasised that a new constitution had to involve all population groups in the country; everyone should have access to South African citizenship; universal franchise should not be emasculated by exclusionary clauses; and minorities should be protected from domination under a new dispensation. Procedurally, he took umbrage at the speed with which the constitution was bulldozed through Parliament, with only 34 of the 103 clauses actually being debated.[43] While he welcomed the fact that the government had at long last risen to the challenge of dealing with pertinent issues, he feared that they had got off on the wrong foot. 'The bungling,' he said, 'began with the very process of creating the constitution.' In his view, 'irremediable flaws' were built into the constitution and these were compounded by the manner in which the government had chosen to proceed. 'In short,' he continued, the constitution 'was unilaterally drawn up, unilaterally ratified and unilaterally tabled in Parliament.' This led to what he called a 'validity crisis'; the constitution was not invalid technically in terms of the authority of Parliament, but rather because of the process through which people were included and excluded.[44]

Slabbert's reservations about the proposed constitution were given further impetus after a discussion with Henry Kissinger, the former American secretary of state. Over breakfast at State House in Pretoria in 1983, Kissinger told Slabbert that they could either exchange pleasantries or discuss the proposals, with him playing devil's advocate defending the new departure and Slabbert rejecting it. Slabbert found Kissinger 'extraordinarily skilful'. What emerged from Kissinger's defence was not actually the need for reform as such but how a dominant minority can manipulate matters in such a way as to maintain control through co-opting new patronage networks. What Slabbert took from this was the idea of co-optive domination.[45] The new dispensation might be packaged as reform, but in substance it was change with no real reform. What the National Party was doing, some analysts pointed out, was to propose power-sharing without the loss of control.[46] Slabbert himself expressed the gist of it by adapting a classic marketing phrase: 'The government was selling the sizzle and not the steak.'[47]

A crucial issue in the referendum campaign was how the question was framed. When Botha announced the referendum date, he also revealed the formulation of the question: 'Are you in favour of the implementation of the Republic of South Africa Constitution Act as approved by Parliament?' Slabbert was strongly in favour of a question with more options, which would have allowed more information on voter preferences pertaining to possible black participation to emerge and positing less of a closed binary outcome. The question, however, was deliberately narrowed down to place the PFP in a predicament: opposing the new constitution with a 'no' vote would make them appear as boycotters of 'reasonable' change, and moreover would lump them together with the Conservative Party, which also supported a 'no' vote but for a completely different set of reasons. Whereas the PFP thought the proposals were wholly inadequate and therefore merited a 'no' vote, the Conservative Party argued that they were too far-reaching and threatened white domination, and therefore warranted a resounding 'no'. The problem of course was that in the final outcome, though the 'no' votes were politically poles apart, it would not be clear which 'no' vote represented which position. This would be the case despite the fact that the Conservative Party and the PFP had nothing in common; Slabbert doubted whether they even shared the 'same planet'.[48] When Slabbert pointed out the ambiguity, he recalled that Botha 'smiled and licked his lips in that familiar way of his. I could see he knew I was in for a beating. It was the kind of political contest he relished.'[49]

The debate about the formulation of the referendum question had a curious twist. Botha realised that if Slabbert were to succeed in reformulating the question to include black people, it would compromise the government beyond a point it was prepared to entertain. Ters Ehlers, Botha's private secretary, mentioned this during a social meeting with sociologist Dian Joubert, who had been one of Slabbert's mentors at Stellenbosch University. Joubert sent a note to Slabbert, indicating that Ehlers had gone further and was 'dead serious' that there should be a 'deal' between Botha and Slabbert. Botha, despite his public antagonism towards Slabbert, was, according to Ehlers, shrewd enough to realise that 'he [Botha] had no natural successor of quality and that over the long term of seven to ten years you [Slabbert] [are] the only man who could prevent a complete political disintegration. All of this was only dependent upon your [Slabbert's] footwork.'[50] Whether this was indeed the case is difficult to ascertain with any certainty, but such political kite-flying is not unknown in the corridors of power.

Be that as it may, the referendum campaign was one of great intensity. Over a three-month period, the number of newspaper articles that appeared on the topic ran into the thousands.[51] There was some scepticism in PFP ranks about the wisdom of deciding to oppose the proposed constitution in the referendum. Harry Schwarz, among others, thought the matter should have transcended party-political lines and the PFP should not have boxed itself into what could be perceived as a negative position. A 'no' vote from the PFP, ran the argument, would confuse the voters, as the party was in the vanguard of the clamour for change, and now that the opportunity presented itself, its leaders were apparently backing off.[52]

The National Party ran a slick campaign, with plenty of newspaper advertising – far exceeding that of the PFP – and plenty of exposure on television. PFP supporters were urged to align themselves with a positive historical shift. The term 'a step in the right direction' as taken by the government was widely bandied about, and a 'yes' vote was seen as essential to strengthen Botha's hand in this new venture. It was also argued that a 'yes' vote would promote consensus politics, enhance international understanding and decrease foreign pressure on the country. Surprisingly, and to Slabbert's chagrin, a solid phalanx of the English-language press bought into the government's message to a far greater extent than the PFP had anticipated. Their basic reasoning was that although the proposals were flawed, they did at least break the existing logjam, and were indicative of more changes to come in the future.[53] Slabbert had no respect for this argument, as the majority of South Africa's people were excluded and there was no compelling evidence for exactly what the government had in mind to change that.[54]

In contrast, the PFP campaign underlined the necessity for 'real' change involving black politicians. Whether this was the best way to approach wavering white voters is a moot point. The party's pamphlets proclaimed: '70 percent of the population would say "no" if they were allowed to do so. So don't be misled. Say "no" to the Nationalists' plan and make them start again with all the people who should have been consulted in the first place.'[55] Given the nature of the contest, this was somewhat off-key. While such exhortations might have been factually accurate, they were misdirected as far as the target market was concerned. Black people, after all, were not part of the referendum, and in any case it was not necessary to convince them of the veracity of the claim; whites, on the other hand, were exclusively involved in the campaign, but their concerns did not feature in the appeals. Slabbert also had an answer for those who thought that at least Botha's initiatives opened up new possibilities: 'Everybody likes a step in the right direction. When you are in a dark tunnel a step in the right direction towards the light can be very nice – except if that light is the light of an oncoming train.'[56] This was a typically off-the-cuff Slabbert comment, laced with a cautionary warning.

For Slabbert, the campaign started rather inauspiciously in Stellenbosch, where he addressed a crowd of about 600 students. He had to dodge three rotten eggs thrown at him, but he continued undeterred and even managed to garner some applause with the retort that 'the legitimacy of the constitution should not be determined by rotten eggs'.[57] More serious, though, as the campaign progressed, was the realisation that the government was cutting into the PFP's support base. Increasingly, the PFP was seen as a negative, boycotting party and the government as the trendsetter for change. Slabbert later described the propaganda as 'thumbsucking and wishful thinking on a large scale'.[58] Shortly before the date of the referendum, he tried to restate the party's position and to counter government accusations. 'We ... have come to the end of an exhausting, sometimes heated, and very often confusing referendum campaign,' he said, and now 'even more so than when it started I wish to urge you to vote "NO" ...' He continued, saying that he did not do so because he was 'bloody-minded' or did not care about reform, but because he sincerely believed that the proposed constitution 'holds very real dangers for the country and we certainly do not need more problems than we have already'.[59]

When the results were announced, Slabbert's worst fears were confirmed. With a percentage poll of 76 per cent, a resounding 66.29 per cent came out in favour of the proposed constitution, while those against lagged behind with 33.71 per cent. While the exact party breakdown of the 'yes' vote could not be determined with any degree of certainty, it was clear that a sizeable percentage of PFP supporters had voted 'yes'.[60]

Slabbert had to admit that the outcome was a serious blow to the party. At the national congress held shortly after the referendum, Slabbert, while regretting the results, stated that given the same set of circumstances he would not have deviated from his original decision. Portentously, he said he was prepared to resign if that was considered in the best interests of the party, but the caucus prevailed on him to stay on.[61] Personally, however, he had earlier told a colleague that he felt 'politically dirty' knowing that he had to participate in what he regarded as a fraudulent system.[62] Nevertheless, government policies still had to be opposed and those supporters who had voted 'yes' had to be wooed back to the party; despite being misguided, they had after all voted 'yes' for 'good solid PFP sentiments' based on expectations of change.[63] For Slabbert, disillusioned at this point, it appeared that there remained just enough worthwhile causes for him to stay on in Parliament.

He had, however, to start from the back foot. Apart from losing the support of the English-language press over the referendum issue, which had to be patched up, the stance taken by big business also demanded his attention. It has long been assumed, often without much evidence, that the English-speaking corporate world was firmly behind the PFP. The 1983 referendum result clearly showed that matters were more complicated. While the PFP had historically received funding from Anglo American Corporation, this was in small amounts relative to the firm's other donations. During the referendum, Harry Oppenheimer had reluctantly voted 'no'. Other corporate leaders, such as Anglo chairman Gavin Relly and Chris Saunders, chairman of Tongaat Sugar (and the top Natal industrialist), voted 'yes'.[64] At a meeting organised during the referendum campaign by Harry Oppenheimer and addressed by Slabbert, there was little enthusiasm for the latter's arguments. He thought that perhaps only two out of the approximately 100 people present agreed with his exposition. They were so keen on change that without too much reflection they grasped at straws.[65] Slabbert was all too conscious of the fickle relationship between politics and big business. By 1981 he was already disillusioned about the way businessmen funded the press. He was fully aware that corporates were 'businessmen before they were politicians'.[66] He later explained that the PFP

> never regarded them [capitalists] as a captive constituency or a monolithic constituency. Their interests were closely tied to government, to power. I never experienced business looking upon the PFP as a protector of their interests. How could we? We had very little power. But they certainly floated towards you when there was disillusionment with government. It was pendulum stuff.[67]

This stance went some way towards explaining why big business had turned its back on the PFP's entreaties during the referendum; the government seemed to be creating a more positive environment for economic growth. Capitalists, however, had in this instance failed to factor in the price of excluding the majority of South Africans; it was an omission that would come back to haunt them.

While the referendum played out in the white political arena, the state's proposed reforms had loosened the props of the wider society, leading to unintended consequences in the extra-parliamentary sphere. The co-optive dimensions of the new constitution and the exclusion of black people galvanised a range of 565 diverse organisations to oppose the constitutional developments under the banner of the United Democratic Front (UDF), launched in Cape Town on 20 August 1983.[68] The UDF was destined to play a major national role in the volatile politics of the 1980s. It was precisely this kind of development that Slabbert, with some prescience, had hinted at in his opposition to the government's reform moves. He was, however, careful not to read too much into the UDF so soon after its launch, and he adopted a wait-and-see attitude. What was clear, he stated, was that the formation of the UDF compounded the problem of legitimacy for the government's plans.[69]

In considering Slabbert's role during the referendum campaign, it may at first glance appear that he badly miscalculated and lost the ground that the PFP had gained up to 1983. After all, the outcome of the referendum and the loss of English-language newspaper support, as well as that of big business, all pointed to a failed political campaign. In this sense, then, he had been truly outflanked. But there was also a wider picture that in the long run vindicated Slabbert's stance. His colleague Ray Swart, from Natal, made the point that although they were labelled as 'spoilers' during the campaign, subsequent developments made them in fact 'realists'.[70] The tricameral parliament became a target for the extra-parliamentary forces, and resistance became much more overt and persistent, which eventually forced the government to declare several states of emergency. In this context, Slabbert's 'no' vote was hailed as prophetic by some outside Parliament.[71] What that held in store for him, however, had yet to be determined.

5
TURBULENT TIMES

Exploring black politics

During the mid-1980s the country went through unprecedented political convulsions on several levels, and the legitimacy of Parliament increasingly came into question. Slabbert, as leader of the official opposition, was to be buffeted from all sides.

The emergence of the UDF, which in some respects served as a surrogate for the banned ANC, foregrounded the position of the disenfranchised in South Africa. Before then, formalised and organised black protest politics inside and outside the country had been, with the exception of the Black Consciousness Movement, more muted, to the extent that Slabbert admitted, early in the 1980s, that he 'knew very little about the ANC and extra-parliamentary politics. I did not know people in the ANC. I had never met them. I never really understood, practically, "the struggle of the people".'[1]

Gradually, however, black politics came into the frame. Slabbert found that a new generation of younger black activists, while justifiably aggrieved, were prone to indulge in revolutionary romanticism and utopian socialist alternatives. They also increasingly questioned the bona fides of white people. To them, the PFP was politically not part of the answer to South Africa's ills, and its proclaimed liberal stance merely 'the icing sugar on the system of oppression'.[2]

The PFP had nevertheless, in the late 1970s, managed to establish a working relationship with Mangosuthu Buthelezi's Inkatha movement (later the Inkatha Freedom Party), which was based in the Zulu homeland of KwaZulu and had a huge number of supporters. The relationship was built partly on the ties between Slabbert, Ray Swart, the Natal PFP leader, and Buthelezi. Both the PFP and Inkatha had expressed themselves in favour of evolutionary change. While the relationship had its tensions, in part rooted in personal misunderstandings, it had the potential to develop into a more potent force. The Buthelezi Commission of the early 1980s, consisting of a cross section of 46 political and other luminaries who punted the possibility of a multiracial federation, was a pointer in this regard. PW Botha, however, soon squashed the idea.³

The UDF presented a different challenge, as it viewed both the PFP and Inkatha as beyond the pale because they operated within the 'system'. During the 1980s starkly rigid lines were drawn between those who were seen to be working within apartheid structures of any kind and those who promoted radical change outside the system. The PFP, however, regarded it as essential to widen its net and reposition the party with an eye to the future, and to claim a place for itself between the two chief protagonists – the National Party government and the extra-parliamentary forces. It was aware of the possibility of being marginalised and therefore sought to extend its reach by recruiting, especially among the coloured and Indian communities. In 1984 Slabbert exhorted the PFP to become the 'largest, most broad-based political party in the history of the South African Parliament'.⁴ In doing so, the PFP was in effect throwing down the gauntlet to the UDF, and not surprisingly was seen to be trespassing on the terrain of the extra-parliamentary movement. Slabbert was warned by their spokespeople that he was sowing further dissension, but he responded by claiming that the PFP was an independent political actor and that there was no reason to restrain the party's forays into 'foreign' territory:

> We cannot expect everybody will like the PFP. We appreciate there will be possible conflict with other groups who do not share our ideals. We are not spending our time finding

out how many people do not like what we are doing. We are rather looking at how many people like it.[5]

In a further attempt to reposition the PFP, Slabbert developed the notion of a national convention movement, led by a convention alliance of anti-apartheid organisations. The strategy was to try and capture the middle ground and establish a new hegemonic political bloc.

This initiative should be seen against the background of increased political unrest, racial tension and, from July 1985, a spate of government-declared states of emergency in 36 magisterial districts. Black communities, some under the banner of the UDF, others not, had started to mobilise on a large scale to render townships ungovernable. Bus boycotts, work stayaways, school protests and mass action had become the order of the day. With the police and later the army occupying townships, protestors were often dealt with harshly, which only served to spark off more protests. The possibility of widespread mayhem loomed on the horizon.[6] To add to the woes, PW Botha's much-publicised 'Rubicon' speech in August 1985, which was supposed to announce meaningful change, turned out to be a damp squib.[7]

Slabbert, who up to this point had been largely a formal House of Assembly politician operating within the mainstream of the system, was now exposed to the rough and tumble of street politics. Peter Gastrow, vice chairman of the PFP, later recalled:

> 1985 was the year of unbelievable turmoil. Slabbert was starting to make his first real contact. My impression was that he was experiencing for the first time the turmoil and the agony, but also the potential within black power … He spoke to political activists. He went to numerous hot places. The whole turmoil sucked him in and I think really broadened his whole perspective about what was happening in black politics.[8]

When Slabbert spoke at the party's annual federal congress in August 1985, a note of near-desperation crept into his speech as he made it clear that the situation was nothing short of a crisis. The 'country was ravaged by unrest', he said, and a 'vision of a herd of gathering swine milling around the edge of a precipice easily comes to mind'.[9]

It had now become urgent, more than before, he argued, to avoid what he regarded as the two extremes – repression and violent upheavals – that were rapidly becoming distinct features of the political landscape. 'We must show that there is a third option,' Slabbert urged. 'An option in the middle, away from violence to change the status quo and away from repression to maintain it. This what I have in mind with a convention alliance.'[10]

Slabbert and Buthelezi jointly convened the first meeting of the Convention Alliance, and the launch in Johannesburg was attended by a significant number of businessmen, who were becoming increasingly frustrated with the government's failed reform attempts. As Slabbert had observed earlier, big business was a fickle constituency, which now, looking for fresh initiatives, sought to renew its influence with the PFP. The occasion, however, promised far more than it could deliver.

The tender alliance plant withered away before it could even be properly watered. It did not have the approval of the ANC, and barely three days before the launch the UDF withdrew its support, arguing that the time was not ripe for such a project. Of course, they also had their reservations about working with Buthelezi, who was seen to be part of the apartheid establishment. Slabbert was aghast. He recalled:

> [T]he thing died just there. But it was too late to stop it. It must have been one of the most embarrassing days of my life in politics. You end up at the Sandton Sun and there you have all these people, but you don't have any substance.[11]

Slabbert was particularly annoyed with certain individuals. One of them was Archbishop Desmond Tutu, who was supposed to be on board but withdrew because he did not want to be associated with Buthelezi. Slabbert fumed that 'that is now our great Christian leader'. He was equally dismissive of the Reverend Allan Boesak of the UDF, who changed his mind after initially agreeing to participate. 'They all took their instructions from them [the ANC],' he railed.[12]

Slabbert was not usually given to such outbursts, and the dismal outcome of the Convention Alliance venture must have rankled. The failure, however, ran deeper than he was prepared to admit. Given the volatility of South African politics at the time, where the fault lines were clearly drawn, Slabbert sought in a rather confused manner to merge his own party's moderate stance with the militancy of the UDF and the ANC. The Convention Alliance's stress on negotiations was also far removed from the political mobilisation priorities and more immediate goals in the townships.[13] The chances of success were slim from the outset.

Slabbert most likely thought the situation had reached such crisis proportions that immediate action was required. Peter Gastrow later trenchantly remarked on the planning:

> It was not canvassed within the Party; it was not discussed in great detail by the Party. This was one of Slabbert's weaknesses. He suddenly became very enthusiastic about the idea and then ran with it at such a speed without doing the necessary networking. At that stage one wasn't familiar with the politics of extra-parliamentary groupings.[14]

Slabbert, disillusioned as he was with the outcome, was still sufficiently fired up to pursue other possibilities. If the ANC happened to be the main player or projected itself as such, closer contact with the organisation, when such an occasion presented itself, would then be logically advisable. 'It was after all they who had destroyed the initiative,' he argued, 'and we wanted to find out for ourselves what they had in mind.'[15]

Such an occasion presented itself through the initiative of Peter Gastrow, who, through a number of intermediaries and much cloak-and-dagger manoeuvring, managed to secure a meeting between some of the ANC leaders and the executive of the PFP. It was not discussed with other members, partly because of the need to maintain confidentiality for security reasons, but also because they did not have a mandate for such a step. The meeting took place on 12 and 13 October 1985 in Lusaka, Zambia.[16]

Thabo Mbeki and other high-ranking members of the ANC attended. It was, as Slabbert recalled, his first meeting with the 'architects of the struggle'. He was more than impressed: 'To say that I was overwhelmed would be putting it mildly.' He was exposed to a 'whole new area of history' and an 'awareness of my insulation in the fight against apartheid, a feeling of intense camaraderie and common objectives'. In retrospect he realised 'how infinitely more accomplished they were as politicians; to what extent it was part of their daily existence to charm a wide variety of people from all over the world and to make them part of the struggle. In a certain sense we were novices and like putty in their hands.'[17]

Socially, Slabbert readily admitted that he was 'charmed out of his pants. Why don't we get together? Love each other,' he enthused. The PFP leadership was well entertained at the Lusaka Polo Club, and, Slabbert remembered, 'we drank South African wine and "snot and trane". Wonderful stuff.'[18] Conviviality reigned, and there were few jarring notes in the discovery of a long-lost common song sheet. Yet for Alex Boraine, though it did not dampen his enthusiasm, there was the nagging incongruity of being so lavishly entertained at the upmarket Polo Club by a group of people who professed to push a revolutionary agenda.[19] Slabbert also later reflected that perhaps they had been naive in their ready embrace of the ANC as long-lost brothers. In trying to understand why the PFP delegation was so responsive to the ANC, Slabbert explained it in terms of the 'internal demonisation that went on', spurred by the government. He described it as 'just heavy, heavy stuff'. What happened was that after 'everything you heard, you read and the fact that it was so non-PC domestically to go and talk to these guys ... you go there and it's just totally different. I mean you just can't believe it and they're reasonable, and they laugh and they chat about the domestic situation.'[20] In his keenness to escape the stereotyping of the ANC in South Africa, Slabbert at this point was particularly favourably predisposed to the movement. This made him more susceptible to their blandishments.

Besides launching an effective charm offensive, the ANC also had the upper hand in political discussions about South Africa. The PFP delegation found it difficult to defend their participation in the parliamentary system, which, as the ANC representatives made clear, was the same system that was responsible for perpetuating apartheid.[21] Slabbert's view, that a peaceful transition would not be possible without involving the government and white people in general, was 'received with polite but dismissive smiles'.[22] The ANC, he realised, had moved well beyond a peaceful solution as its first priority. He found that their arguments were mainly predicated on the morality of the struggle and less on strategy and tactics, apart from emphasising the futility of working within the system and a commitment to the armed struggle. In retrospect, Slabbert felt that this was the first point at which he should have realised that he could not be part of the struggle except on the ANC's terms.[23] There was belated reassurance on strategy, though in a private discussion between Mbeki and Slabbert on the way to the airport, Mbeki indicated that on the issue of violence, on which Slabbert held strong views, the ANC might well still consider a two-pronged approach, which might include negotiations. 'Talking is always better than killing,' Mbeki claimed.[24]

Back in South Africa, Slabbert appeared energised by the visit and he proceeded in an almost messianic fashion, expressing himself forcefully in fiery speeches.²⁵ He regarded it as 'totally immoral to sit on our hands when South Africa is sliding into an escalating crisis'.²⁶ The crisis had to be averted, and he believed, following his conversation with Mbeki, that it was still not too late to start talking about negotiations. For that to happen, however, apartheid first had to be abolished. He now also professed to have a better understanding of the armed struggle, and that as long as the conditions persisted that had given rise to the armed struggle in the first place, the ANC could not readily abandon it. This was in contrast to his earlier unqualified outlook, which condemned all political violence from any quarter.²⁷

Slabbert had clearly changed his position. Since his full immersion in white politics during the 1981 election and the 1983 referendum, the dynamics of black politics in 1985 had increasingly become a major factor. The predicted legitimacy problems with the tricameral Parliament, and the recurring cycles of increasingly harsh repression that in turn prompted even more volatile protests, caused him to reassess precisely how he and his party could still play a worthwhile role. He had now moved beyond a point of mere parliamentary protest (although he realised the importance of this) and political manoeuvring to affect the balance of power in Parliament to a more urgent insistence on the immediate need for dialogue. 'Anything else,' he later recalled, 'was just an insult to my intelligence.' By late 1985 the Botha regime had become anathema to him. 'Short of violence,' he said, 'I would have done anything to undermine it. I made no bones about it.'²⁸

The important shift in Slabbert's thinking, and that of the PFP, was reflected in the subsequent discarding of the idea of constitutional power-sharing and a minority veto in favour of individual rights and an independent judiciary. These were major moves, prompted not only by the unstable situation in the country but also by Slabbert's exposure to black political organisations, which drove the message home to him that any such brakes on constitutional power would not be tolerated.²⁹ The Slabbert of 1985, who took the lead in these developments, was not the Slabbert of the pre-1983 referendum, when politics outside Parliament was not as volatile. He was chastened by events but managed to hold the party together. There were, however, powerful centrifugal forces at work, and the increasing militarisation of the 1980s further contributed to this.

Caught in the crossfire

The stark realities of militarisation in South Africa during the 1980s could not but infuse the nature of political discourse and presented Slabbert with a number of awkward issues. As the official parliamentary opposition for most of the period, the PFP was not in a position to define the terms of the debate, as the agenda was set by the National Party under PW Botha. Botha had served as defence minister from 1967 until he was chosen as prime minister in 1978, and he became president in 1983 under the new constitutional dispensation. Under Botha and his handpicked minister of defence, General Magnus Malan, the interests of the military were assiduously promoted.

At the heart of the ideology of militarisation was the notion of a total strategy to counter what was perceived to be a 'total onslaught' emanating from South Africa's enemies. These enemies were first and foremost communists – backed by the Soviet Union and its satellite state, Cuba – who used Angola as a base and a springboard for incursions into South African-controlled South West Africa (Namibia), since 1966 the focus of a nationalist insurgency led by the South West Africa People's Organisation (Swapo). South Africa, it was argued, stood largely alone in this struggle, as the liberal West was perceived to be too pusillanimous to assist. Conveniently underplayed in this outlook was that apartheid in itself was a major destabilising factor that attracted worldwide negative attention.[30]

The idea of a total onslaught seeped into the very fabric of white society and inevitably resonated in party-political terms. The PFP, as the opposition to the left of the National Party, was concerned about its pervasive effect. Colin Eglin, the senior PFP parliamentarian, said in 1983: 'Every attack on South Africa, every criticism of its policy or actions, every move to exclude or boycott, every proposal to disinvest is seen as a part of the Total Onslaught. Foreign governments, international organisations, church bodies, trade unions and political activists which criticise or act against South Africa are seen to be part of the Total Onslaught, whether as initiators, agents, allies or simply as dupes in the Total Onslaught strategy.'[31]

The PFP tried to mediate the total onslaught approach by seeking to separate what it regarded as 'legitimate security considerations' from 'wholesale panic which bordered on paranoia'. It was not convinced that, in terms of realpolitik, the Soviet Union had grand designs of imposing communist rule per se on southern Africa, but it considered the Soviets to be opportunistic in taking advantage of targets that might present themselves, with a view to increasing their sphere of influence.[32] Such a nuanced understanding, while it might have had a certain appeal in rarefied political circles, was difficult to convey effectively in the cauldron of everyday politics, especially at a time when Cuban forces were massed on the northern frontier of South West Africa, bombs were exploding in public spaces in South Africa, and the country was seething with black unrest, requiring several states of emergency to be decreed. Nor were matters helped by the blood-curdling pronouncements made by the ANC in exile that, in order to advance their cause, it was necessary to develop a 'hatred of the enemy', and, reaching back into history, that one of the reasons 'our forefathers fought so heroically against the enemy was that they hated them'.[33] It was within these prickly political parameters that the PFP had to operate.

Given the pre-eminent place accorded to defence matters in white society, the PFP was careful not to convey the impression, in Parliament or further afield, that it rejected the enhanced role of the military. On the contrary, Harry Schwarz, who was particularly hawkish on defence issues, made it clear that the South African

Defence Force (SADF) had a legitimate task and that it should be supported: 'If you are a South African, if you believe in peace and if you seek protection against violence and terror from our defence and police forces, you must be prepared to assist in that defence.'[34] Similarly Philip Myburgh, the PFP spokesperson for defence, argued in 1983 that as far as the military was concerned, 'the greatest possible measure of agreement should be reached', and that the 'security and defence of South Africa are one of our prime considerations'.[35]

Apart from the personal convictions of these speakers, this point of departure was also meant to convey to the public that the PFP as a party was not 'soft' on security, as National Party members often averred.[36] It was a point that needed repeating often. In May 1987, before the general election, Brian Goodall, then PFP spokesperson for defence, made it clear that it was 'nonsense' for the government to say that the PFP refused to acknowledge the threat against South Africa. Even if the PFP was in government, he continued, 'there would still be a threat. We would, however, deal with it much more effectively than this government has.'[37] Such a message was essential for the PFP to try and establish its credentials with the voting public, as well as to create manoeuvring room in Parliament. Otherwise it could far too easily be sidelined on the basis of perceived 'disloyalty'.

In 1974, soon after the start of his parliamentary career, Slabbert had tried to exploit the available space to extract information from the government on military matters. His concern also had a personal angle, as his half-brother, Sean Taylor, was a conscript involved in Operation Savannah, the SADF's ill-fated covert incursion into Angola in August 1975. Slabbert was part of an official parliamentary delegation sent to the border in January 1976 when the news of the Angola operation was revealed. He was not only worried about what might happen to Taylor but also aghast at the foolhardiness of invading Angola in what turned out to be a futile attempt to influence local politics. The operation meant that the principle of non-interference in the affairs of other countries, which South Africa had advocated for so long, had been violated. As information about Operation Savannah was classified, Slabbert was not allowed to raise the issue in Parliament, but he nevertheless tried to circumvent the restrictions by posing a hypothetical scenario of where conscripts should be allowed to be deployed.[38]

As the ideology of the total onslaught gained greater traction, the dividing lines between state and party became more porous. Slabbert was concerned that what started off as a 'total strategy' was in the process of becoming a 'totalitarian strategy'.[39] The incident that sparked this remark was a report leaked to the *Sunday Times* newspaper in March 1980. It revealed a plan by the SADF to manipulate the news media in order to counter opposition criticism of PW Botha. In Parliament, Botha viewed the accusation as of minor concern and was loath to admit that the SADF had crossed the fine line between state and party by trying to shield him from PFP criticism. Slabbert stated that the SADF should take care not to become involved in partisan politics, and that if the idea took root that the 'Defence Force is simply the National Party in uniform, this country would split from top to bottom'.[40] In a lengthy critique of the leaked document, Slabbert consistently argued for a clear and rigorously observed division between party and state.

It is a moot point whether Slabbert really believed there was, in the first place, such a substantial difference between party and state. There was some criticism that he was naive in even thinking that there was anything to choose between the two.[41] The political reality, though, might well have been that, in line with PFP general strategy, it was publicly necessary to foreground such a divide, as it provided a way of drawing the National Party into debate and keeping the government accountable. General Jannie Geldenhuys, chief of the SADF in 1985, later stated that Slabbert's opinion did indeed carry some weight in certain government circles.[42]

Debates on defence matters could derail easily. In response to Slabbert's comments on the revelations of SADF involvement in party politics, the irascible Botha described Slabbert's speech as a 'tirade' and likened him to a 'young rhinoceros bull'. Slabbert's response was measured: he regretted that a senior member of the House, with years of service, should speak to a junior member in such a manner, and he hoped that he would not ever have to stoop to the level at which Botha had addressed him.[43] Relations between Botha and Slabbert remained strained. A senior National Party member later let slip the root cause of the animosity: 'Slabbert is too clever; PW hates him.'[44]

Furthermore, it could not be taken for granted that when the leader of the opposition addressed the House on military matters, suitable attention would be paid. In 1985, while speaking on the complexities of conscription, he found himself rudely interrupted by two National Party MPs who, for some unknown reason, started to argue among themselves – the one calling the other *dikkop* (blockhead) – and had to be reprimanded by the Speaker before Slabbert could continue.[45]

Most of the time, Slabbert preferred to shy away from name-calling or ridiculing his opponents. There were exceptions, though. Magnus Malan's stonewalling tactics, or what Slabbert regarded as the defence minister's hypersensitivity to criticism of the SADF, could occasionally become exasperating. Slabbert compared Malan to a turkey that he had encountered on the farm in his youth. When teased, the turkey would start cackling, and after a while it became so conditioned that as soon as someone approached, it would start cackling, without even being provoked. This, said Slabbert, was the 'cackling politics' of the minister of defence.[46]

Despite such exchanges, not all was lost in Parliament. Through diligent committee work, the PFP at times succeeded in changing or watering down the more extreme National Party defence proposals. Thus a 1983 Bill on conscription was changed in several respects after PFP interventions. One of the proposals in the Bill was that religious objectors should be given the option to buy themselves out of further military service after they had completed their first stint.

The PFP argued that this would privilege the well-off and that nobody should be exempted from service because they could afford it.⁴⁷

While the PFP sought as far as possible to maintain a united front in Parliament, defence issues in the turbulent 1980s spilled over into the deliberations of the party. These revolved mainly around the question of compulsory military conscription and conscientious objection, and, from late 1984, the deployment of troops in the black townships.

The terms of who qualified for military exemption on religious grounds were narrowly defined and did not leave much latitude for those who objected to conscription on the basis of what was described as an 'unjust war'. Moreover, the penalties for those who refused to do military service were severe and could include a jail sentence of up to six years. As the country became increasingly militarised, the period of military service was extended accordingly. Compulsory military service for all white males was first introduced in 1967 with a stretch of nine months. This was extended to twelve months in 1972, and in 1977 to a two-year period of compulsory service. In tandem with these obligations, the lengths of time spent doing annual camps after the initial period of service were also increased: in 1972 it was 19 days' camp for five years; in 1977 this rose to 30 days for eight years; and from 1983 the requirement was to serve a further 720 days spread over 14 years.

This was not the end of it. The member was then transferred to the Citizen Force, where he was expected to serve 12 days annually for another five-year period, and he could be recalled up to the age of 55 years before finally being placed on the national reserve for a further ten-year period.⁴⁸ The stringent call-up regulations could, in theory, mean that white males were beholden to the defence force in one way or another for most of their adult life. The scope and extent of these demands catapulted the issue of conscription right into the centre of the political arena. Conscription was no longer a minor issue of young men being called up for a limited period; in the 1980s it started to assume the form of mass mobilisation.

TURBULENT TIMES

The deployment of white troops, under state emergency regulations, in black townships where unrest occurred was equally a quantum leap for the defence force. Although there is evidence that some black people preferred the troops to the police in the townships – the latter being regarded as more vindictive and ill-disciplined[49] – the impression was that South Africa was descending into civil war. The border was no longer in the north of the country, but had moved into the towns and cities. Once the defence force moved into the townships to help quell anti-apartheid protests, it compromised its own claims, debatable as they might have been, to neutrality. These developments added a sharper edge to the way in which political parties positioned themselves.

It was against this background that Slabbert opened the PFP federal congress in Durban in 1985. He stated frankly:

> Defence issues have always been controversial within the PFP, and rightly so, because they involve matters of life and death. I prefer a controversial, heated but honest debate to the kind of pseudo-patriotic posturing which so often typifies political comment on these matters. It has been stated I ... am too uncritical or even 'jingoistic' in speaking on behalf of the PFP on defence matters. I obviously disagree with such sentiments.[50]

In general terms, without always being mutually exclusive, there were three groupings on defence issues within the PFP. In the centre, there was some consensus on the need for political reform instead of increased defence spending as the preferred way to ensure stability. In addition, there was a fair measure of agreement that a larger professional defence force, consisting of career soldiers rather than conscripts, was desirable. On the left, a grouping with anti-militarist tendencies held sway. On the right, there was more readiness to accept the need for conscription and a greater willingness to accept the government's assurances of why the defence force should play a central role in South African affairs, with the proviso that this should not become an end in itself and should be accompanied by meaningful political reform.

The position of shadow minister of defence in the PFP had a reputation as one of the more controversial major portfolios in the party, and it was here that underlying tensions surfaced.[51] The hot seat was frequently vacated as defence spokespersons followed each other in rapid succession: Harry Schwarz, Roger Hulley, Philip Myburgh, Slabbert himself, Brian Goodall, Peter Gastrow and, by the end of the decade, Nic Olivier.

Those parliamentarians on the left of the party included people like Helen Suzman, Graham McIntosh and Alex Boraine. (One of Boraine's sons, Jeremy, went on the run from the military police for failing to report for camp duty.[52]) More to the right were Harry Schwarz, Philip Myburgh, Alf Widman, Dave Dalling and Reuben Sive. Three of these had actual military experience, which might well have influenced their outlook. Schwarz, whose family came to South Africa as Jewish refugees from Nazi Germany in 1934, felt deeply loyal to South Africa as the country had provided his family with opportunities at a time of need.[53] He had served in the South African Air Force during the Second World War; Philip Myburgh volunteered for army service in 1958 and some of his immediate family had also served during the Second World War; and Sive carried the title of major for service in the Union Defence Force.

Internecine clashes could at times be unedifying. Graham McIntosh, who at one point refused to report for military duty, was at loggerheads with Schwarz, who regarded it as the duty of every South African to obey the law. McIntosh retorted: 'I don't take his [Schwarz's] comments very seriously. Mr Schwarz has a political erection every time anybody mentions the defence force and with that his rationality disappears completely.'[54] McIntosh was considered to be particularly volatile when it came to defence issues. He was also berated by Slabbert

TURBULENT TIMES

for implying that there was no or little difference between the SADF and the terrorists. 'Hyperbole, exaggeration and emotional utterances,' Slabbert cautioned, 'are detrimental to a satisfactory and constructive debate on defence matters and cause alarm.'[55]

The issue of conscription specifically caused considerable debate within PFP circles. While not all that urgent during the 1970s, the question assumed greater political proportions with the dramatic increase in the length of military service during the early 1980s and the more prominent role of the defence force. Heated arguments for and against conscription became a hallmark of PFP congresses and had the effect of clouding the practicalities of what was possible at the time. The issue caused Philip Myburgh to resign as defence spokesperson. He considered an idea put forward by the left wing of the PFP, that conscription should be abolished immediately, as impractical and irresponsible. This could not be done without having a suitable alternative in place, the lack of which would seriously weaken the defence force precisely at a time when it was needed as a buffer to allow political reforms to take place under peaceful circumstances.[56]

Slabbert had to step in as defence spokesperson. He was buffeted from all sides. At one point he even threatened to resign (again) as party leader should the caucus fail to resolve the controversy.[57] Gradually tempers cooled, though it is hard to say whether this was due to Slabbert's threat or time for more reflection on the issue. Eventually, Slabbert was able to pass a resolution, described as a 'personal triumph' for him, to the effect that 'as the expansion of the fulltime non-racial professional defence force and volunteer reserve arm progresses, so also progress can be made with the phasing out of conscription as part of the military organisation until it is no longer necessary'.[58] With this formulation Slabbert tried not only to appease the warring factions of his party but also to provide a firm directive on the issue of conscription. He furthermore made it clear that the party was in 'no way going to actively oppose military service, nor in any way undermine the role of the defence force'. At the same time, he was alert to the fact that while it seemed that conscription was a burning issue, it was also the way in which troops were used by the military that sparked negative reactions.[59]

This was particularly the case with the deployment of conscripts in black townships. The military argued that their role in the townships was not to arrest ringleaders but to protect innocent people who preferred to stay out of politics. It was only in extreme cases of conflict that they were supposed to intervene.[60] It was, however, a very fine line. Slabbert could not but observe: 'I do not think it helps to say the defence force will only be involved in a supportive capacity. The temptation to go further and intervene is inescapably great.'[61] While the prescriptions on the use of the military in the townships might have been difficult to observe and easy to exceed, the situation also had worrisome policy implications for the PFP, as it militated against the view that the SADF should be an impartial guardian. The defence force had, in effect, become a key player and could be perceived as promoting the status quo. As a result, Slabbert noted, it would be 'impossible to present it [the defence force] as a neutral shield behind which orderly reform can take place'.[62] With this development, the credibility of a much-peddled PFP argument came under severe strain.

To add to Slabbert's woes, the SADF conducted a series of cross-border raids into Mozambique, Botswana and Lesotho. He experienced a sense of déjà vu, similar to the way he had been deceived by the military at the time of the incursion into Angola in 1975–1976. Under the cloak of national security, he was bypassed and left in the dark, whereas the normal parliamentary protocol was to inform the leader of the opposition of such developments. He could barely conceal his resentment: 'If the … minister of defence and his department do not trust me or my party, let them say so clearly and not inform me confidentially about anything. I will learn to live with that, but I prefer that to being lied to.'[63] It was not surprising that Slabbert started to lose faith in the military. This became clear to Philip Myburgh, who, in an effort to establish a better working relationship, arranged for informal meetings between Slabbert and senior military personnel. Slabbert only attended two of these meetings and declined further invitations.[64]

Steadily, then, as military matters started to loom large during the 1980s, the PFP had to position itself on two fronts. It had to counter the government's view of the total onslaught without being perceived as 'soft' on security by the voting public. Moreover, it had to contend with differing views on military matters within its own ranks. It fell to Slabbert to steer the ship through treacherous seas with a squabbling crew. And, as if this was not enough of a challenge, new clouds were gathering on the horizon in the shape of another organisation with its sights set on military matters.

Sniping from the white left: The End Conscription Campaign

The End Conscription Campaign (ECC) was founded in 1983 with the aim of pressuring the government to end compulsory military service. Additionally, it sought to stimulate awareness of the extent of South Africa's militarisation; to oppose the presence of the SADF in South West Africa; to campaign for alternative forms of national service; and to work for peace and justice in South Africa. Of all these, the main thrust was the objection to compulsory military service. In doing so, the ECC sailed legally close to the wind, as it was punishable by law to encourage men to refuse service. It therefore claimed that it merely provided conscripts with 'accurate' information about SADF activities, allowing them to make up their own minds.[65]

Such a fine distinction was, however, not always observed in practice. Not surprisingly, the organisation was on a collision course with the government. Over and above attacks in the press, it also had to deal with 'dirty tricks' and harassment aimed at discrediting the campaign.⁶⁶ The ECC was banned in 1988 on the basis that it improperly influenced young men and thereby broke the law, as it was aware that certain members worked underground for the banned ANC. At the time, the ECC understandably sought to deny any link to the ANC, but after 1994 it emerged that such connections had indeed existed.⁶⁷

There is a tendency in the historiography of oppositional forces in the 1980s to foreground the ECC as a significant player in the politics of the day.⁶⁸ Without wishing to deny its uniqueness, we have to bear in mind that its influence can easily be exaggerated. Just because the ECC happened to be on the 'right' side of history in the post-1994 era does not necessarily mean that it was very important in the 1980s. At its peak, it had no more than 1 580 active and fully committed members in nine regions. The ECC's organisational reach was restricted to the major cities, and it failed to make significant inroads into the Afrikaans campuses; at Stellenbosch, for example, it only had a 2.1 per cent following. In the English-speaking community, its support was mainly drawn from the middle-class liberal intelligentsia, church organisations and civic bodies such as the Black Sash, which had a hand in establishing it in the first place. Although much was made of its supposed success in influencing young men not to register, it is hard to prove that the ECC was, except in highly publicised cases, actually instrumental in all refusals. Young men also stayed away for reasons other than the political objections advanced by the ECC. Overall, despite some fluctuations, reporting figures stayed relatively constant.⁶⁹ What the ECC lacked in actual influence, it made up for in a highly visible and creative countercultural drive, including cartoons and posters mocking the SADF, which had the effect of raising its public profile considerably.⁷⁰

The ECC also raised the ire of Magnus Malan, who did not take kindly to the lampooning of the SADF. Moreover, he claimed that the ECC's funding came from abroad and the organisation was less concerned about conscripts than it was about undermining the

SADF, which according to him served as a bulwark against revolution.[71] In addition, he sought clarity about the PFP's attitude towards the ECC; to his mind, the party was being too circumspect. 'Why does the PFP not clearly state that they reject an organisation like the ECC?' he asked. 'Is this another one of the PFP albatrosses?'[72]

While the ECC might not quite have been an albatross for the PFP, it did put the party on the spot, and presented it with an explicit challenge from the extra-parliamentary white left. Some ECC members considered the PFP's view that conscription could only be phased out once a viable alternative was in place as a vote for the continuation of apartheid.[73] Max Ozinsky, later a prominent ANC leader in the Western Cape, recalled that he and other like-minded youths regarded the PFP stance as hypocritical, as the party was quick to criticise but not prepared to make any real sacrifices to end apartheid. He joined the ECC and later uMkhonto we Sizwe, the armed wing of the ANC. This stood in contrast to what he considered the 'fake liberals of the PFP', who had become 'completely irrelevant to a generation of white youth who were expected to sacrifice their lives [in the SADF] so that their parents could continue enjoying the benefits produced for them by apartheid'.[74] Although not employing the same strident tone, the PFP youth wing at the time also edged closer to ECC rhetoric. It started to question the validity of the claim that conscription could only be phased out gradually, as well as the idea that the defence force was a shield for the implementation of necessary reforms.[75]

The PFP sought to inject what it considered to be a measure of realism into the debate. Philip Myburgh recalled that the ECC was more intent on publicity than about finding working alternatives. The military authorities, he claimed, although they had to act against the ECC, were not really given to unseemly and ongoing public squabbles with a section of the country's youth. As a result, in certain cases, it was possible to come to a compromise solution with young men who had serious qualms about military service, perhaps by allowing them to serve in noncombatant roles. The ECC, however, did not buy into this, as even noncombatants were still seen to be part of the 'apartheid war machinery'.[76]

Slabbert, notwithstanding his increasing disillusionment with the military, had, as he said in 1985, 'not yet lost all my idealism'.[77] He did his best to hold the official PFP line, and at the same time also expressed his misgivings about the ECC. In public debates he berated them for targeting the defence force without providing an alternative. All such a strategy did, he argued, was to provide ECC supporters with 'a kind of moral superiority which allowed them to call other people bad names'.[78] Although he could agree on certain points with the organisation, especially as far as the presence of troops in the townships was concerned, overall he considered its position too glib, even 'dangerously romantic, extraordinarily naive and counterproductive'.[79] The ECC, he explained, was more given to vilification of the defence force than to understanding the complexities of the matter. He found it

> totally illogical to use the issue of conscription in order to in fact attack the SADF, and the role it plays in South Africa. The Defence Force can do away with conscription tomorrow completely (which no doubt would help a great many morally anguished and privileged White South Africans), but would in no way affect the negative and counter-productive role that the Defence Force can play if not called to account or controlled in society.[80]

It was easy, he said, for the ECC to polish 'platitudes in front of a supportive mass rally', but it was another matter to try and engage the top echelons of the SADF with realistic alternatives.[81]

Slabbert's reservations about the ECC echoed on the Stellenbosch University campus, where similar concerns about the organisation were raised.[82] The demeanour of, and the arguments advanced by, ECC spokespeople also piqued some Afrikaners, who considered the organisation to be 'enveloped in a haze of intellectual and moral superiority'.[83] Slabbert also refused 'to partake in any propaganda attempt which tries to present every youngster in uniform as a goose-stepping fascist intent on preserving apartheid and killing blacks'.[84] In this respect, he was on solid ground. Conscripts on the whole were not driven, bloodthirsty belligerents; the majority merely sought to survive military service unharmed, and they were more animated about concluding their obligations than revelling in military exploits. Even PW Botha had no illusions about the enthusiasm of conscripts and thought that only between 20 and 30 per cent were highly motivated.[85]

While Slabbert adopted a clinical approach in dealing with defence matters, the vexed issue of conscription also affected him more personally. He raised this concern early in 1986: 'I have a son who is 15 years old. I am motivated by one predominating question … whether I have done everything in my power to prevent it being necessary for my son to take up arms against one of his fellow countrymen.'[86]

In some respects, the personal had now become the political, and it was only one example of the wider impact of the military situation. The PFP was literally caught in the crossfire: on the one hand the government was quick to describe the opposition as unpatriotic and anti-South African, while on the other the ECC made strident if not very carefully considered calls for an immediate end to conscription. The position was bound to have an effect on the internal dynamics of the party.

In all of this, Slabbert had to try to straddle different positions. He had to make a real effort to keep accountable a government intent on usurping more power; he had to cauterise the wounds inflicted by the internecine strife within his party; and he had to deal with a rumbustious ECC. At the same time, he had to keep the bigger picture in mind and consider the long-term effects of the government's total onslaught ideology.

The pressure was undoubtedly mounting on Slabbert. Not only

were military issues increasingly challenging, but by the mid-1980s he had also been through a disconcerting referendum defeat, the embarrassing failure of the Convention Alliance and a series of government-decreed states of emergency, which posed their own problems. He also realised that without a fuller understanding of black politics and incorporation of new legitimate role-players, South African politics – and with it the PFP – would remain in the doldrums. On the basis of what he had experienced up to this point, he had to decide what the future held for him and the PFP.

6
RESIGNATION

Exit moves

While Slabbert always had lingering doubts about the political career path he had embarked upon, he drowned these by dint of hard work and full immersion in the cause of the PFP. Yet, at the end of a tumultuous 1985, these misgivings slowly became more prominent, to a point where he felt he had to raise the possibility of his leaving Parliament with some of his colleagues. One of these was the redoubtable Helen Suzman, the MP for Houghton and the PFP's longest-serving parliamentary representative. Suzman dismissed the idea out of hand.[1] The two did, however, discuss the matter again in early 1986, when Suzman tried to dissuade Slabbert from taking any rash action.[2]

Slabbert also discussed the matter with Colin Eglin during an extended overseas tour late in 1985. After an exhausting 17-hour flight from Cape Town to Sydney, the two settled down in the hotel restaurant for a meal and some good red wine. Within earshot of where they were sitting, they observed carefree young Australians enjoying a disco. This prompted Slabbert to remark: 'On waking up in the morning a young [white male] South African would say to himself: "I wonder what future there is going to be for me in South Africa?" Or: "I wonder if I will be conscripted to do military service on the border?" In contrast to this, a young Australian waking up would say: "I wonder what the waves will be like at Bondi Beach?" Or: "I hope I didn't make my girlfriend pregnant last night."'[3] It was at this point, quite unexpectedly, that Slabbert told a stunned Eglin that he was considering resigning from Parliament.[4] It is not inconceivable that the effects of jet lag or the red wine, or the thought of his own son, Riko, being eligible for military service, were preying on him. This in turn, might have foregrounded the issue of his own function in a Parliament that seemed incapable of effecting the required changes that would render military service unnecessary.

Whatever Slabbert's exact reason, an exhausted Eglin tried to convince him to stay the course and pointed to domestic and international reappraisals that might still work towards meaningful change. Slabbert was less than convinced, but agreed to Eglin's suggestion that he sit down with PW Botha and have a frank, face-to-face discussion on South Africa's future.[5] They made the arrangements the following day.

The meeting took place on 25 November 1985 at the Union Buildings in Pretoria. Slabbert proceeded directly to the seat of government after a long flight from Canada, to where he had travelled after Australia. Unbeknown to Slabbert, Botha taped their conversation, and later released the transcript to counter Slabbert's version of the discussion. Botha's taping of the meeting without Slabbert's knowledge was perhaps a piece of less-than-honourable sleight of hand, but it was not completely surprising when it came to politics of this order. The transcript of the interview revealed that Slabbert was not as critical of Botha as he later claimed, namely, that Botha's intransigence left him with no hope for the future.[6]

Indeed, if one reads the interview cold, it does appear that the two men had more in common than what transpired later. However, Slabbert's strategy should also be factored in. Knowing Botha's volatile temperament, Slabbert adopted a deferential attitude, carefully refraining from saying anything that could cause Botha to erupt and destroy the possibility of a calm and rational discussion. He felt that a 'courteous, conciliatory approach' would be better than the confrontational exchanges they had had in the past.[7] Slabbert therefore spoke to him in the time-honoured Afrikaner manner, where the necessary respect is shown to an elder. 'I pleaded literally as a nephew before an uncle,'

RESIGNATION

Slabbert later explained.[8] If this approach is not taken into account, the interview can easily be misread as Slabbert's kowtowing to Botha. It might also well have been at the back of Slabbert's mind to convey to Botha that he was available as an interlocutor and as a negotiator in his own right should talks with the ANC get off the ground.[9]

The discussion dealt with the way in which future political changes might affect white people, and Botha made it clear that their position and 'way of life' should not be compromised. Slabbert tried to shift the ground to black politics, which had become so dominant in the 1980s. In particular, he sought to foreground the ANC as an essential role player that needed to be incorporated into negotiations. Knowing Botha's aversion to the ANC, he carefully phrased his suggestion in a manner the president might just relate to: 'The problem with the ANC is ... it is a myth. No, it is not a myth, it is a romantic image to the world ... I honestly think – and I say that from experience in the matter – you can pull the teeth of the whole ANC story.'[10] (This, Slabbert later pointed out, was precisely what the De Klerk government tried to do in 1990, when the ANC was then also sufficiently pliable to agree to negotiations, though at the time the transcripts were released the ANC took umbrage at Slabbert's remarks.[11]) Botha responded that Slabbert had his permission to talk to his advisers on the matter. He also required Slabbert's help with the release of Mandela. Slabbert, however, pointed out that Mandela could not be freed in isolation and that the ANC had to be involved.

While there were moments of promise in the discussion, little could be taken for granted. An exasperated Slabbert found this out when Botha, at a time of unprecedented black unrest, made the outlandish claim that he enjoyed the majority of black support. Botha grinned and smacked his lips as he said this. Slabbert was incredulous. He later recalled: 'Perhaps that was the moment that I finally decided to resign.'[12]

He contacted Eglin after the interview: 'It was as I thought it would be ... I could make no progress with Botha. He won't agree to the minimum steps which I believe are essential if we are to save South Africa from the consequences of apartheid.'[13] After the release of the transcript, Eglin commented that despite Slabbert's earlier remarks, the interview seemed to have gone better than what Eglin had thought earlier.[14]

It may well have appeared so, but only because the hidden anxieties were not fully apparent in the discussions, and the overall tenor of the meeting created the misleading impression of an agreeable exchange of views. The only substantial aspect of the discussion relates to Botha's woefully inaccurate assessment of his own political position, which served to emphasise the gaping chasm between the two men. If Botha was so misguided, all hope was lost. Even the far-right Reformed National Party (Herstigte Nasionale Party), not known for its realistic appraisal of what was politically feasible, found it disconcerting that someone with such a lack of realism could be head of state.[15] Once it dawned on Slabbert that Botha had no inkling of what it would take to effect relative peaceful change, it was no wonder that he felt a 'pervasive sense of despair and helplessness.'[16] His twin sister, Marcia Haak, who saw him soon after the meeting, recalled that his 'eyes were listless, he looked exhausted. He said that he thought he and the State President were on different planets.'[17]

Slabbert nevertheless followed up on Botha's invitation to talk to the minister of constitutional affairs, Chris Heunis, and the head of the National Intelligence Service (NIS), Niël Barnard. The latter received him courteously and listened attentively, without expressing an opinion. Heunis, as was his wont, was more loquacious and given to his usual elaborate and at times convoluted explanations. At one point, however, he dropped his guard and bluntly interrupted Slabbert's plea for voluntary political association outside an apartheid frame: 'Van Zyl, you must understand. If people expect us to sacrifice the group basis of our politics, we shoot.' Slabbert observed that he 'was not angry or threatening, but simply stating a fundamental non-negotiable for the government'.[18]

RESIGNATION

Slabbert not only tested the waters with white parliamentarians and officials; there is also evidence that he was in contact with Thabo Mbeki.[19] The academic and political commentator RW Johnson later argued that a deal was struck between the two that involved Slabbert's leaving Parliament before public talks with the ANC could proceed.[20] Whether that was indeed the case needs to be explained. Slabbert was a strong individual, and although he had a very good relationship with Mbeki, it is unlikely he would have allowed Mbeki to dictate his career path and whether he should stay in Parliament or not.[21]

Yet, in a letter to Slabbert in January 1986, which Slabbert apparently received the very day he was to make his announcement,[22] Mbeki adopted a rather prescriptive tone and suggested he was already aware of Slabbert's plans. Revealingly, he told Slabbert: 'The decision that you have taken has the potential to make a very important impact towards the kind of society which we all seek. We think it is therefore very important that your announcement should measure up to the importance of the occasion.' This was followed by the injunction that 'it is necessary that you emerge as a man of vision whom it is said is lacking in white politics'. In addition, he was told, almost instructed, that as 'to your future conduct it would be important to say that you only sit as a representative in a democratic institution. For present purposes you could stand again on a democratic platform and, when elected, not take your seat.'[23]

Slabbert had also tried to sell to the PFP the idea that members should retire from their seats, and, if they happened to be re-elected, refuse to sit in the House until the Population Registration Act of 1950 was rescinded. Eglin was aghast that someone as adroit as Slabbert could come up with such a 'flawed and fanciful scheme'.[24] Slabbert later acknowledged that it was 'a bit far-fetched'.[25] He was probably at his wits' end, causing him to deviate from his usually sober deliberation, and Mbeki's influence in this specific respect is conjectural. This is about as far as one can go. As for his actual resignation, Mbeki, in the letter, mentions that the decision to resign is Slabbert's. This is independently corroborated by Alex Boraine.[26] What happened afterwards was that Slabbert probably informed Mbeki, who saw in this a potentially positive development for the ANC. Slabbert himself later refuted the idea that Mbeki persuaded him to leave Parliament, describing it as 'common fiction presented as fact'.[27]

Seven members of Slabbert's inner circle, which included politicians and academics, met him privately in early February 1986 to discuss their leader's imminent resignation. In a wide-ranging and intense discussion, the idea that MPs should resign and if re-elected refuse to take up their seats was raised again and rejected out of hand. Besides being impractical, it could also not be assumed that those who left would gain greater credibility – if that were the intention – with black people over the long run. They would at first be applauded, it was argued, and then forgotten – 'no voice, constituency or clout'.[28] Due allowance was made for what they called the *gatvol* (fed-up) factor on the part of Slabbert. It was recognised that he had put far more effort than most into the PFP and had made greater sacrifices. In order to address this, it was suggested that his parliamentary duties be scaled down and he be released from some party obligations to enable him to become more involved in extra-parliamentary activities.

This middle-of-the-road suggestion did not find favour with Slabbert. Nor did he agree with the observation that his resignation would leave the party in the lurch. His reply was that 'if they had put their hope in an individual rather than a party, then he had failed in his duty as leader'.[29] He did, however, end the meeting with a parting comment that he would give the matter further thought. This was most likely said out of a sense of collegiality rather than out of conviction. In a way, Slabbert's conduct uncannily resembled his response to the approaches of the United Party some 13 years earlier, when they tried to persuade him to stand as a candidate: he showed interest but then rapidly switched to the PFP to follow his own instincts (see Chapter 2). This time around it was the PFP that was to be at the receiving end of Slabbert's change of mind.

In the week of the no-confidence debate in Parliament, set to reach its climax on 7 February 1986, Slabbert showed little outward signs of stress. Journalist Ken Owen, who visited him in his office, found him 'unusually relaxed, a man at peace with himself ... The easy charm was undiminished, his ability to see into the heart of South Africa's problems unaffected'.[30] He had all but made up his mind, though there was an outside chance that he might still change course. He had hoped almost against hope that the dramatic events of 1985 would cause the government to reconsider the fundamentals of apartheid. A glimpse of such a possibility would have been PW Botha's speech to open Parliament and the no-confidence debate.[31]

Slabbert played his cards close to his chest, and few outside his immediate circle were aware of his intended course of action. He only told Eglin of his final decision in the morning. Eglin realised that there was no point in arguing with him, though he advised Slabbert to inform Helen Suzman accordingly. She was furious when he told her and accused him bluntly of deserting the cause.[32] He looked grim and tense when he informed the full caucus of his decision, only 45 minutes before the afternoon session, which started at 2.15 pm. He did not allow time for any discussion.[33] The press had no inkling; after all, it was a Friday afternoon and it was most unlikely for any MP to raise anything controversial so late in the week.[34]

Botha's traditional opening speech as state president was predictable in that he essentially confirmed the status quo. There were no surprises here, but what did cause a stir was the way he castigated the minister of foreign affairs, the unconventional Pik Botha, who had the temerity to suggest, in the most convoluted of terms, that South Africa might well have a black president in the future. This, however, turned out to be a sideshow. Ironically, the president was more favourably disposed towards Slabbert. Although Botha took Slabbert to task about earlier sharp critiques relating to Botha's supposed lack of understanding of the interrelationship between politics and economics, overall he had some appreciation for Slabbert's role. He said that he was not accustomed to Slabbert's behaving in a derogatory manner. 'At the outset,' Botha continued, 'the two of us were somewhat at loggerheads, but I thought we had subsequently developed a reasonably good understanding.'[35] It was not the first time Botha's judgement had failed him. High drama was about to follow.

When Slabbert took the floor, he routinely but trenchantly assailed government policy before coming to the heart of his speech. 'I wish to conclude on a more personal note and without acrimony and bitterness,' he cautiously informed the House. He then paid homage to his colleagues for their part in opposing apartheid. 'There is, however,' he continued, 'another aspect of opposition which has a momentum and life of its own … That aspect is political leadership in opposition. This too has to be judged, but on different grounds, and the most important judge is the person himself.' This meant, he said, that a person had to decide 'when the tension between analysis and practice is no longer bearable for himself: in other words, he has to decide when the moment has arrived to go.' He considered that the 'magic moment for any political leader is to find the right time to go. I believe it is perhaps slightly less painful to go when people want one to stay [than] when people want one to go. I have decided the time has come for me to go.' Listening to the state president's speech, he claimed, had finally clarified matters for him.[36]

Parliament was stunned. The House went silent. The president appeared shocked and stared impassively straight ahead. Senior ministers glanced furtively at their leader. Rina Venter, minister of health and social services (and the National Party's first and only female cabinet minister), whispered to a colleague: 'Now politics in South Africa has changed for ever.'[37] Several PFP members looked grim-faced and anguished.[38] Slabbert's family members were also present. Marcia Haak, who was in the know, 'felt for him at the moment but

I knew it was the right thing for him to do'.[39] With the no-confidence motion predictably defeated, Botha rose and slowly strolled towards Slabbert, shaking his hand and exchanging formal courtesies. It was only once the ceremonial proceedings concluded, and the initial shock had subsided, that the parliamentary lobbies became hubs of excitement and rumour.[40]

Slabbert made clear his resolve to break with all parliamentary matters when he failed to attend the farewell occasion Parliament had planned for him. Although he had originally intended to participate, he later explained, in a carefully worded letter to the Speaker, that, as his resignation was deemed so controversial, he did not wish to add further fuel to the fire and would therefore rather absent himself. Hendrik Schoeman, the leader of the House, regretted this decision. While political opponents and leaders of parties seldom saw anything positive in their opponents, Slabbert was an exception: 'He commanded respect as a man of integrity and intellect'. Given Slabbert's standing, political commentators were at a loss to explain his move. They had to admit: 'We are no nearer to solving the mystery of the Demise of the Golden Boy of Politics.'[41]

Rationale

Slabbert's central concern was whether Parliament could in any way be relied upon as an effective tool to transform the political system. Tinkering with apartheid was not a solution; the whole system had to be abolished. He had the firm impression that this realisation still had to dawn on a National Party leadership irrevocably mired in group thinking. Despite their best intentions, this fundamentally worked against change.[42]

He particularly regarded the tricameral parliamentary arrangement as a huge obstacle to transformation. The 1983 referendum, he recalled in Parliament, was one of the 'most painful periods in my political life'. He badly wanted to see change, but, he continued, 'out of deep conviction I had to be critical and negative whilst with everybody else I would have liked to believe we were getting out of the mess'.[43] Instead, as he later argued elsewhere, the system became one of the key factors polarising the situation. He 'felt trapped in an institution that had to generate an alternative and in fact was seen as a problem rather than a solution itself, and I couldn't see how one could break out of that.'[44] He was clearly back as a sociologist, wary of self-serving systems riddled with tautological justifications.

He made it clear that he did not object to Parliament as an institution per se. He appreciated the protest role that PFP members played, and it was precisely because he respected the institution that he wished to see it function optimally. The way Parliament operated under the Botha administration, though, diminished its efficacy. He elaborated:

> I left Parliament because it had become a waste of time. A waste of time for what? For promoting the idea of a non-racial democracy in South Africa and then building up a parliamentary party that could effectively bring it about. Perhaps it was a mistake for me to believe that this was possible in the first place. But at least it was worth a try.[45]

If Botha had shown sufficient insight to dismantle apartheid structures through Parliament, Slabbert would have seen his way clear to assisting him unconditionally. In the absence of such insight, he felt that he could not continue working in an institution where apartheid laws were regarded as non-negotiable.[46] In more outspoken terms, he related that what he had seen and heard had 'been a sort of macabre ballad of people too scared to peer over the ramparts of their trenches and to see what the reality was outside'.[47] Later on, he recalled that he regarded Parliament as 'literally a machine that thrived on the political grease of patronage. It was in its own world, totally removed from the daily struggle going on in the rest of our society.'[48]

RESIGNATION

Although Slabbert's critique of Parliament, expressed with his usual eloquence, can be well understood, the timing of his open disaffection is of interest. In his 1985 book *The Last White Parliament*, there is little firm evidence that he regarded Parliament as being redundant. He steadfastly believed in evolutionary change and real political negotiations, of which Parliament was to be an integral part. Admittedly, he did have reservations about how to measure the success of such a strategy, but the strategy as such was not in doubt. He could therefore say, with some conviction: 'I have no difficulty trying to explain why I am in Parliament and what I am trying to do and why I am encouraging others to do the same.'[49] In an article for the *Financial Mail* in November 1985, he argued that protesting in the streets and 'howling at the moon at an English-speaking campus' had their place, but did not exclude engaging in a rational and robust debate with a cabinet minister.[50] It was self-evident that Parliament could not simply be bypassed, but in order for Parliament to facilitate change, the 'only useful purpose' the tricameral constitution could serve was 'to get rid of it'.[51]

As we have seen, it was precisely his encounter with Botha at the end of November, and the later meeting with Heunis, that caused him to reconsider the role of Parliament. So within a month his lingering reservations about his role as a formal politician surfaced with a vengeance, his doubts multiplied, and his beliefs became seriously eroded. His questioning academic outlook now trumped the politician in him and predisposed him to act upon increasingly nagging qualms. It all happened within a very concentrated span of time. In this respect, it can also be noted that Slabbert was known to be impetuous at times, and once he made up his mind he could be stubborn.[52] However, this does not imply that he took such an important decision on a whim.

Besides these issues, he felt seriously undermined by the disdain with which the military treated Parliament. As defence spokesperson for the PFP, he came to realise that despite government undertakings, such as the Nkomati Accord of 1984, to stop the destabilisation of neighbouring Mozambique, the process continued virtually unabated. He made this discovery during a special visit to Maputo early in January 1986. He met President Samora Machel, who presented him with the diaries of one Colonel Vass, a Renamo soldier, which incontrovertibly bore testimony to such transgressions. Yet the higher echelons of the military denied any such knowledge and through subterfuge tried to deceive him. The incident, which he was sure Botha was aware of, left a sour taste; he felt the president abused him with impunity. He rejected emphatically the cynicism with which the government treated the traditions of Parliament:

> The whole ritual of loyal opposition, honouring the House, consulting the Leader of the Opposition was so much hogwash. It was a constitutional charade which they indulged in to suit their purposes. They had no compunction to lie, misinform or disinform Parliament and members associated with it, if they thought it necessary.[53]

While Slabbert's increasing revulsion towards Parliament loomed large, there were other factors that should be considered. Some of these related to friction within the PFP. During the meeting with his close colleagues shortly before his resignation, he spoke with feeling about his frustration with the 'petty squabbling and jostling which went on in the topmost echelons of the party'.[54] Besides interpersonal rivalry, the differences between the left- and right-wing factions of the party on matters such as defence policy created further tensions.[55] Moreover, he also felt that English-speaking businesspeople had turned their backs on him and he had lost the support of the Southern Transvaal region, the party's wealthiest. In addition, there were snide rumours that he was no longer as committed as he used to be and that 'the political iron had left the Slabbert soul'.[56] While such internecine concerns contributed to his disillusionment, they can at best be viewed as secondary considerations for his resignation.[57]

It is furthermore necessary to place Slabbert's departure within the wider context of the political landscape at the time. The turbulence of 1985, and the dramatically altered pattern of South African politics, did not leave the PFP unaffected. The dynamics within a changed constellation in which the ANC and the UDF now featured more prominently than before meant that the PFP message to its traditional white constituents had to be adapted accordingly. It ran the risk of becoming an umbrella party trying to satisfy everyone and in the process satisfying no one. In terms of system politics, the party's position had also gradually come under threat. The PFP could no longer lay claim to being a party of the future, as the UDF had simply supplanted the party's usual 'forward scouting' role. Squeezed by the National Party and the Conservative Party on the right, and for the first time by extra-parliamentary forces on the left, the PFP had to operate in an increasingly airless environment.[58] The PFP, it was reported, was akin to the metaphorical man who badly wanted to join a heated debate but nobody had the slightest interest in his opinion. The only way he could become part of the conversation was to align himself with one of the other two parties.[59] Moreover, on the right there were indications that the Conservative Party seemed poised to overtake the PFP as the official opposition. These were ominous signs for Slabbert. He knew exactly what he did not want – to be relegated to the back benches again.[60] If he had to choose a time to depart, strategically he could not have chosen a better one.

Commentators have often tried to explain Slabbert's departure by referring to a supposed fatal flaw, which was essentially thought to be a lack of tenacity. Insinuations of this kind flew fast and furious. Ken Owen led the pack by stating, shortly after Slabbert's resignation, that 'he had it too easy. He brought no constituency with him, no political dowry, except a fine mind, a handsome face and a trim figure.'[61] Along similar lines, Slabbert was accused of lacking 'staying power', of being a 'self-indulgent Afrikaner glamour boy', and of having 'an unreliable, unpredictable streak'. These were, Slabbert thought, 'simplistic and pejorative psychoanalysis'.[62] Such opinions were nevertheless bandied about, he said, by 'some editors and crusty cognoscenti who frequent the Rand Club and pose as amateur psychoanalysts and who claim that I do not have the … stamina for politics'.[63] He took exception to a narrative that depicted him

> simply as a self-indulgent dilettante, indifferent to the feelings of others, untrustworthy, unpredictable, a political lightweight simply waiting for the moment he could shrug his shoulders and walk off leaving a devastated party behind. Perhaps he had even been planning this all along so that he could walk out in a blaze of self-indulgent sensationalism.[64]

He strongly countered such interpretations by claiming that while he was in parliamentary politics, he worked harder than at least 80 per cent of the caucus members in addressing meetings, fundraising and promoting the party. He further argued that he had a very good idea of how many members spent their time: 'For most MPs politics is no sweat – you do not need stamina, just the ability to ride out rituals and boredom until you can pursue your own affairs again.'[65] He could also point out that on his watch the PFP had grown, and that in the 1981 general election it had garnered 21 per cent of the votes.

Slabbert, unlike some of his colleagues, had little truck with the rituals and clubby atmosphere of Parliament, nor did he regard the position of leader of the opposition as a life sentence. After the 1983 referendum, he indicated that he would have preferred not to participate in the tricameral constitutional arrangements, but was prevailed upon to continue. Once he made that commitment, he was prepared to go in 'boots and all'. However, it could not be business as usual and they had to show some progress in helping to dismantle apartheid.[66]

RESIGNATION

During the ensuing three years, there was little cheer to be had. He developed 'a very real sense of 'having had enough', especially as 'things' had worsened and not improved'. Slabbert was fully aware that frustration was an integral part of the political scene, but he felt much more than mere routine frustration. He understood the political game only too well and realised that politics 'inevitably involves compromising one's personal integrity', and that one reason 'politics is called the art of the possible is because politicians have to justify their compromises'. But here was the rub. 'For me,' he said, 'a time had come where my justifications simply could no longer square up to my compromises. I was beginning to feel obscene.'[67] He realised that it was a private problem and that politicians usually found their own way of coping with the contradictions, but personally he regarded such deceptions as no longer tenable. It all appeared to have become quite futile and he felt he had become redundant. In Parliament he explained:

> It is bad enough when one's opponents start taking one for granted – either as a political punch bag, or a nice guy to have around but not to be taken seriously – but it is worse when one feels one is starting to take oneself for granted; in other words when one feels that this is where one is going to be for the rest of one's life.[68]

This awareness prompted him to reflect more deeply on the nature of the occupation. 'Politics is necessary,' he argued, 'but it is not a business or a profession or even a vocation.'[69] The only way it could be meaningful was for political leadership to be a proactive career. It could not be 'a safe route to a retirement gratuity and pension', he said.[70]

In some sections of the Afrikaans press, Slabbert was stringently criticised as merely being unable to communicate his views effectively and garner support. 'The friendliest remark one could make,' *Beeld* weighed in, 'is to say that he was a spectacular failure.

Influential and powerful forces supported and mollycoddled him. But at the end he was just not enough of a politician.'[71] The issue, however, was not essentially his feistiness and durability as a politician; after all, he could mix it with the best of them. At the heart of the matter was the fact that he was not enough of a career politician of a certain kind, who could without too much exertion survive from year to year on a staple diet of parliamentary debates and party and committee work. He was a politician of a different order, who pursued a broader vision and equitable outcomes with intent. He argued that he 'could think of better vantage points [for] viewing the developments than being trapped in a position of futility that I was experiencing'.[72]

For Slabbert, there was an additional moral element involved. In an interview, he made it clear that it was more than just politics per se. 'My obligations,' he explained, 'are simply wider than those of people who believe that it is your responsibility to be leader of your party in Parliament for ever and ever amen. My moral obligation relates to the country …' He felt he should ask: '[A]m I making any contribution towards resolving the crisis? Am I really doing the best I can to get rid of apartheid?'[73] These reflections had a messianic ring to them, and recalled his youthful commitment to the church and the need to make a decisive impact on other people's lives. As opposed to what now appeared to him as the increasingly tawdry world of politics, he was searching for a more meaningful engagement where he could make a difference. The historian Hermann Giliomee later raised the possibility of what might ultimately have been Slabbert's goal: 'What could be more noble and exciting than abandoning Parliament to pursue the ideal of a negotiated settlement along liberal-democratic lines. It was an ideal worth devoting all his energies to, even his career.'[74]

Related to the moral dimension of Slabbert's decision was the observation by colleague Graham McIntosh that deeper metaphysical concerns might also have been at work. Writing to Slabbert, he suspected that this was 'an imperative based on a frame of reference'

RESIGNATION

and that the idea of 'existential self-authentication' was the best way to define it. He continued revealingly:

> If one discounts a possible undisclosed political purpose there seems no rational basis to your decision and as you have always passionately and, in my view, consistently sought to be always true and rational, your decision, in this case must be based on a philosophical commitment. It is the kind of irrational rock against which the dean of the kweekskool [seminary] was powerless when you told him you had lost your calling. It is the same kind of imperative that takes men into religious life. On an existential basis your action is entirely explicable and I find I can digest it.[75]

Slabbert's response is not available, but McIntosh's observation has a certain validity. Slabbert had a philosophical streak in him and was given to reflecting upon existential matters and the purpose of life.[76] It would have made perfect sense for him to view and question his role in Parliament in such terms.

What emerged was that being a politician in the apartheid Parliament in the mid-1980s was not what Slabbert could any longer regard as a higher-order calling that imparted meaning. So on both an elevated and a practical political level he was driven to question the sense of his existence. At the start of his career he might have had more of a calling instinct (see chapters 1, 2 and 8), but in 1986, as a result of the context in which he found himself, this had started to wane. He commented that earlier he had seen Parliament 'as an opportunity that had to be explored'. However, he had now 'done so and that's it'.[77] In a wider sense, Slabbert's outlook in 1986 evokes a pointed observation by Max Weber, the founder of modern sociology. Writing generally on politics as a vocation, Weber said: 'Only he has a calling for politics who is sure that he shall not crumble when the world from his point of view is too stupid or too base for what he wants to offer. Only he who in the face of all of this can say, "In spite of all!" has the calling for politics.'[78] Such a life sentence without reprieve did not appeal, and was most unlikely ever to appeal to Slabbert's temperament.

His alleged lack of endurance was often linked to the view that he had a 'five-year attention span' and after the initial flush of enthusiasm was inclined to lose interest in a project.[79] His earlier abandonment of his theological studies and his truncated academic career are then brought to bear on the issue of his parliamentary retirement. However, this chink in his armour, if it was that, assumed a different form. It was not the absence of determination, but rather a tendency to overreach and want to achieve too much. It was not a case of doing things by half measures, but rather of wanting to do everything by full measures. Former Democratic Alliance (DA) leader Helen Zille, who was a journalist on the *Rand Daily Mail* during the 1980s, recalled a conversation with Slabbert in which he asked her what she considered 'a really existential question: what is the purpose of my life, here and now in South Africa?' From the tenor and slant of the conversation, she concluded that 'he felt he should be in executive office, and that he aimed for the very top'.[80] Of course, he fully realised that objective conditions being what they were, it was illusory to think along such lines. Yet the idea never completely disappeared from his thinking. In 1985, when the PFP organised a large-scale fundraising drive with a view to driving effective change with Slabbert as party leader, it came to him that despite the grim outlook, the reasoning behind aiming to reach more ambitious goals was not completely wayward. 'Nevertheless,' he explained, 'there was an inescapable kind of logic to it all. If the PFP was going to "change things", and that was why we were asking people for money, then as leader of the PFP, I had to present myself as a plausible threat to the present incumbent of the highest office of the land.'[81]

Slabbert rarely advertised himself in this way, but it does demonstrate that he was not without his own ambitions, and that despite adverse conditions he held out certain hopes. Particularly after his

RESIGNATION

depressing encounters with Botha, it seems that he was no longer prepared to be second best, and if he stayed in Parliament his prospects of achieving more would evaporate rapidly. So if he could get out and explore other possibilities, given the rising tide of extra-parliamentary activism and prospects, his chances outside might not be worse than inside Parliament. Such a calculation might not necessarily have been uppermost in his mind, but there might well have been an awareness that if he could achieve a senior position in a new democratic dispensation, both his personal, often-hidden yearnings and his political convictions would be addressed. However, while Slabbert was looking forward to a new dawn, and could perhaps even see himself coming through the mist into the first rays of daybreak, it was not yet assured. Nor, realistically, could Slabbert's place in the politics of a possible new order be predicted.

Shortly after Slabbert's resignation, *Beeld* posed the following question: 'Was it one small event that led to a nervous political breakdown, or was it merely a growing sense of futility that eventually crystallised? The Slabbert saga indeed contains all the ingredients of a political detective hunt.'[82] The answer to this is that it was not necessarily a political meltdown, nor a simple either/or situation, but rather a combination of factors. These involved his long-standing critical attitude towards closed systems, his temperament and quest for meaningful fulfilment, his personal frustrations and visions, and ultimately his reading and interpretation of the politics of the day.

This does not imply that the logic was necessarily always flawless. Stanley Uys, the noted political analyst, took Slabbert to task for what he regarded as an important oversight in failing to deal with the question of raised expectations. Slabbert's 'whole academic training', he said, 'should have told him that frustrations are at their most acute when they are closest to being released, when fulfilment is approaching ... Parliament is not all that different. It too is seething with expectations. For Slabbert to pull out at this juncture, at this moment of impending crisis, boggles the mind.'[83] While this was a sharp rebuke, it is a moot point whether Slabbert's limited leeway to effect change was sufficiently considered. Slabbert argued that he had given the matter enough thought, and according 'to my own light and wisdom I have done whatever can be done with the available opportunities, and to continue as before I would be bluffing myself and others'.[84]

Fallout

A week after Slabbert's departure, Alex Boraine was the only colleague who, after some speculation that he might actually succeed Slabbert, also tendered his resignation, and for very much the same reasons as Slabbert. Apart from the political commentaries, the press focused on the pension payouts and gratuities the two were about to receive. It was estimated that Slabbert would receive an immediate payment of about R100 000 and a monthly pension of approximately R3 600. These sums, it was claimed, would allow him to live in 'reasonable comfort'.[85] Slabbert was not so sure. Although he actually received R120 000, he had to use the money to pay off a housing loan he had received from the Oppenheimers. All he knew was that after 12 years in Parliament, he was left with only R2 500 in his pocket and he had to find a job.[86] A part-time teaching position at UCT and the University of the Western Cape was in the offing, though.

Slabbert and Boraine had no fully worked-out fallback position, either financially or politically. They discussed their options at length. Boraine later recalled that they did think it was necessary to consult black leaders inside and outside the country to find out from them whether 'they thought two middle-aged white males had any contribution to make'. Other options were to simply sit on the sidelines or leave the country. The thought also occurred to them that perhaps they should try and make some money for the first time in their lives.[87]

RESIGNATION

More immediately, they had to deal with the political fallout, which was much stronger than they anticipated, including the responses of some of their colleagues. Colin Eglin recalled:

> The emotions generated by the departure of the leader they had admired and trusted were soon manifest in PFP ranks. Members outside the parliamentary caucus were bewildered, while within the caucus there were a few members, who, being close to Slabbert, took his resignation stoically and with understanding. For the rest, reactions ranged from anger to disbelief and disappointment.[88]

Slabbert was only too painfully aware that he had angered many of his former colleagues, and he drafted a letter that he asked Eglin to read at the first caucus meeting. He assured them that his resignation was a political statement and not merely an act of self-indulgence, and he hoped that once the anger had subsided they would be able to talk politics again. This did not mollify feelings.[89]

One person who was particularly furious with Slabbert was Helen Suzman, as noted earlier. When he told her, just before his farewell speech, that he had already served 12 years in Parliament, she responded that she had already served 26 years and 13 of those on her own. His compliment that she had a 'built-in survival kit second to none' did not clear the air.[90] There was not much that Slabbert could do to change her mind. He approached her again in March 1986, but she held firm to the view that he had been a huge disappointment and had walked away from his commitment 'so casually that it was breathtaking'.[91] Suzman, according to the journalist Max du Preez, had also earlier, unbeknown to Slabbert, injected an unfortunate ethnic element into the argument when she remarked to a PFP member: 'What do you expect of a bloody Afrikaner?'[92]

Politicians are inclined to make much of the sacrifices they have had to endure, and tend to judge others by that yardstick. Suzman was no different. She justifiably foregrounded her contribution to Parliament, but in her exchanges with Slabbert she failed to mention that in 1973, when the Progressive Party was at a particularly low ebb, she also had toyed with the idea of resigning. At the time she thought that if the party did not improve its showing in the 1974 election, it would be better if they disbanded and directed their finances and energies into extra-parliamentary work. Eglin had had a similar idea,[93] which did not differ much from Slabbert's reasoning 13 years later. However, by then, partly through Slabbert's endeavours, the party's fortunes had improved, and with that came convenient political amnesia.

Such was the outcry against Slabbert that one newspaper commentator observed: 'Van-bashing seems to be the favourite sport these days.'[94] Another reporter concurred, stating that there seemed to be a 'lynch mob after Van Zyl Slabbert'. He was aware that South African political behaviour was not known to be particularly edifying, but the reactions to Slabbert's resignation reached new levels of incivility. The PFP, in this case, reminded him 'of very small children dispossessed of their beach ball. Complaints seldom got as shrill, nor does malcontent rise to such querulous heights.'[95] Some former colleagues, however, did have the grace to reflect upon their earlier disillusionment. Douglas Gibson, for instance, described by Alex Boraine as a 'nasty character', wrote to Slabbert about a fortnight after the latter's resignation saying that, although he had been angry initially, he had upon reflection come to the realisation 'that there was a definite purpose to the resignation and that it was not simply a quixotic impulse'. Slabbert expressed his gratitude for such understanding.[96]

Slabbert's departure nevertheless left the PFP in an invidious position. The party had embarked on a major fundraising drive and obtained the services of a professional fundraising consultant, Everald Compton, an Australian who conducted the campaign along slick, Madison Avenue lines. Slabbert was the face of the campaign, and Compton argued that Slabbert's image and leadership qualities

RESIGNATION

were worth millions if packaged properly.[97] This happened despite Slabbert's repeated objections. Personalising the campaign in this manner also meant that for many fundraisers, it was not the PFP that was to drive change but Slabbert himself. 'This kind of cultish naiveté,' he later said, became 'a very severe source of moral and intellectual compromise for me.'[98] Such exposure, embarrassing as it might have been, was of course the price of politics. Besides, it should be factored in that Slabbert's shock resignation was equally awkward for the party. The campaign had to be redirected and the party ran the risk of being accused of misleading donors.[99]

In other respects, although the party was in disarray after Slabbert's announcement, it soon regrouped under Colin Eglin, who resumed the leadership. Buoyed by encouraging public support from Harry Oppenheimer, Eglin emphasised that the party had to move beyond Slabbert and act in a cohesive manner in order to regain momentum. He rapidly set about restructuring the party organisation.[100]

Party organiser Neil Ross later recalled that a while after Slabbert's departure, an unintended positive consequence became apparent. He explained:

> His [Slabbert's] leaving allowed the party to become more pragmatic, get its feet down on the ground and, in fact, to crystallise its viewpoint. Because Slabbert straddled people's viewpoints they were able to in fact go along with things because it was Slabbert ... And some of the people we lost, ... you know the old thing of purging the party to strengthen it, I think in this instance it was true. In fact, we had spanned too wide a span in terms of people's political viewpoint and in many ways I think Slabbert's departure from the Parliament was a blessing.[101]

Ross was not alone in this kind of thinking. Helen Suzman, despite her earlier criticism that Slabbert's resignation had rent the party asunder, felt in late 1986 that the 'shock of his leaving has actually drawn people closer together. There is a far better spirit in the caucus, and much more cooperation and a willingness to work together.'[102] While these observations may be seen as a case of making a virtue out of necessity, the party seemed to have dealt with Slabbert's departure effectively. It was more difficult to convince the electorate of the PFP's political credentials now that a leader such as Slabbert had deserted the party. The litmus test for the overall standing of the party would come with the 1987 general election.

The PFP was pleasantly surprised when opinion surveys revealed that by the end of 1986, it had regained the percentage loss suffered after Slabbert's resignation, and as much as 37 per cent of the white electorate indicated that they were broadly supportive of the party's principles and policies. They had reason to hope as polling day (6 May) approached. The dynamics of the election, however, worked against them. PW Botha was intent on curbing the influence of the Conservative Party, which was gaining ground. He not only hammered the Conservatives as being out of touch with political reality but also tainted the PFP as fellow-travellers of the ANC, portraying the National Party as centrist and the only party responsible enough to be entrusted with the country's future. Botha's propaganda worked and the PFP emerged in tatters, losing seven of the 26 seats it had picked up in 1981. To top it all, the Conservative Party replaced the PFP as the official opposition.[103]

The party's heavy defeat inevitably raised the question whether the drubbing had anything to do with the absence of Slabbert. One of the party's research consultants claimed that this was indeed the case. The party failed to get its message across because it did not have skilled communicators like Slabbert.[104] It was an assumption that Slabbert irritably dismissed as misdirected 'individualistic nonsense'. He then proceeded to list all the variables between the 1981 and 1987 elections: a different constitution, massive extra-parliamentary mobilisation, farcical coloured and Indian elections, riots and unrest on an unprecedented scale, successive states of emergency and a powerful executive president.[105] The political landscape had changed dramatically and, not surprisingly, the outcome of the 1987 election was a much more complicated matter than justified merely singling out one individual, however influential that person might have been earlier on.

Besides the nuts and bolts of election outcomes, the PFP had more fundamental concerns. The issues of direction, strategy and potential that Slabbert had grappled with and acted upon were now squarely in the lap of the party. There were no easy answers, nor was the leadership in a position to suggest creative pathways out of the predicament. Slabbert's departure had called into question the legitimacy of the tradition in which the PFP was used to operating. The very foundation of the party's liberal *raison d'être* and its gradualist approach were in fact now under threat.[106] In relinquishing the leadership role, Slabbert had inadvertently laid bare the PFP's more deep-rooted problems.

The National Party took umbrage at Slabbert's wholesale condemnation of Parliament, effectively impugning the institution in which the party reigned supreme. Slabbert's actions were also seen as a blow to the government's reform efforts and damaging to South Africa's standing abroad.[107] Nevertheless, the National Party quickly found its balance and, after some damage control, emerged in an even more favourable position. It now had to deal with a weakened opposition on the left, and it was a welcome relief to be rid of Slabbert's withering attacks in Parliament.

Black spokespeople welcomed Slabbert's resignation and encouraged other parliamentarians to do the same.[108] The ANC, through Mbeki, was particularly effusive:

> Never in the history of our country has a White establishment political leader confronted the iniquity of the system of White minority domination as Dr Slabbert has done

today. We salute his courage, his honesty and his loyalty to a common South African nationhood … Today millions of our people, of all races, will acclaim Dr Slabbert as a new Voortrekker.[109]

Local white communists were, however, less fulsome. Given to suspicion and inclined to think predominantly in structural terms, they thought that Slabbert was part of a Trojan Horse-type plot to defuse the 'struggle' from within.[110]

In reviewing the fallout from Slabbert's resignation, it can be argued that if his departure did not actually help to loosen the props of apartheid society, it did force various groupings to take stock of South Africa's prospects. In rupturing the familiar parliamentary discourse, he foregrounded the need for more meaningful political engagements. Slabbert never regretted leaving Parliament when he did, though he was remorseful about the impact it had on some of his colleagues.[111] Overall, the fallout from his resignation did not render Parliament impotent, and it remained an essential institution. All roads still led back to Parliament. To Slabbert, though, these routes led to a dead end.

It also meant that once negotiations started in 1990, after President FW de Klerk, Botha's more pragmatic successor, unbanned formerly proscribed political movements, Slabbert had no official standing. Although he had all the attributes of a skilled negotiator, he was unable to play a significant part in the negotiation process. De Klerk later thought that had Slabbert stayed on as a parliamentary leader, he could have played a meaningful role.[112] Whether that would have made much of a difference in the ultimate outcome, however, is purely speculative. Slabbert, though, credited Colin Eglin, who did participate, as having 'punched above his weight'.[113] Outside the realm of conjecture, it can be said with certainty that Slabbert's resignation brought the issue of Parliament's role sharply into focus. Seldom in South Africa's history had the voluntary resignation of a parliamentary leader caused such a furore.

7
INTO A BRAVE NEW WORLD

Taking political stock

With Slabbert's departure from Parliament, he moved tentatively into the less predictable, more volatile world of extra-parliamentary politics. It was not an overnight process and called for much reflection as to how he should position himself. It represented, not only in form but also in substance, a different emphasis from the kind of political thinking that had informed much of his parliamentary career. At the same time, though, he was freed from the constraints of party-political procedures and could follow his own instincts more readily.[1]

Slabbert changed course insofar as he reconceptualised the terms in which the South African dilemma was construed. He placed less weight on the conflict in South Africa being of a racial nature, with a white-led government squaring up against a black oppositional movement for control over the state. Subscribing to such a fixed view did not leave much manoeuvring room. Instead, he increasingly saw it as a struggle between despotism and democratic concerns that went beyond the usual binary-oppositional racial terms. Primarily, it was democracy as such that was at stake, and the issue was to find ways in which this outcome could be assured. In 1988 he stated: 'I have made no secret of my faith that the cause of democracy is served better by the majority struggling against tyranny than among the minority keeping it in power.'[2]

He moved from earlier Prog positions, which had evolved from dispensing with a qualified franchise and a minority-white veto to flighting various power-sharing arrangements, to a personal position that favoured majoritarianism. This, admittedly, may have compromised traditional liberal views on the need for pluralism. The question, however, was what to do once it became clear that such a belief had failed to effect meaningful change. It was no longer possible, he thought, to maintain the convenient position of benign observation, neutrality and the occasional well-meaning but ineffectual intervention. 'The primary question now that liberals are forced to face,' he said, was '"Where do you stand in the struggle? For freedom or stability?" They may refuse to choose by calling a plague on the irrationality of both houses and hover around in a fit of sullen irrelevancy. If they do so, the struggle for freedom will become the exclusive preserve of the revolutionary, and the maintenance of stability the preserve of increasing repression.'[3] The choice before liberals had become so stark, he argued, because of the successive states of emergency and increasing international pressure, that one could no longer afford the luxury of thinking that the impasse would merely be resolved by people of goodwill.

This implied that what had passed as the 'standard' liberal political creed, with its presumed assumptions of cultural and political superiority – liberalism with the haughty sneer of those accustomed to having an automatic right of way – had to be interrogated. What was required was to develop a particular strain of liberalism commensurate with local needs and circumstances. The onus was on 'standard' liberal thinking not only to come to terms with universal suffrage, but also, ideologically, to show 'a concomitant willingness to demonstrate that liberalism is consistent with majority aspirations'.[4] This inflection went beyond the assumption that liberalism as defined up to this point was the only norm; it too had to adapt. What has been described as 'Slabbert's liberalism' tried to show 'that liberal ideas and values can work for all of us'. It did not have to be restricted to certain political parties or groupings, and it sought to construct alliances rather than to erect walls, and hoped to persuade rather than to coerce.[5]

In general, it was a hallmark of Slabbert's thinking that he was not ideologically hidebound; more often than not he went against the grain and refrained from boxing reality into a specific framework.[6] Conceptually, this allowed him to pursue different routes in the attempt to abolish apartheid. However, the absence of political orthodoxy could also provide a less than surefooted point of departure as far as future political systems were concerned. What was missing, or not given sufficient weight, was that in a deeply divided South Africa, majoritarianism could turn democracy into a liberal veneer for racial domination. A system in which most of the leaders and public representatives are chosen on the basis of their race, it can be argued, is substantially different from a democracy in which voters, regardless of race, choose according to their beliefs and interests. Slabbert did not pay much heed to the possibilities of such an eventuality and seems to have thought that a strong constitution and entrenched human rights would be a sufficient antidote to the abuse of power. He was aware, though, that if this was not the case, he would be called upon again to stringently oppose a possible new system of domination.[7]

Besides refiguring the liberal calculus, Slabbert also had to adapt to the nature of black mass-protest politics in the late 1980s. He was not by inclination or conviction given to street politics. That much he made clear when he announced in Parliament upon his resignation: 'I am not a radical, a revolutionary or a violent protester.'[8] It was, however, important for him to understand the dynamics of these protests beyond the government's usual dismissal of black political activists as being ill-informed, subversive and indoctrinated youths. He was fully aware that mobilisation politics involved grassroots organisations that often had well-defined strategies in place and particular aims in mind. What concerned him, though, was that so often objectives were obscured by sloganeering, excessive rhetoric and revolutionary romanticism, characterised by an overly optimistic belief that the state was about to be overthrown, so that mass protest meetings then became ends in themselves. Although he was reluctant to prescribe strategies to those in the trenches, he was insistent that mobilisation for its own sake, which could easily degenerate into chaotic and anarchic destruction, only strengthened the government's hand.[9] Mobilisation was a card that had to be played carefully to have a measure of success.

He similarly sought to place the ANC in perspective. The organisation was seeing a visible upsurge of support in the townships as a liberation movement, and assumed a position, along with the UDF – for all intents and purposes its internal running mate – as the most implacable oppositional grouping to the government. He realised that the ANC's commitment to violence was problematic, but that the organisation could not easily retreat from that position, especially with apartheid still in place. Once apartheid was off the statute books, however, he thought the ANC's threats of violence could be politically nullified. The mystique that enveloped the ANC, as a banned organisation, could be pierced once it was allowed to operate and compete in the open political market. It would then be presented with a set of new challenges that it did not have to confront while in exile.[10]

Forever the academic, Slabbert sought his intellectual moorings in the work of the Austrian-born philosopher Karl Popper, whom he held in high regard. He was particularly impressed by Popper's *The Open Society and its Enemies* (1945) and *The Poverty of Historicism* (1957). Writing in the aftermath of the Second World War, Popper systematically questioned the claims of large-scale social engineering and opted instead for changes initiated by individuals and social agencies in a less prescriptive manner. In the mid-1980s, Slabbert sought to align Popper's ideas to the South African situation, especially as they related to apartheid:

> Utopian engineering has to do with mobilising society's resources in pursuit of the 'grand plan'. This plan is usually

> nothing else but the vision of a very powerful and small interest group in society that uses its position of power to control the lives and resources of society in pursuit of this plan. The plan becomes the only goal that is to be pursued, to the exclusion of all others. Popper was vigorously opposed to such 'grand plan' politics. And in its place, he proposed piecemeal tinkering. This approach tried to avoid the mistakes of the past, rather than formulate grand goals for the future. It argued that one had to use one's experience of the knowledge available at the time to improve the quality of life systematically and on a wide range of fronts of society, that room should be left for human ingenuity and creativity in looking for new ways and means of avoiding old mistakes, rather than giving all power to a small minority to force society in the direction of only one set of goals determined by that small group of people.[11]

It was within this wider framework, which allowed for initiatives other than those pertaining to the 'grand plan', that Slabbert sought to find a niche that would enable him to express agency in a new context.

This was not necessarily surprising. He had a history of continuously rejecting structures that seemed to weigh him down: formal administrative requirements in academic life, the strictures of the Dutch Reformed Church and, of course, ultimately the constraints of Parliament. Moreover, personally he was given to excelling in situations in which he had free rein to pursue his own course. Wilmot James, who knew him well and worked closely with him in several capacities, commented:

> He was a role model in autonomy, Van Zyl. If an institution or organisation did not work for him, he wasn't afraid to step out of it, and create something of his own. He believed

in human agency and worked tirelessly for it. He would craft a niche; find a place where his exuberance and intellect could always thrive, and where his ideas would rapidly take shape.[12]

The time away from Parliament allowed Slabbert to free up his thoughts, to reconsider his political trajectory and to plan accordingly. The entry into a brave new world, however, would not always be plain sailing.

Flesh to the bones

Initially, after resigning from Parliament, Slabbert and Boraine had no clear idea how they should proceed politically. Nor was it the case that they were to be automatically embraced by anti-apartheid activists. In fact, some were quite sceptical and advised Boraine, and by implication Slabbert, that as white liberals they should rather concentrate on finding ordinary employment outside politics.[13] Earning a living was indeed an issue, and Slabbert turned to political consultancy and intermittent university teaching to generate an income. He was, however, still intent on making a political difference.

For eight months, Slabbert and Boraine, with the financial help of the Norwegian consul general, toured the country. They engaged with a wide variety of political leaders, community activists and other influential figures, sounding them out on possible future directions they could pursue. These included people like Cyril Ramaphosa, general secretary of the National Union of Mineworkers, who was quite sympathetically inclined towards them.[14] They were also in contact with the ANC, which initially had assumed (wrongly, as it turned out) that after leaving Parliament they would join the movement. Nevertheless, through Thabo Mbeki the ANC was favourably disposed to the idea, flighted by Slabbert and Boraine, of an independent institute or foundation that could promote dialogue. There was one proviso, though: they should discuss any notion of establishing an organisation with existing anti-apartheid role players in the country. Given the states of emergency, such arrangements called for considerable cloak-and-dagger manoeuvring and clandestine meetings with masked township activists before possible cooperation could be assured.[15]

With the groundwork completed, the Institute for a Democratic Alternative for South Africa (Idasa) was founded in October 1986. Slabbert liked the acronym; it had, he claimed, an African ring to it. The first branch office opened in Port Elizabeth on 1 November. The eastern Cape Province was chosen in particular because it was one of the most politically volatile areas in the country, with constant unrest, consumer boycotts and a dangerous standoff between black and white. If the new institute was to have any impact, it was argued, it had to go where it was needed most.[16] Idasa was destined to have a long and in many ways illustrious life for a non-governmental organisation, and only closed down in 2013, over the years skilfully reinventing itself and negotiating the rapids and often watersheds of politics. Slabbert and Boraine laid the foundations well.

The organisation started off modestly enough, though, with house meetings between black and white, arranging discussion groups and other forms of interaction. The ignorance and prejudice, Slabbert recalled, were perturbing. Yet the enthusiasm was not wanting, and it was difficult to keep up with the demand for such encounters.[17] The first major public launch was held in Port Elizabeth in May 1987, with a conference on democracy. Over 400 delegates attended a programme of lectures and workshops. Many of the participants were black, suggesting that the country's future was no longer an insular discussion among predominantly white people attending a standard political meeting. Boraine regarded the conference as unique for its time and the mixed audience 'gave the occasion a concrete sense of reality'.[18]

It was not Idasa's intention to compete with any political party or movement, nor did it seek confrontation with the government, despite its fundamental objections to apartheid policies. Instead, it was closer to a think-tank, committed to a non-racial democracy for South Africa, and sought to focus on what the meaning of such a dispensation could and should be. Idasa's concerns were outlined by Slabbert:

> Is it possible and how does it come about? What does a non-racial democracy mean for health, law, education, land use, local government, housing, conservation, religion and yes, central government in South Africa? Is it possible to generate an idea of a post-apartheid non-racial democratic South Africa that is so compelling that most South Africans would rather work to bring it about than fight against or cling to the present one? This is the challenge Idasa hopes to meet.

In dealing with the term 'non-racialism', Slabbert sought to explain it as not denying the existence of racial groups in South Africa, but rather believing that these should not be used in 'any formal constitutional or legal sense to determine the nature of an individual's political, social or economic participation'.[19] In expressing such a formulation, which at the time appeared to carry a redeeming message, Slabbert could not have foreseen the way in which it would be flouted for more than two decades after the advent of black majority rule, to advance affirmative-action policies according to race.

Idasa regarded a democratic constitution as an essential political prerequisite for peace, and this became a common theme in all political discourses to the left of the government. The concept of democracy, however, needed to be disaggregated and different interpretations and inflections explored. To this end, Slabbert hoped that joint workshops, seminars, conferences and projects involving white and black participants would introduce a new element into the prevailing political discourse, creating a groundswell of opinion crucial for further change. These events were well attended by delegates from across the political spectrum.[20]

Idasa, as it was explained by former staffers, was 'born out of a mission to educate'. Operationally it had especially the white population in mind, in order to counter what was regarded as 'a systematically imposed ignorance'. The initiative came from white people and was in aid of white people and carried, it was said, the support of the largely black anti-apartheid movement. 'The theory', it was contended, 'was that change could occur if white resistance to change was overcome.' It was therefore regarded as strategically important to involve the white community in the 'struggle for non-racial democracy out of their self-interest in change, not mainly by moral exhortation'. Whites had to be coaxed out of their insulation in order to work towards a greater goal.[21] A confidential internal report indicated that the Afrikaner power base at universities and in the churches was targeted in particular, as these institutions were seen to produce the emerging leaders of the future.[22]

This kind of outreach should be seen against the background of what Idasa regarded as the pervasive fears, mistrust and stereotypes – on both sides of the fence – that needed to be addressed in order to effect change.[23] The survival of Afrikaners, it was argued further, was not dependent upon their remaining an immovable structure like the Voortrekker Monument. Slabbert regarded this as the 'fallacy of misplaced concreteness'; what was required instead was greater flexibility and channels through which politically aware Afrikaners could be informed of alternative options.[24]

The focus on the Afrikaner was of course not a completely new point of departure, and it was redolent of the PFP, which also assiduously wooed the Afrikaner vote with less than tangible success. The emphasis, though, was different; a change in thinking was presented as being in the self-interest of Afrikaners rather than as merely contributing to the electoral standing of a political party. Slabbert was fully aware of the obstacles. In 1987, in response to a question about what whites feared most about black majority rule, he said: 'Loss of status, loss of privilege, the deterioration of living standards and the quality of life.'[25] To assuage these fears would call for sufficient assurances and precautions in a new dispensation. Ultimately, however, he regarded it as an irrational fear given the alternative reality that with the continuation of apartheid and concomitant political upheavals and financial sanctions, whites also ran the risk of losing much. He argued that it was not really a question of when 'are we *really* going to be in trouble' but rather that 'we are in trouble *right now*'.[26]

Slabbert and Boraine went on extended trips abroad to try and raise funds for Idasa. Boraine recalled that for all his other qualities, fundraising was not Slabbert's strongest suit: 'He was decidedly embarrassed, gazing at his shoes, looking out of the window; on more than one occasion, when I was at the point of mentioning the amount we were asking for, he would asked for the directions to the men's room.'[27] Slabbert indeed did not relish such tasks. During his PFP days, he was most upset when hotel tycoon Sol Kerzner refused to even consider a request for funds, saying abruptly that he did not give money to communists. Afterwards, Slabbert pointedly remarked that in future he would not even think of asking Kerzner for five cents to go to a railway toilet.

The duo's fundraising trips sometimes ran into heavy weather, as potential donors were not always convinced that two white men could make a difference; it was, after all, perceived to be a black struggle. Others were more understanding, and eventually Idasa received generous and regular financial support from the Scandinavian countries in particular.[28]

Idasa expanded rapidly: more staff were appointed and regional centres opened in all of South Africa's major cities. Slabbert, however, declined to become a permanent staff member. He became the first chairman of the board and also acted as a part-time director of planning, with Boraine as the full-time executive director.

Slabbert never drew a salary from Idasa, but he was paid for expenses incurred while doing Idasa work. This arrangement seemed to suit him, as he preferred not to be weighed down by day-to day activities and saw his role as more issue-orientated.[29] Given Slabbert's high profile, it was perhaps not an ideal situation, as the press interpreted it as his preferring to distance himself from the organisation. He tried to ease such reservations, however: 'My stepping down as co-executive director does not affect my scope or involvement with Idasa and its activities and in fact it creates an opportunity to become more involved.'[30] This was a neatly phrased explanation designed for public consumption, but it also glossed over differences between Slabbert and Boraine over the direction and rate of expansion of Idasa.[31] Such disagreements did not affect their working relationship or friendship.

In considering Idasa as an organisation, it is instructive to move beyond its structures and aims and consider its underlying dynamics. Beyond the obviously political, there was a glimpse of proselytising intent akin to missionary work. It was run by Boraine, who came from a church background as a Methodist minister, and Slabbert, who once was very serious about entering the Dutch Reformed Church ministry. It was, as Wilmot James observed, 'because of the theologian in Slabbert' that he wanted to persuade, never to bully people.[32] Although the comparison between religion and Idasa's activities should not be overdone, as the differences between the sacred and the secular are obvious, it can be argued that there was a connecting link, which can be picked up in the endeavour to convert whites politically and in doing so to save the 'unenlightened'. Without wishing to put too fine a point to it, it is almost as if such a transference happened unwittingly, and that Slabbert's original sense of religious calling, though often well-hidden and subsumed under layers of other considerations, could emerge in another context. Or, to put it more bluntly: on a meta level, Slabbert could, with Boraine's help, become the dominee he never was; through

Idasa, he could now cultivate his own secular flock outside the usual formal constraints.

History has generally been kind to Idasa; it is seen as an organisation that was ahead of its time, and it added lustre and status to Slabbert as one of its founders. This does not, however, imply that the organisation was not criticised. Sections of the Afrikaans press in the 1980s rejected it out of hand as an irrelevant talking shop, and Slabbert was seen as a dubious political go-between.[33] Helen Suzman, still aggrieved after Slabbert's departure from Parliament, had similar reservations and pointedly asked: 'What has he been able to achieve since he left – conferences, meetings, speeches to foreign backers? No doubt he has fulfilled a useful role in keeping open the lines of communication between black and white. But he was doing that before he left Parliament.'[34] Of a different order were the suspicions among some extra-parliamentary groupings that Idasa might perhaps siphon off anti-apartheid donor money intended for them.[35] Idasa, in turn, was apprehensive that the state, as a counterstrategy, might block its funds from entering the country.

Another level of critique, from the Marxist left, was that Idasa promoted a form of elitist democracy from which the underclasses would be excluded. This view was reinforced by the financial backing the organisation received, and the criticism became particularly severe when it later transpired that Slabbert had received funding from George Soros, the Hungarian-born investor and philanthropist. Soros, like Slabbert, was influenced by the work of Karl Popper and this common interest helped to cement a friendship that would last for many years.

Criticism relating to Idasa's financial backers was based on the assumption that the imperatives of the funders narrowed down the debate on how democracy should be structured. Idasa, it was said, shied away from notions of 'popular democracy', with the masses fully incorporated into post-apartheid political structures, and veered towards a form of democracy in which the state arrangements favoured the elites. Through Idasa, Slabbert was seen to advocate an agenda that centred on the 'defence and isolation of the "new political space" (occupied by both the old and newly emerging elite) from the influence of the masses'.[36] Slabbert did not directly answer these criticisms, but he had grave intellectual reservations about Marxist analyses in general.[37] On a practical level, separate from the structural arguments and suppositions, Idasa's documentation reveals that the organisation was adamant that donors had no decision-making status.[38] Whether or not the influence of donors as such was a consideration for those in charge remains a moot point.

Slabbert's entry into the extra-parliamentary world was mediated through Idasa. It had the advantage of imparting a certain degree of independence yet also aligning itself selectively with oppositional forces outside Parliament. In doing so, Slabbert had in fact devised an excellent strategy to ensure that he did not get fully embroiled in the political turmoil of the time, where on the left often nothing less than complete commitment was expected. By maintaining a certain distance, he created some room for manoeuvre. Thus, in contrast to the blanket call on the left for disinvestment in South Africa at the time, Slabbert believed it to be 'counter-productive, over-evaluated and it has a stultifying or paralysing effect on change inside South Africa'.[39] Idasa also provided him with a springboard to launch new projects, of which the visit to Dakar by a contingent of selected whites to meet ANC luminaries in 1987 turned out to be particularly noteworthy.

A new Voortrekker: The Dakar initiative

The idea of organising a conference in Senegal originated when Slabbert visited the country in June 1986 as a guest of France Libertés, a foundation run by Danielle Mitterrand, wife of French president François Mitterrand. A meeting to discuss the possibility was held on the island of Gorée, off Dakar, from where thousands of slaves were transported to the Americas during the Atlantic slave trade. Also in attendance was Slabbert's friend Breyten Breytenbach, the noted Afrikaans author and poet, who had spent seven years in jail for anti-apartheid activities. Slabbert 'enjoyed being a white African in another totally strange part of Africa so much, that I thought it would be wonderful if other South Africans could have this experience'.[40] He and Breytenbach enthusiastically discussed the idea of arranging a conference between the ANC and Afrikaners; they thought it was risky, but it might just be the catalyst to break the logjam at home. 'Create the facts,' Breytenbach said, 'and then work with the consequences.'[41] It was only through poetic inspiration, a journalist later remarked, that such an unusual initiative, outside the channels of formal and 'realistic' politics, could be launched.[42] Slabbert was also spurred on by an incident at a conference he had attended in New York, when an ANC member made an emotional attack on Professor Pieter de Lange, a former rector of the Rand Afrikaans University and chairman of the Broederbond. He thought at the time that there was so much confusion that it called for a 'good hard debate' between Afrikaners and the ANC to clear the air and outline the differences clearly.[43]

Slabbert and Breytenbach then set about making the idea a reality. They obtained funding from various sources, including George Soros, the Friedrich Naumann Foundation, Lufthansa and various Scandinavian governments. Breytenbach, through his contacts at France Libertés, took care of arrangements in France and French-speaking West African countries, while Slabbert and Idasa organised matters domestically.[44] The government had strong reservations about funding coming from abroad. Slabbert, though, found it absurd that the government could think of acting against them on this score: 'Surely what you do with the money is far more important than where you get it. We have been paying out of our own pockets for years to implement apartheid. Surely that is far more objectionable than using foreign funds to explore an alternative to violence and apartheid.'[45]

Slabbert's ANC counterpart was Thabo Mbeki. Initially, Mbeki had some reservations and doubted whether the event could be pulled off, but eventually, after meetings in London and Madrid, he and other ANC members were won over. 'These guys are really serious,' Aziz Pahad of the ANC had to admit.[46] Mbeki was kept fully informed of all the arrangements and the proposed structure of the conference. The ANC, probably for security reasons, organised their travel schedule and accommodation separately from the Slabbert group.

Slabbert indicated to Mbeki that he had high hopes for the encounter. 'This can become an historic meeting of great significance,' he wrote. He hoped that Mbeki would be able to bring his 'heavyweights' along; if this could include the organisation's president, Oliver Tambo, even if only for a day, it would be so much better.[47] By March 1987 most of the logistics were in place. Slabbert was careful to keep it as simple as possible and did not want any large official function in Paris before they left for Dakar. Informally, he wrote to Breytenbach that a cocktail with the 'auntie' (Danielle Mitterand) would be more than sufficient and 'then we fokoff to D (Dakar) with as little publicity as possible'.[48] There were real fears that the venture might be derailed, and Breytenbach and Slabbert, as the latter recalled, played at being spies and communicated in code language: 'The flowers have arrived and are in the vase' meant that the money had been banked.[49]

Looking after the organisational part of the proposed conference was one thing, assembling the touring party was another. Slabbert had decided upon the following criteria: he had to know everybody personally; they had to be trusted to keep quiet; they had to be politically conscious; and they had to speak Afrikaans. For security reasons, Slabbert and Boraine approached individuals personally.[50] In total, the group consisted of 61 people. As always, who and what exactly was an 'Afrikaner' was problematic. Those approached and who agreed to go could not really claim to represent Afrikanerdom as such, but the majority of them did speak Afrikaans and come from Afrikaans backgrounds. Some occasionally published in the Afrikaans press, but they lacked any real influence in the inner circles of Afrikaner power. Among them were academics, teachers, journalists, artists, directors, writers and professionals. There were also several coloured Afrikaans-speakers and a sprinkling of English-speaking businessmen and academics, as well as three foreign political scientists working on South Africa.[51] There were very few women, and some of those who went did so in the slipstreams of their male companions. It was an oversight, which Slabbert later rued and unconvincingly tried to explain away by saying that he did not know many politically conscious Afrikaner women who met his set criteria.[52] On the ANC side, there were 17 delegates under the leadership of Thabo Mbeki. Although Oliver Tambo did not attend, the individuals selected carried considerable weight in ANC circles and came to occupy high-ranking positions after the transition in 1994.

In formulating the aims of the meeting, Slabbert made it clear that they had no mandate, nor were they in a position to negotiate on anyone's behalf. They were solely intent on exploratory talks with the ANC on African soil, and on obtaining first-hand information on the organisation's policies and strategies. It was a message he had to repeat often. He took umbrage at criticism implying that he would be talking at the wrong time and in the wrong place about issues over which he had no control. He was also accused of meddling in matters that, although admittedly important, were best left to those in power. If he wanted to play the role of 'National Fixer', it was said, he was on his own trajectory, but as he did not represent anyone, it was little more than show business.[53] On another level, apart from engaging with the ANC on questions of national concern, he had three other aims: to expose Afrikaners to Africa; to introduce Afrikaners to an important political organisation; and to 'make Africans aware that not all Afrikaners go around shooting blacks'.[54]

The government initially maintained a stony official silence on the trip. In all probability Slabbert's stature played a part, though it was just as likely a calculated move to avoid giving publicity to such an event and adding to its status. However, what the government did not do, the Afrikaans media in general did for them. The Dakarites came under heavy fire, and were portrayed as pawns in a bigger game they did not understand, as parvenus and para-politicians, or, damningly, as Lenin's 'useful idiots'. It was only later that the government responded by threatening to put measures into place that would make it much more difficult in future to embark on such unauthorised meetings with 'terrorist' organisations.[55] On another note altogether, it was rumoured that the NIS had discreetly supported the venture, but this was a fabrication that Slabbert dismissed out of hand.[56]

It was on 6 July 1987 that the intrepid travellers to Dakar met at Jan Smuts Airport in Johannesburg (today OR Tambo International). Jacques Kriel, a medical doctor, had a 'strange, eerie feeling – like some cloak-and-dagger spy film'. There was at this point still much insecurity regarding the government's strange silence and the reception they would receive in Senegal. Once he spotted his travel companions, he felt more at ease. He was now in company and experienced a 'common excitement – and a common uncertainty', which helped to establish a sense of camaraderie destined to last a long time.[57] Journalist Max du Preez recalled the departure along similar lines:

> If one looks carefully, one will notice the nervous ones amongst the people moving through passport control and customs. They are all white and male and Afrikaans, and most of them glance furtively over their shoulders. They all say that they are going to London, some for work, others for holiday. But it is a lie and most of the okes have never lied to an official before, only to their wives. Few of them can spell 'clandestine'.

It was only once they were safely in the departure hall, 'that there is a sense of exhilaration. Even a giggle. It is after all a great adventure. They are going to talk to communists and terrorists; partying with the total onslaught.'[58]

After a 30-hour flight, which included a detour, the South Africans arrived in Dakar somewhat disorientated, to be welcomed with great fanfare, with Slabbert treated almost like a head of state. They were whisked through the streets with sirens wailing and all other traffic halted. The president of Senegal, Abdou Diouf, received them warmly. Mbeki and Slabbert embraced one another like long-lost brothers. The delegates were put up in the luxurious five-star Novotel hotel, which was also to be the venue for most of the discussions.[59] This was no hardship African safari for the down-at-heel; with such warm acclaim from their Senegalese hosts and almost international status bestowed on the visitors from the south, the scene was set for some serious discussion and convivial circumstances for bonding.

Some revelled in the social dimensions of the event. It was outside the formal discussions that they could really meet their fellow South Africans in exile. Max du Preez recalled that alcohol was the great leveller. Boisterous parties continued late into the night, marked by much bonhomie and fuelled by brandy, wine and whisky. It was not long before tears, nostalgia, singing, raucous declarations of burning patriotism and lifelong brotherhood materialised as binding agents.[60] These occasions clearly gave vent to much pent-up emotion.

Mbeki claimed that the ANC did not want to play upon the emotions of the Afrikaner delegates and emphasise their 'sins'.[61] Perhaps it was not necessary to do so. Some of the Afrikaners at Dakar needed little prodding to bare their souls. Journalist Chris Louw later related that he was a bit naive:

> There was a kind of bravado among the younger Afrikaners. They were tired of the stereotype of the rigid racist

INTO A BRAVE NEW WORLD

> Afrikaner ... We wanted to show that we were even more African than the ANC; in that sense the meeting was more performance than substance. We were ashamed of our government, for PW Botha's boorish behaviour, for the hotpotch of National Party policy, that we gave in to the temptation to choose the side of the ANC and its ideology ... We wanted to create as much distance between the National Party and ourselves as possible.[62]

These delegates were easy pickings, even before the politics of redemption could properly kick in. Slabbert's aim of exposing Afrikaners to different ways of thinking succeeded only too well. They became filled with the zeal of the newly converted. In a way, it can be argued that Slabbert's missionary impulses also played out in this context, though he might not quite have perceived it that way. He was furthermore a tad too trusting; for example, he was taken in by the performance of Mac Maharaj, who limped about with a walking stick, claiming it was because of the torture he had suffered in South Africa. Only later, at a multiparty conference in 1990, did Slabbert discover that Maharaj was 'milking us' at Dakar, feigning injury to extract sympathy. When Slabbert asked him about his back, Maharaj replied: 'Ohhh, I don't need that kind of thing any more.'[63] Nevertheless, Slabbert was not oblivious to the euphoria that Dakar created and warned against the possibility of a 'false consensus' emerging, especially among younger participants, and he saw the need for the more senior intellectuals in the group to maintain a critical distance from their ANC discussion partners.[64]

After all the delegates and ANC members had introduced themselves, Mbeki opened the proceedings with a memorable, simple yet powerful statement: 'My name is Thabo Mbeki. I am an Afrikaner.' It was more than an icebreaker; it was closer to melting the iceberg.[65] Mbeki's biographer remarked: 'You [could] actually see, in the relief of his broad, broken-toothed smile as the audience bursts into applause and laughter, the stakes in this game he is playing: wooing white South Africans away from apartheid while maintaining his credibility among comrades already suspicious of his intentions.'[66] While the effect of Mbeki's opening statement cannot be denied, the formulation and style of delivery were not necessarily all that original. There is evidence to suggest that he had copied the use of such epigrammatic opening lines from a brilliant English literature lecturer at Sussex, where he had studied, and that he was so impressed that he resolved to emulate it in public life.[67]

Slabbert's speech at the opening thanked the hosts for an overwhelming welcome and then proceeded to outline why there could not be a solution possible in South Africa without the ANC. Despite their differences in approach to the South African dilemma, he was hopeful that the situation could be resolved. He ended on an emotional note: 'There is sadness that we have to meet so far from our common fatherland. This in itself is a tragic commentary on the history we share.'[68]

The main themes during the ensuing discussions were strategies for change, the problem of national unity and the structure of a liberated government and economy. Strategies for change, and more specifically the armed struggle, as well the issue of national unity and the position of Afrikaners in a future dispensation, were foregrounded. André du Toit of the University of Cape Town outlined the vexed problems of armed struggle and especially attacks on so-called soft targets, while Maharaj and Mbeki explained why armed resistance was a central plank in their overall strategy, and the difficulties they had in exerting full control over all their cadres in South Africa. Apart from this, Breytenbach raised a concern pertaining to future policy directions. He introduced a cautionary note, making the point that in a number of African countries, post-colonialism had been marked by an uncritical adoption of communist principles. This issue was not pursued by any of the internal South African delegates.[69] Turning to the question of national unity,

ANC speakers emphasised the need to discard ethnic thinking in favour of building a non-racial society. Hermann Giliomee of the University of Cape Town had serious reservations about the viability of non-racialism and advocated a compromise position of bicommunalism that would heed specific Afrikaner concerns. In propagating this, he was seen as being out of step with the other delegates and was described by the ANC as the 'Boer in the woodpile'. The ANC, ever watchful, also observed the seating of the participants and noted that Giliomee mainly sat in the company of those regarded as being on the conservative flank, and that it would be difficult to shift him ideologically.[70]

Through all of this, Slabbert maintained a low profile, apart from the occasional summing-up or press release. The reason may have been that his views were well known, or that, as an organiser of the event, he was being careful not to play too prominent a role.[71] He was struck by the intensity of the debates. 'One thing is quite evident about this conference,' he remarked, 'it is not just a gentle chat; there is a deadly seriousness underlying the overt friendliness.'[72] Slabbert succeeded, however, in floating above the skirmishes and smoothing over disagreements.[73] He established a particularly good relationship with Mbeki, to the extent that he later remarked that he 'would die for that bugger'.[74]

Not surprisingly, though, he found the event emotionally taxing. On one occasion, he was seen splashing around frantically in the hotel pool and laughing uncontrollably, probably in an attempt to release pent-up tension.[75] He would have been even more agitated had he known that during the Dakar event and subsequent trips to Burkina Faso and Ghana, he was tracked by members of the South African Communist Party (SACP), who reported on him. While they regarded Dakar as a 'good thing', as it could 'weaken' the enemy, and Slabbert himself was considered to be 'intellectually competent', he was not to be trusted as he was 'an opportunist', a 'showman', 'intellectually dishonest' and had an 'inflated view' of himself.[76] The world of extra-parliamentary politics had its own quota of surprises.

Slabbert did not join the others for the return flight to South Africa but instead went to Spain for a break from politics. In contrast to the warm welcome they had received in Dakar, a hostile reception awaited the group upon their homecoming in Johannesburg on 21 July. Members of the unreconstructed right-wing Afrikaner Weerstandsbeweging (Afrikaner Resistance Movement, AWB) filled the arrivals lounge, baying for the blood of the 'traitors'. The Dakar flight had to be diverted to the end of the runway and the passengers spirited away under police escort.[77] PW Botha had apparently thought of arresting the Dakarites on their return, but thought better of it after consulting with the NIS.[78]

To add to the returnees' woes, soon after their arrival a bomb exploded in Johannesburg at the SADF's Witwatersrand Command headquarters, injuring 68 people. In the public mind, this placed a huge question mark behind the Dakarites' claim that they had gone to meet the ANC in an effort to promote peace, and it provided grist to the government's mill that the Senegal venture was an abject failure. Upon his return, Slabbert expressed his deep disappointment with this development, and hinted that it might have been a rogue act that did not necessarily reflect the official ANC position.[79] This argument did not carry much weight among those sceptical of the ANC and the Dakar venture. *The Citizen* newspaper asked pointedly: 'Now who does Dr Slabbert think was responsible? The man on the moon? Only the ANC uses car bombs, limpet mines and landmines.' He was considered to be 'completely bonkers'.[80] More scathing comments were to follow. If Slabbert had to write a book, it was said, it should be called 'The Great Trek to Dakar: The new Voortrekkers'. It would be written in 'the blood of numerous people who have been liberated from this earth by means of limpet mines, car bombs and landmines' and would be the magnum opus of 'Leader, Herr Frederik von Slaghuis von Gotterdammerung'. These new Voortrekkers were regarded as completely spineless, and instead of fighting the enemy preferred to 'talk their way into surrender, their motto being: "Hands up and hand over"'.[81]

Slabbert, despite such criticism, sought to place the bombing in context and stated that 'it was patently ridiculous to use the continuing violence on all sides as a reason for describing Dakar as a failure'. He argued that it was 'only the government of South Africa which could reduce the violence or stop the armed struggle. No "safari" or visits by any delegation from South Africa have the power to reduce the violence or stop the armed struggle.'[82] Coming from a different angle, he had some support from Giliomee, who pointed out that bombings, instead of obviating the need to engage with the ANC, actually underlined the importance of dialogue on the issue of violence.[83] Oliver Tambo later apologised to Slabbert for the ramifications of the bomb, which had not been planted to embarrass the Dakarites.[84]

On a number of counts, the Dakar venture was a risky one for Slabbert. So much could have gone wrong: the government could have halted the expedition before it even started; the ANC could have withdrawn at the last moment; the discussions could have gotten out of hand; and the group might have been arrested upon their return to South Africa. He might have calculated, though, that on a balance of probabilities these eventualities might not occur. There was nevertheless something intrepid about the whole enterprise, especially at a time when few white South Africans chanced it outside South Africa's borders. The fact that he pushed ahead demonstrated a keen determination without a firm promise of reward. He could not benefit from the safari, either personally or financially. In a general sense it might have raised his political profile, but as he had no formal political ties it was not possible to hope for advancement or repositioning in any such direction. Perhaps the motive can once again be traced to a missionary sense of the need to persuade people to follow a certain creed, to subscribe to a cause bigger than oneself, and to commit to that goal. However, exactly what fruit the initiative bore was only established later.

Legacy

A joint statement was issued at the end of the Dakar trip, with Slabbert emphasising that each delegate left the meeting with more accurate information, that stereotypes had been broken down, and that they had moved towards a 'common search for peace' and away from 'blind prejudice and obduracy'. It was, however, not an exercise in negotiation but an initial exploration of the field.[85] He later also warned against manufacturing a 'spirit of artificial consensus', and, equally so, 'over-exaggerating' the initiative on the one hand, or 'rubbishing it as cheap lefty politics' on the other.[86]

The venture attracted considerably more media attention than Slabbert had anticipated. 'We started riding a donkey and ended on a tiger,' he remarked, and the experience meant that 'we are going back as changed people'.[87] Several individuals gave personal testimony on the importance of the trip. Theuns Eloff, a young minister at a conservative Afrikaans church in Pretoria, recalled that at the beginning of the talks with the ANC, he was a bit wary and kept his distance, but he soon realised that they were not beyond the pale. He then proceeded to impress the meeting with his sincere and forthright contributions. Eloff was not too concerned about who extracted the most out of the encounters. 'Of course, they used us, and we used them,' he said, 'but that did not matter.'[88] Both parties learnt from each other. Eloff's career trajectory also changed after Dakar: because of his participation in the trip he was suspended by his church; he then became involved in the business world, played an important role as facilitator at the negotiations between the ANC and the government in the early 1990s, and was later appointed rector of North-West University. Other Dakarites, such as Lourens du Plessis and Johann van der Westhuizen, both law professors, as well as historian André Odendaal and filmmaker Manie van Rensburg, regarded the trip as a seminal moment in their lives.[89] Slabbert himself admitted to the effect of Dakar and how he had to adjust to 'reintegrate the experience' in his daily life.[90]

Moving from the individual to the wider ramifications of the venture, one has to assess its general impact. A common and persistent claim is that Dakar was a central event in bringing about South Africa's negotiated settlement in the early 1990s.[91] This is speculative and a case of reading causation in history backwards, presuming linkages that need to be proven. Dakar's importance was contingent upon a range of factors, some of them emanating from government initiatives. Without these, and taken on its own, Dakar might simply have slipped into history's black hole as a boondoggle.[92]

What is more credible is to link Dakar to a circumscribed and less ambitious outcome. The deluge of media coverage of the expedition very pertinently injected a new dimension into South African politics. While polls before and after Dakar showed that many whites were against negotiating with the ANC,[93] the event nevertheless unsettled the ruling discourse. Sociologist Ian Liebenberg, one of the Dakarites, explained:

> Dakarites had no power to put pressure on the PW Botha government but their voice. They could not leverage South Africa into normal politics. They could assist at most in a small way to influence public discourse through a disruptive moment with the hope that other actors would take a cue for future negotiated transition from authoritarian rule to a democratic order.[94]

In this sense, then, Dakar had a restricted role. It was, as Breyten Breytenbach argued later, a trigger for thinking differently about the South African dilemma.[95] Intriguingly enough, none other than Niël Barnard, then head of the NIS, also later recalled that generally Dakar 'played an important role in psychologically preparing the grassroots of this whole process'. This did not necessarily imply that at the time the public was actually converted to negotiations, but, more modestly, that the possibility of negotiations now featured more generally in public discourse. Other than that, however, Barnard resented that the government was being prescribed to 'by clerics, academics and the private sector as to how we should conduct the political business of this country'.⁹⁶ It was not possible, though, to put the genie back in the bottle. A series of further encounters with the ANC, held under the auspices of Idasa, and dealing with various topics including culture and economics, followed in Europe and Africa.⁹⁷ Although these attracted some attention, the exposure did not nearly match the level of interest of Dakar; it was almost as if the Idasa talks with the ANC had become normal and the public gradually came to accept them as such.

But unbeknown to the public and to the Dakarites, outside the media spotlight and on a different level, the government had developed its own communication channels with the ANC. This was an important development, and placed the significance of the Dakar venture in a different perspective. At the core of it was the reality that whereas the Dakarites had no power, those in government had the power to determine outcomes. By definition, then, the impact of the latter would eventually, in terms of historical consequences, weigh more heavily. André du Toit later commented that, in a certain sense, 'contacts with the ANC only really became of political significance once people close to the National Party had become involved'.⁹⁸ Barnard claimed that even before 1986 they had planned contact with the ANC, and that talks between government officials and the ANC were ongoing from at least 1987.⁹⁹

Structurally, then, what was at work was in effect a two-track approach to negotiations, but with each initiative acting independently. Mike Louw, the second-in-command of the NIS, recalled that in terms of substantive negotiations, they were at cross-purposes with the Dakarites and other such efforts. This had a negative effect, he claimed. The NIS had carefully tried to move PW Botha towards a negotiating positioning that would include the ANC, but the more he learnt about the attempts of the Dakarites, the more intransigent he became. Louw explained:

> Now all these people were doing this and coming back and trying to put pressure on him [PW Botha], trying to represent themselves as facilitators, there is no way he would have followed that path, he would have gone his own way and done it in his own manner or he wouldn't have done it all. And we really thought these things were retarding the process instead of accelerating it.[100]

PW Botha's status as state president, Louw emphasised, was also at stake: he would 'never have walked in Van Zyl Slabbert's steps to Dakar. That would have been the last thing he would have done in his life.'[101] The government, according to Louw, only started making progress with their strategy 'once they got the other people involved, sidelined – because one of the first things we said to Thabo and company when we met overseas was: please let's get rid of all these middlemen and facilitators and what have you, we are not going to make any progress with them'.[102]

From the government's side, then, Slabbert and his party were only muddying the waters. In terms of realpolitik, such a perception virtually nullifies the role of the Dakarites. It does, not, however, sufficiently take into account the sense of shared identity and destiny generated at Dakar, which, one can safely assume, also worked to the government's benefit in its dealings with the ANC, especially at a time when the government had yet to establish firm and credible contacts. In this respect, Willie Esterhuyse, professor of philosophy at Stellenbosch, who was often involved on the government's side in exchanges with the ANC, and who had his reservations about the Dakar venture, nevertheless thought that the Dakarites had succeeded in deconstructing the perception of the ANC as the enemy – an important element in all peace drives.[103]

Although placing Dakar in a wider context has the effect of diminishing its overall importance, its utility value should not be underestimated.[104] In line with this, the German historian Ulrich van der Heyden has recently come to the conclusion that the Dakar conference 'was no panacea. It was only a small step within a specific political context. It was a thoroughly humane attempt to steer public discussion towards negotiations and towards the establishment of a democratic state based on a constitution.'[105]

Slabbert himself had a sober view of the outcome of the talks. He was not impressed by emotional outbursts and spoke out against the 'hysterical' reaction to Dakar.[106] He thought it had achieved what it had set out to do – 'a serious workshop between seasoned social scientists from the Afrikaans community and a delegation of the ANC on critical issues relating to the conflict in South Africa'.[107] He further thought that the contact assisted in undermining outdated paradigms and helped to legitimise the idea of talking to the ANC. The ANC also left with a more positive view of Afrikaners and hoped that a mutual resolution could be found.[108] Slabbert would not be part of the government's initiative in having talks with the ANC; when news of this filtered through to him later, he had no inclination to find out more.[109]

Slabbert's name is indissolubly linked with the Dakar venture. It constituted a high point in his career, even though he did not foresee its outcome. But he did not seek to bathe in the attention and publicity that Dakar generated at the time, nor did he seek to overinvest in its historical significance. It is not that he was merely being modest at the time or apathetic later on – he did not, as noted, dismiss its importance altogether – but he saw no point in inserting himself into the centre of the narrative.[110] 'I felt very isolated at Dakar,' he later recalled.[111] He was nevertheless fêted by funding agencies, which before Dakar had been inclined to give him the cold shoulder. Dakar, he recalled, was the 'magical moment' for Idasa in terms of fundraising.[112] Apart from that, the reasons for Slabbert's reticence, besides possible personal predilections, are best sought in the wider political area. It has been suggested that rather 'being a comfortably situated player in the game of power politics, Slabbert was more of a political dilettante, driven most fundamentally, … by a visceral distaste for racial injustice originally reflected in his early inclination towards a religious vocation …'.[113] One should not, of course, altogether discount his sense of power politics,[114] and should also bear in mind that his initial foray into theology actually turned him away from the Dutch Reformed Church and its racial practices. Nevertheless, there was a sense in which he transcended the normal patterns of South African politics and seemingly preferred to place himself outside the formal arena. Two friends, Heribert Adam and Kogila Moodley, commented: 'Slabbert's status and influence was greatest not when he was leader of the official opposition, but, paradoxically, when he held no formal positions of power.'[115] If one accepts this proposition, it becomes clear why Slabbert did not need endorsements of his Dakar exploits. Such affirmations made little sense to him, as he was on a different track, where the usual political accolades did not matter as much.

Besides the nature of Slabbert's politics, there were also other legacy activities subsequent to Dakar, notably, the establishment of the Gorée Institute. In addition, the idea of an independent Afrikaans newspaper, later to be named the *Vrye Weekblad*, with Max du Preez as editor, also germinated during the trip.[116] The Dakar undertaking, then, had a number of unintended spin-offs, both at home and further afield. Moreover, Slabbert remained remarkably busy. His diary for 1988 was packed with meetings with academics, politicians and businesspeople. He seems to have been in constant demand.[117]

In the post-apartheid period, Dakar's durability, brittle as it might have been from the outset, went through various permutations. Every ten years, many of those who had gone to Dakar marked the anniversary at the Spier Estate, close to Stellenbosch. The 1997 meeting was characterised by an abiding sense of optimism for South Africa's future, but bubbling beneath the surface of clinking glasses and nostalgic reunions was an undercurrent of political concern. Some Afrikaners felt that Afrikaners in particular were being marginalised in terms of the maintenance of their language and culture. One delegate explained: 'We went to Dakar to find hope, liberation and freedom. Funnily enough we have landed up in a situation where we now need to be liberated.'[118] Hermann Giliomee argued that the government had become increasingly elitist and that Parliament was being bypassed by a select group of high-ranking politicians and other bodies that did not consider themselves beholden to democratic practices.[119] Mbeki, as vice president and soon to be president, sat quietly through the discussions, making copious notes. In a short speech he spoke favourably about Afrikaner integration in the civil service, and on language matters he advised Afrikaners to cooperate with other minority indigenous language groups.[120] In all of this, Slabbert chose to stay aloof from the specifics of language, but he bluntly declared that 'unless the ANC can succeed in consolidating this democracy and create a competitive market economy, there will be no rights for Afrikaners, Xhosas, Zulus or anyone else'.[121]

Ten years later, at the 2007 reunion, the concerns mooted in 1997 had become more strident. While Mbeki still valued the technical and professional expertise of some Afrikaners in the state and private sector, as an interest group they no longer featured prominently in his agenda. As a seasoned strategist, he realised that he could very well do without them politically. Increasingly, Afrikaners felt alienated and a widening gulf developed.[122] Mbeki did not attend the 20th anniversary of Dakar, nor did any of the other ANC discussants, although Bheki Khumalo, Mbeki's former spokesperson, was present. Chris Louw was acutely aware that in a new context there were other factors determining political preferences and choices. They clearly had to deal with an ANC quite different from 20 years earlier. Succinctly, he explained: 'The ANC needed us then. Now it is no longer the case. We were the useful idiots ... More cynical: liberation was the ANC's main aim, not democracy. More correctly: the African majority wanted the power. Democracy was an unavoidable by-product, never the aim.'[123]

Breyten Breytenbach had indicated before the reunion that he was equally disillusioned. The dreams they had at Dakar of a 'vibrant pluralistic political life' that did justice to South Africa's diversity had all but evaporated, and instead South Africa had for all practical purposes become a 'one-party state, with the state as an agency for a patrimonial party'. As to 'nation building', his crusty response was: 'Eish oke! Were you that stupid to believe in such a utopia?'[124] Some months later, Slabbert said he was particularly concerned about Mbeki's dense rhetoric regarding the national democratic revolution, drawing upon outdated communist concepts and practices. Mbeki spoke in obtuse language, he said, instead of formulating 'practical policies that ordinary folk can understand and be mobilised to make real in their daily lives'.[125]

If the shine had gone off the memory of Dakar by the 20th reunion, the 2017 gathering left the impression that the once-inspiring legacy had virtually imploded. In the wake of Jacob Zuma's debilitating presidency, Breytenbach launched a withering attack on developments under the ANC. 'The situation is now worse than ever,' he said, 'because intellectual, moral and ethical leadership has not been created to pave the way forward.' Breytenbach was particularly scathing about the ever-diminishing role of Afrikaans in official life.[126] Other speakers followed suit in debates that were occasionally cast in emotional terms. It was clear that, despite the attempts of Dakarites such as André Odendaal and Aziz Pahad to salvage the situation, and the ANC's reputation, the writing was on the wall.[127] Dakar, so it seemed, had served its purpose. Perhaps it was not all that surprising. To all intents and purposes, the ANC had already abandoned the ideological Dakar crutch far earlier. In 1994 Joe Slovo, the influential head of the SACP, even went so far as to state that as far as the ANC was concerned, the Dakar meetings and other similar occasions had no significant effect on the movement in exile.[128]

It would be unrealistic to expect Dakar to have kept its gloss over a period of 30 years in a rapidly changing society. It was, after all, not a marriage, nor a 'love fest', as sections of the Afrikaans press chose to refer to it, but more of a blind date with no firm outcome guaranteed. Not surprisingly, the relationship soured over time. Slabbert might have regretted it, but he was also realistic enough to appreciate the advances that had been made, despite shortcomings, over the intervening period. In 2003 he recalled what he had experienced at Dakar and a host of other venues during the late 1980s:

> In these discussions I was particularly keen to understand the theory of change underpinning revolt, the resources available to achieve it, and the ideological ends that were to be achieved by success. The more I listened, the more depressed I became. The rhetoric of revolt was simply the flipside of the rhetoric of repression. Each defined success as the total elimination of the other – only then could the ideological be achieved. I could see endless attrition at enormous cost to the country and its people.[129]

If Slabbert's assumptions were correct, even if somewhat exaggerated, the fact that such an eventuality could be avoided would in the long run have meant much more to him than the vanishing appeal of Dakar.

8
TRANSITIONS

A new dawn

In the last week of January 1990, Slabbert was on a Fellowship at All Souls College in Oxford when his friend Dick Enthoven contacted him to say that President FW de Klerk wished to talk to him. De Klerk had taken over as state president from the ailing PW Botha in September the previous year, following a long battle over the succession. Slabbert duly phoned De Klerk, but their conversation left him none the wiser. The new president was in an affable mood, mentioning that there would be a slight acceleration in policy and that Slabbert was welcome to come and talk to him – but not before 2 February.[1] On that day came the dramatic news: in his inaugural parliamentary address, De Klerk unbanned all the formerly proscribed political movements – the ANC, PAC and SACP – and announced that a new constitution was to be negotiated.

Barely three months earlier, in November 1989, Slabbert, while admitting that De Klerk seemed to have adopted a more tolerant attitude towards political marches, had warned against assumptions that any major changes were imminent. The National Party was known for creating false expectations, he said, and there was an enormous difference between less restrictive control and negotiations for democracy.[2]

Now, in one fell swoop, it seemed that much of what he had argued for in his political life was about to come to pass. 'I ... could not believe what I was hearing,' he recollected.[3] What really surprised him was the scope of De Klerk's sweeping changes, which were announced without first having informed his party as a whole.⁴ It was obviously of far greater consequence than the slight quickening of existing policy that De Klerk had hinted at. Slabbert was also surprised that the ban on the SACP had been lifted. Representatives of the NIS, without giving much away, had earlier visited him in Oxford to ask his opinion on developments in South Africa. He got the impression that even in the event of major changes, there would be no unbanning of the Communist Party.⁵

Nevertheless, for once there appeared to him to be real reason for euphoria, though, as always, Slabbert was wary of the media frenzy that erupted. Writing from All Souls on 15 February, after the dust had settled somewhat, he said:

> In twelve days South Africa went into a new political orbit and the world developed a virulent strain of Mandelitis. Modern communications have the ability to trivialise complex and complicated situations and in this instance often managed to reduce the De Klerk-Mandela relationship to a soap-operatic gunfight at South Africa's political corral. If only FW and Mandela could square up and shake hands everything would be OK and we could all continue the barn dance. Even if one realises it cannot be so simple; one cannot but be overwhelmed by the enormity of events during these 12 days that have changed and shaped South Africa's destiny.

Therefore, he continued, 'for the moment let us bask in the political magic that has hit us. Six months ago all of this would have been beyond realistic contemplation. Now that it has become real, the idea that tomorrow could be another country is more than probable.'⁶ Slabbert was equally aware of the shortcomings of academic predictions of South Africa's future. It was sobering to reflect that all 'the "paradigms", "analytical frameworks" and hackneyed references that were used to predict the "inevitable" that was about to happen in South Africa now appeared ridiculous. Suddenly we could with our own eyes look at our country and ponder upon the possibilities which were dwarfed by our fears and prejudices."[7]

Slabbert had a personal interview with De Klerk shortly after the latter's watershed speech. He asked him one simple question – why? De Klerk replied that he had had a 'spiritual leap', and, after a pause, added that the fall of the Berlin Wall and the collapse of communism in Eastern Europe in 1989 had afforded him the opportunity to act decisively because of the ANC's loss of East German and Soviet patronage. He had presumed that this development would give him the upper hand in negotiations, an assumption that Slabbert thought was not entirely unrealistic. However, Slabbert felt that De Klerk had miscalculated on two important issues: the level of popular support the ANC could command in the country, and the local and international prestige accorded to Nelson Mandela, which surpassed De Klerk's own standing as a major reformer.[8]

In Slabbert's own understanding of these seismic changes, he thought it would first be necessary to clear the undergrowth in order to dismiss the idea that change was inevitable; instead, change had been precipitated by deliberate political choice and a set of external and internal structural conditions.[9] The external conditions included the collapse of communism, South Africa's increasing international isolation and the deleterious effects of sanctions as well as global pressures on several other levels, and the settlement in Namibia and Angola, which freed up space to address South African issues more urgently. Internally, rapidly worsening economic conditions, increasing internal polarisation – marked by violent political unrest, along with strikes and labour unrest, which were difficult to quell – and the change in leadership from PW Botha to FW de Klerk all helped to shape the outcome.[10]

Slabbert had an ambivalent view of De Klerk. In part, this stemmed from his parliamentary days, when De Klerk had been assigned to counter Slabbert's analyses of the shortcomings of apartheid. Hermann Giliomee recalls Slabbert often mentioning to him 'how De Klerk with the slightest of smiles would rise to his feet in Parliament after a Slabbert speech, dismiss his analysis, and go on to present apartheid, with all its defects, as the best policy option for the country. The memory rankled.'[11] This was indeed the case, as Slabbert later indicated in a review of De Klerk's autobiography: 'For twelve and a half years I sat and listened to him as he defended apartheid. With such a cynically wry smile he explained how a liberal democracy (precisely what he helped to launch) would be disastrous for South Africa and why "Multi-ethnic Separate Development" was the only solution for South Africa.' It remained a mystery to Slabbert how all those arguments had disappeared and how De Klerk simply failed to explain convincingly the logic of his earlier justifications.[12]

Yet, for all this, he had a great deal of respect for what he regarded as De Klerk's 'extraordinary and decisive political act', which called for 'considerable personal bravery' and which 'irreversibly changed the future of South Africa and its people'.[13] Similarly, Slabbert was impressed with the way De Klerk handled the 1992 white referendum on the question of whether negotiations should continue. He won by a resounding margin of 68.6 per cent. It was 'high-risk politics', for which De Klerk should be commended.[14] Although Slabbert could not easily forget the president's past history, he was clearly impressed by De Klerk's fortitude in charting a new path.

Politically, Slabbert was not well placed at the time of De Klerk's momentous announcement. He was caught off-guard, not least because he was inclined, often with good reason, to dismiss government modifications of apartheid in the second half of the 1980s as being superficial or cosmetic, but without always taking fully into account the wider ramifications of the changes. A case in point was the 1986 abolition of influx control, which effectively scuttled the idea of homelands and, concomitantly, recognised the black population as permanent South African citizens. Legally, this was a major breakthrough, even if it only seemed to confirm what was happening on the ground anyway.[15] Added to this, in the circles in which Slabbert moved before 1990, there was a heavy emphasis on the dynamics of future negotiations. This would have preoccupied Slabbert to a greater extent than simply mulling over what to all intents and purposes might have appeared, somewhat misleadingly as it turned out, as yet another round of Nationalist tinkering. At a stroke, De Klerk had managed to make formal politics relevant again, and the ANC, which was surprised by the move, had to reorientate itself. Slabbert found himself in neither camp; he was in no-man's land, not part of any constituency and therefore shut out of formal proceedings.

Nevertheless, shortly after February 1990, Slabbert's name was bandied about in the press as a strong contender for a mediating role in future negotiations. He indicated that, if so required, he was prepared to 'get his hands dirty helping to build a new South Africa'. He was wary, though, of landing an invidious middleman position at the beck and call of all and sundry. He would have been happier to consider a more circumscribed role that called for a 'grandstand view' of developments and in finding solutions to possible deadlock situations.[16] This came to nought, as both the National Party and the ANC indicated to him that negotiations would mainly take place solely between these two entities and that his help was redundant. He found it strange that some had blithely assumed that he expected a position to be offered to him.[17] Although Slabbert was not completely deaf to the siren call of higher-order formal politics in the new dispensation, he had developed a built-in resistance to submitting too easily. Equally, he had a thick enough skin not to be too perturbed by rejection, subtle or otherwise. This was to be a recurring theme in the post-apartheid period.

With the gate to a return to the political arena apparently closed, Slabbert became a productive commentator on developments. He assumed an independent position and provided realistic assessments of the obstacles on the road to a satisfactory settlement. Knowing the strengths and weaknesses of the two major political parties, he was quick to notice excessive demands or spoiling tactics.[18] Intellectually, he was intrigued by the way politics unfolded. 'It is just fascinating to be plugged into what is happening in this country on so many levels,' he said. 'If you want to talk about people having hobbies, trying to understand the transition is my hobby.'[19]

One way of coming to terms with what was happening was to go beyond the platitudes about democracy that marked so much of the South African discourse. To this end, in 1992 he produced a booklet titled 'The Quest for Democracy', dealing with the transition. He especially drew upon concepts such as 'contingent consent', the assumption that no party will use its dominance to permanently exclude losers from the possibility of attaining power, and the idea of 'bounded uncertainty', accepting the unpredictability of politics but contained by clear constitutional principles.[20] What is remarkable about 'The Quest for Democracy' is that 28 years later, these concepts still seem to inform some of the deliberations of the current Democratic Alliance, the spiritual successor to the Progressive Federal Party.[21]

Slabbert not only commented on matters pertaining to the negotiating process, but later on the Truth and Reconciliation Commission (TRC) also appeared on his radar. The TRC, which operated between 1995 and 1998 and released its final report in 2003, aimed to establish the truth about extreme human rights abuses under apartheid, and, through full disclosure and the granting of amnesty, hoped to reconcile victims and perpetrators. It was a highly ambitious project fraught with a variety of methodological, moral and emotional issues. The past was not to be tamed easily. Professional historians, many of them aware of the pitfalls of such an undertaking, generally gave the exercise a wide berth.[22]

Although there was no doubt in Slabbert's mind about the need for reconciliation in the country, he had serious reservations about the efficacy of the TRC enterprise. His objections primarily centred on the notion of truth as employed by the commission, which, in the absence of due legal processes to determine veracity, he regarded as questionable. He also found problematic the assumption that so-called truth would necessarily lead to reconciliation. He provided an in-depth and extended analysis of his position, but in typical Slabbert fashion, he also pointedly formulated the core of his argument. A simple visit to the divorce courts, he said, might have disabused the luminaries of the TRC of the idea that there is a necessary correlation between truth and reconciliation.[23] To Slabbert, the TRC was little more than a political instrument. Although the commission might have revealed hidden facts, overall it still remained within the political ambit and should therefore be judged accordingly.

In his criticism of the TRC, he came up against his good friend Alex Boraine, who was deeply involved in the process and eventually served as deputy chairperson of the commission. Although they differed fundamentally, it did not affect their friendship. Slabbert respected Boraine, he said, because, among other reasons, Boraine was one of the few people he knew capable of antagonising a wide spectrum of people.[24] (Others thought Boraine had an authoritarian, Methodist streak,[25] implying a certain doggedness in pursuing justice with a semi-religious mandate.) Slabbert was far less enamoured of Archbishop Desmond Tutu, the TRC chairperson. While he found him charming and affable, and respected his role in the anti-apartheid struggle, he had no time for Tutu's theology, which he regarded as the 'God is a Disprin variety; a multipurpose placebo.' He had even harsher words for Tutu's philosophical outlook, which he found 'sh-t boring and amazingly superficial'.[26] It is a moot point whether Tutu's failure to support Slabbert's National Convention drive in 1985 still rankled.

The opening of South Africa after 1990 was in many ways a fulfilment of what Slabbert had fought for earlier. The manner, though, in which some changes subsequently took shape did not necessarily carry his approval. The TRC was a case in point. It was, moreover,

A youthful Barbara Slabbert, Van Zyl's mother.
(Source: courtesy of Tania Slabbert)

One of the first photographs of Slabbert, circa 1942. He is in the foreground, with his mother and Marcia behind.
(Source: courtesy of Tania Slabbert)

Marcia and Van Zyl Slabbert as head girl and head boy of Pietersburg High School in 1958. At left is Marcia's boyfriend.
(Source: *The Last White Parliament*)

Slabbert as a young Stellenbosch MA graduate in 1964.
(Source: Slabbert Collection, Stellenbosch University)

Slabbert married Mana Jordaan in Stellenbosch in 1965. The marriage lasted until 1983. Slabbert's paternal grandfather is at left.
(Source: Slabbert Collection, Stellenbosch University)

Climbing the academic ladder: Slabbert as head of the sociology department at Wits University, 1973. (Source: Slabbert Collection, Stellenbosch University)

The way we were: Slabbert and his young family in the early 1970s – Mana, Riko (3), Slabbert and Tania (7). (Source: Die Burger, 4 May 1974)

Slabbert burst onto the political scene in the 1974 general election, when he ran as the Progressive Party candidate for Rondebosch. (Source: The Last White Parliament)

In an echo of his early missionary impulse, Slabbert made efforts to investigate the plight of those living on the fringes of Cape Town. He reported on this encounter in the mid-1970s when he asked a resident of an informal settlement: 'What is this place called?' The man replied: 'Lourdes Farm. You know – like the place of the holy water.' (Source: The Last White Parliament)

The pleasures of friendship: a boating trip with Alex Boraine and his family on the Knysna Lagoon, circa 1979. Slabbert is at the stern, Boraine at the bow.
(Source: courtesy of Jeremy Boraine)

The politician as sportsman: Slabbert was a keen road runner, and is shown here competing in the Peninsula Marathon in the late 1970s. On the right is Mike Tarr, then a PFP MP.
(Source: The Last White Parliament)

Afrikaners of different political stripes: PW Botha of the National Party, Frederik van Zyl Slabbert of the Progressive Federal Party and Andries Treurnicht of the Conservative Party.
(Source: The Last White Parliament)

Goodbye – forever. Taking leave of Parliament in 1986.
(Source: Weekend Argus, 8 February 1986. Editorial cartoon by Mynderd Vosloo)

Departing for Dakar to meet representatives of the African National Congress in 1987 – but leaving officialdom guessing.
(Source: PW Botha Collection, Archive for Contemporary Affairs, University of the Free State)

Dakar 1987: Afrikaans-speakers from the University of the Western Cape with the leaders of the delegations. Seated (from left) are Jaap Durand, Slabbert, Thabo Mbeki and Jakes Gerwel. André Odendaal and Ampie Coetzee are shown standing.
(Source: Rashid Lombard Photo)

Slabbert and Jane, whom he had married in 1984, at their beach cottage at Boggomsbaai on the southern Cape coast in the early 1990s.
(Source: courtesy of Rudolf Gouws)

The end of a life. Slabbert's memorial service was held in Johannesburg on 27 May 2010. Pictured from left are political analyst Harald Pakendorf, Tania Slabbert, S Smirren and Jane Slabbert.
(Source: Gallo Images/Foto24/Christiaan Kotze)

also a period of adjustment for him; whereas he had fought apartheid tooth and nail, he now had to carve out a new role, a task not made any easier because of the absence of a firm foothold in the emergent formal higher-order politics.

Facilitator

Slabbert nevertheless stayed active and his diary was even more congested than during his parliamentary days. 'In Parliament you could be busy,' he explained in 1992, 'but you have a fairly fixed ritual. What I am involved in now covers such a wide spectrum of activities.'[27] He networked a great deal and often acted as a consultant and corporate speaker. He also put people in touch who had no previous acquaintance. One such case was arranging for Ali Bacher of the then South African Cricket Board to meet the ANC spokesperson for sport, Steve Tshwete, allowing for sensitive discussions on cricket unity after 1990 to get off the ground.[28]

In 1991 Slabbert became a significant role player as chairman of the Central Witwatersrand Metropolitan Chamber, which was established following negotiations between the Transvaal Provincial Administration and the Soweto People's Delegation, under the leadership of Cyril Ramaphosa. Slabbert only agreed to this position on condition that both parties were in favour of his appointment. The Chamber was a mediating body intent on ending the rent boycott in Soweto, started under apartheid, in exchange for incorporation into a new non-racial metropolitan structure and a common tax base. The complicated process involved at least 19 different organisations from across the political spectrum, including civics, city councils, Eskom, regional service councils and the Council of Business.[29]

From his vantage point as chairperson, Slabbert learnt a great deal of the practical grassroots problems confronting the democratic transition. 'I saw at first hand,' he said, 'how sound local democratic practice is linked to immediate problems concerning the daily quality of life – water, sewerage, electricity, refuse removal, housing, transport …' It was precisely at the disjuncture between low and high politics where the friction was likely to occur: 'Lofty pronouncements about the virtues of citizenship in a new democratic constitution will fall on deaf ears if these problems are not attended to at a local level.'[30]

Slabbert thought the best way to resolve questions of service provision was to take the political sting out of the issues, but it was not that easy. Appointing technical experts to oversee changes would have facilitated problems and helped to depoliticise service delivery, but organisations with vested interests were not prepared to surrender control. Slabbert was often caught betwixt and between various factions, and divisions were aggravated by tendentious press reports. It took almost three years to reach an inclusive agreement and an official end to the rates and rent boycott, just in time to avert a complete collapse of services and the exhaustion of the Chamber's finances.[31]

His work in this respect was well recognised. 'In a country as torn as South Africa,' a reporter observed, Slabbert's adroit footwork spoke 'volumes for both the man and the political animal. Not that the two are easily separated.'[32] He was also singled out for holding the Chamber together in what was described as 'a glorious experiment in participatory governance'.[33]

Despite the pressures and long hours, Slabbert seems to have found the work fulfilling. In an interview midway through his tenure he told a reporter:

> The Metropolitan Chamber has become a bit of a passion for me. It's the best contribution I could make to breaking the political logjam. I've achieved more in my 18 months here dealing with real issues than I did in my 12 years in Parliament. Here you sense that you're involved in something that could begin to change lives.[34]

Slabbert might have exaggerated somewhat, as the two occupations varied so much that a comparison was bound to be skewed. Nevertheless, it is clear that the work at the coalface of democratic transition suited him. Perhaps, one may surmise, it was the fact that after intensive effort he could actually see the fruits of his labour.

His spell at the Chamber had a rather bizarre interlude in 1993 when, out of the blue, De Klerk appointed him chairperson of the board of the South African Broadcasting Corporation (SABC). The ANC, including Nelson Mandela, was immediately on the case and told him he would damage his reputation by accepting the position. Slabbert was not asked whether he was interested, nor did he have a particular inclination to serve in such a capacity. De Klerk, desperate to resolve the situation, prevailed on him in a private meeting to accept the position provisionally just to get the board off the ground. Slabbert found it hard going. He soon discovered that despite his assurances that he did not regard the position as a sinecure, and was continuing under duress, some ANC-aligned board members were plotting to get rid of him. Fatima Meer, a sociologist whom he had known for years, told him frankly that despite his 'contribution to the democratisation of South Africa, the people would not tolerate a white Afrikaner male in that position'.[35] He resigned immediately.

He was succeeded by the ANC's Ivy Matsepe-Casaburri. She was appointed in exactly the same manner – without consultation – but he commented that she had 'the correct political birthmarks: a woman, black and part of the struggle'.[36] Described by one author familiar with the history of the SABC as a 'self-serving would-be apparatchik', Matsepe-Casaburri had a less-than-inspiring tenure as chairperson, and was soon shown the door.[37] Slabbert rejected criticism that he had compromised himself in accepting a post offered by De Klerk. He retorted: 'My own sense of personal integrity was never dependent upon frothing politicians, crusaders and charlatans. I sleep very well.'[38] What he learnt from this, he later recounted, were the ambiguities that from early on would rule in post-apartheid South Africa, despite earnest protestations of non-racialism: 'Mandela did not want me because I was not "a loyal servant of the ANC" and was a "white Afrikaner male". De Klerk wanted me because I was "not a loyal servant of the ANC" and was a "white Afrikaner male".' Likewise, patriotism was easily bandied about if it served one's interests. A few days after Slabbert's resignation, Mandela phoned to thank him and congratulate him on his 'patriotic act'.[39] But it was certainly not patriotism that had prompted Slabbert to terminate his relationship with the board.

After the SABC board debacle, Slabbert admitted openly that he was inclined to be drawn too easily into being chair of any organisation in which he showed an interest, and that he should be careful to avoid such entrapments in the future.[40] It was not long, though, before he agreed to be co-chair of the Local Government Elections Task Group, which was appointed to oversee the local government elections held in November 1995. It was a substantial task. To one reporter he said: 'You are now looking at a man who is bleeding from the inside.'[41] The elections proceeded smoothly, and Slabbert demonstrated his ability to manage such a huge exercise. He explained that he had taken the job 'not because I wish to hold public office or because I suffer from status anxiety, but because I am completely convinced that if we do not democratise at the local level as soon as possible, our transition is dead in the water.'[42] This interest was likely reinforced by his experience at the Witwatersrand Metropolitan Chamber, where the importance of practical everyday issues on the local level had been impressed upon him. Allied to this was an awareness and sensitivity that what happened at the grassroots level was a signifier of meaningful change.

Less satisfactory was his chairing of the Electoral Task Team, which investigated alternative electoral systems for South Africa during the early 2000s. In line with the certification of the 1996 Constitution, following on from the 1993 Interim Constitution, the electoral system had to be reconsidered after the 1999 election. The prevailing system consisted of proportional representation on a closed list, in which the party bosses decided who could go to Parliament. In the absence of defined constituencies, there was little accountability to the voters at large. Tony Leon, the leader of the Democratic Party (DP) – soon to become the DA – argued that the 400 MPs just drew a salary and supported their parties without fulfilling any meaningful oversight role.[43] A cabinet committee unanimously agreed on Slabbert as chairperson of the task team but dragged their feet in ratifying the appointment. Not surprisingly, he found it exasperating; time was running out and task team's work had to be completed well in advance of the next election, due in 2004. He did not wish to present a 'hurried and incomplete report', and in the back of his mind also wondered whether some members of the cabinet, despite their unanimous decision, had reservations about his suitability for the position.[44] Eventually his appointment was confirmed a year after he was first approached. In the meantime, President Thabo Mbeki misleadingly informed Parliament that the work of the task team was well under way, whereas it was not even out of the starting blocks.[45]

The inauspicious start notwithstanding, Slabbert assembled a number of notable local and international experts on voting systems to assess the South African electoral system. A majority report of the committee came out in favour of a 'mixed' system, with the suggestion that constituency-based voting should account for 300 representatives to the National Assembly and 100 members should represent special-interest groups on the existing list system. The minority report basically supported the status quo.[46] At the core of the matter was the question of accountability; the 'mixed' system, it was argued, lent itself better to assuring such an outcome.

The cabinet, however, paid scant regard to the report, with Kader Asmal, then minister of education, being especially dismissive, according to Slabbert. Asmal later denied this and claimed that the Slabbert proposals were simply too complicated to be implemented timeously.[47] Be that as it may, the system as it existed, with party bosses exercising power and ensuring pliant MPs, served the interest of the governing party, and therefore there was no real political incentive to change. Slabbert was most annoyed, if not infuriated. 'I have never felt so used, abused and insulted,' he said. 'It started off badly and ended worse.' It was, overall, 'a disgusting and eminently forgettable experience, except for the excellent contributions of some of my colleagues'.[48]

While Slabbert found the Electoral Task Team experience quite unsavoury, the actual report had a significant afterlife. Since 2003 it has featured prominently in literature and debates on the topic of electoral reform. The recommendation in the majority report pertaining to the need for a 'mixed' system in particular attracted attention. It was seen as more likely to come closer, in terms of accountability, to the much-vaunted ideal of a 'people's parliament' than the prevailing arrangement.[49] As late as 2019 the report was still a central point of departure in discussions about South Africa's electoral system.[50] Even more significant as a testimony to Slabbert's vision, in 2020 the Constitutional Court ruled in favour of an electoral system that incorporated voting constituencies.[51]

In considering Slabbert's career after 1990, it is clear that he was less in the limelight than during the apartheid years, but circumstances in the 1990s were so altered that, inevitably, new role players had to emerge. The fact that he was less prominent during this period should not create the impression that he had all but disappeared. He remained active in fields where he thought he could make a difference, though the SABC board debacle and the shenanigans with the Electoral Task Team – as it turned out, his final official sortie – left him dismayed. It was certainly not the way he would have wanted to end his governmental work. On the other hand, his experiences with the Metropolitan Chamber and the Local Government Elections Task Group enthused him. But at this point he did not seek more. In fact, just before the local elections in 1995 he confided to a reporter that he wished to become 'obscure' again.[52] It was not so easy. Over time, he had developed too much of a political profile to simply disappear without a trace.

Slabbert and the ANC in post-apartheid South Africa

During the latter part of the 1980s, as noted earlier, Slabbert had had regular contact with ANC leaders. At conferences and meetings he established close relations with Thabo Mbeki, with whom he felt comfortable. Intellectually, they were on a par and given to quick and humorous repartee. Slabbert later recalled that some of their meetings, while Mbeki was in exile, were 'hectic with partying and carousing'.[53] These early encounters with the ANC alerted him to the lifestyle and outlook of some of the ANC leadership core, as well as to the differences and rivalries between various factions. Despite, or perhaps because of, the high political stakes at the time, there were enough opportunities to relax. He recounted that '*in vino veritas* discussions took place frequently and passionately'. The temptations were many for exiles as they moved 'from one hotel and conference to the other, with sex, adulation and alcohol readily available'.[54] He was nevertheless impressed with their overall camaraderie and goodwill, which he found infectious.

Slabbert's contact with ANC leading lights at the time allowed him to see the organisation in its various guises. Upon the ANC's return to the country, he did not view all the returning exiles through rose-tinted glasses. He commented later:

> Although the lives of many who went into exile were cruelly disrupted and they suffered greatly, there were others swanning it in luxury hotels, pummelling tender Scandinavian consciences for 'struggle money' and coming back as self-styled 'MK generals' who fought in every battle and 'won the military war' against apartheid. I don't owe them a sweet farthing. The real struggle was here at home and many perished unrecognised and their families unrewarded.[55]

Before the 1990 breakthrough, he was also well aware of ideological positions that favoured armed struggle as a priority over negotiations.[56]

Slabbert doubted the overall efficacy of armed struggle but realised its importance within the ANC's discourse as an element in maintaining morale in the ranks and in pressurising the South African government. In the first quarter of 1989, during a combined academic and political visit to Moscow, he went so far as to state that the only alternative to the ANC was chaos.[57] If Pretoria had to spurn overtures of possible negotiations, the Soviet Union should continue to support the armed struggle.[58] It is clear that as the 1980s drew to a close, Slabbert, despite certain reservations about the ANC's strategies, could well understand the organisation's overall importance in the context of political developments in the country, and even tacitly support it. Given the circumstances, he was at the time perhaps not sufficiently mindful of what seasoned observers of the ANC, especially in Moscow, had identified as 'democratic centralism' within the organisation, including an intolerance of opposition.[59]

The ANC, having come to power through negotiations, did not have a free hand in shaping the new Constitution. After 1994, with the establishment of a Government of National Unity, it followed the standard constitutional protocols of a liberal democracy. Slabbert observed in 1997 that, on balance, with the eyes of the world on South Africa, there was a tendency more 'to observe and interpret the spirit of liberal-democratic principles than to subvert it'.[60] What was increasingly problematic, he realised, was that outside the orbit of formal constitutional observance, 'the dynamics of transformation may prove a far more serious threat to consolidating a liberal democracy in South Africa than the intent of those who negotiated it and now have to practise it'.[61] At stake, he said, was a commitment to a democratic culture, which included a wide span of activities and attitudes, such as financial accountability, an insistence on due process of law, payment for services and general administrative efficiency.[62]

In the early 1990s, Slabbert hoped that the ANC would make judicious use of talented South Africans to turn the giant ship of state around. He later admitted that he was naive in this respect and gave little heed to those who warned him against the ANC. Among those were Helen Suzman, with whom he reconciled after their ways had parted in 1986. She told him, early in the 1990s, and he now had to concur, that the internal dynamics of the ANC dictated complete loyalty to the organisation and that independent opinions were easily distrusted.[63]

Although Slabbert was careful not to admit to any personal ambitions in the new South Africa, there was a sense in which he thought he could play a significant role. Privately, he admitted as much to friends, but also added that the ANC was not really interested in having him on board. He was told that he should join an ANC branch and work himself up through the organisation.[64] This was as clear a message as could be wished for; he was not high on the ANC's list of priorities and his earlier commitments did not count for as much as he might have thought.

In any case, by the end of the decade he had become thoroughly disillusioned with, and outspoken about, the movement in general:

> Ultimately, just as with the old regime, it is all about the power of patronage and favouritism; about clientelism and protectionism; about the circulation of the elite and new public servants and sycophants, the whole utterly boring lot of them. Privilege, status, power and pomp become the barometers of change and transformation, and the same tired, hackneyed, racist, pseudo-patriotic arguments are used to establish the boundaries of loyalty and inner-circle favouritism.[65]

All of this, he recounted in 2007, had a deleterious effect on good governance. 'Instead of preserving as much competence as was available,' he said, 'the government felt obliged to reward ... party loyalty over competence; to confuse authority with intelligence while dealing with corruption highly selectively, if at all.'[66]

During the late 1980s, he had turned down attempts to inveigle him back into white party politics.[67] However, in the new dispensation, and shortly before the 1999 election, he briefly toyed with the idea of a comeback. He discussed the matter with DP leader Tony Leon over dinner. Also in attendance was Lawrie Schlemmer, the well-known social scientist and pollster.

Slabbert indicated that he felt he might 'have one more campaign left in me', and the possibility of his standing for premier of the Western Cape was aired. The idea appealed to him, but he told Leon that in the case of a hung parliament in the Western Cape, he would insist that the DP align itself with the ANC and not the National Party. It was a deal-breaker, Leon said, as Democratic Party supporters would not countenance such an arrangement. Slabbert's revulsion towards the National Party was still so strong, Leon observed, that he could not bring himself to consider the idea of cooperating with them in any guise. The following day, Slabbert informed Leon that he would not pursue the matter any further.[68] It would appear that Slabbert's loathing of the National Party was stronger than his often-articulated misgivings about the ANC.

Slabbert occasionally commented on ANC luminaries such as Mandela. He understood the universal respect Mandela commanded, and was in general agreement with the fulsome admiration bestowed on the prisoner turned president. Yet he was not completely beguiled by the Mandela 'magic'. While he could appreciate Mandela's reconciliatory role and some advances in service delivery, he had his reservations about the president's overall hold on government policy-making, implementation and administration. He was furthermore concerned that in making some cabinet appointments, Mandela had not risen above the temptation to follow the 'jobs for pals' route, regardless of demonstrable incompetence.[69] In short, he thought that Mandela's presidency was marked by 'too much charisma and not enough governance'.[70] On a personal level, he also experienced a different side of the usually amiable Mandela. This happened when Mandela asked Slabbert to approach George Soros for funding for Mandela's planned African peace initiative. Soros required further details and indicated that he did not sign blank cheques. Slabbert tried to explain this as gently as he could to a visibly upset Mandela. But it was to no avail. Mandela just glared at Slabbert and subsequently refrained from any friendly interaction with him.[71] Despite this, Slabbert still held Mandela in high regard as a unique leader, and as a person who could 'charm the milk out of your coffee any day of the week'.[72]

Slabbert's frosty relationship with Mandela had a more elaborate reprise with Mbeki as deputy president and president, and became a topic of some speculation. When Mbeki returned to the country from exile after 1990, Slabbert assisted him in obtaining a penthouse apartment in Johannesburg. The cordiality, warmth and open intellectual exchanges that had marked their relationship under apartheid, however, started to wane. Slabbert revealed how their first full conversation proceeded after a chill of three years. They met at Mbeki's residence, where he had moved since vacating the penthouse. Mbeki had just been appointed as deputy president. With a number of people keen to be associated with him, Mbeki appeared awkward and out of place. When Slabbert eventually had the opportunity to talk to him, he told Mbeki that he did not want any rewards but was available for service, and that Mbeki should feel free to use him if he was so inclined. Mbeki then asked Slabbert what he would do if he was in his position. Slabbert replied that he would set up several commissions of experts in key areas for advice and to 'tell me how much I have to learn and how stupid I am'. Mbeki seems to have taken offence at this, Slabbert recalled: it 'was the end of our comfortable relationship. He is the only person I know who has demonstrated to me that my friendship was expendable.'[73]

Several years later, Mbeki claimed that at the time he had no inkling of exactly what Slabbert required of him.[74] A confidant of Mbeki who was present at the occasion remembered that Mbeki, who was still basking in the afterglow of his appointment as deputy president, was taken aback by Slabbert's frank approach, which he deemed inappropriate.[75] Although such exchanges carried a latent political charge, in that Mbeki might have thought that Slabbert was implying that black people were not fully capable of running the country on their own, at the core of the matter was a diametrically opposed conception of what friendship entailed. Mbeki, though appearing affable, could ultimately be calculating and distant.[76] Slabbert was more gregarious and set considerable store by friendship. He was, as political commentator RW Johnson remarked, so 'big-hearted and large-spirited himself, he probably didn't allow enough for the fact that other people might not be the same'.[77] For Slabbert, then, friendship rose above the political, and he considered reciprocity a key element in nurturing a common understanding. Mbeki did not view relationships in the same way.[78] From the outside it appeared to some that 'Mbeki might be leading Van up the garden path or, possibly, that Van was leading himself up it'.[79] If this was indeed the case, Slabbert after some time fully realised his mistake.

There is a neat irony here if one delves into the past of both individuals. They shared similar childhoods: from a young age, Slabbert's difficult home background forced him to cope on his own; in Mbeki's case, politics meant that the enforced absence of his father, Govan Mbeki, on Robben Island contributed to Thabo's often detached and undemonstrative outlook.[80] Each, however, dealt with a similar set of circumstances differently.

Slabbert initially appreciated the difficult balancing act Mbeki had to perform as president to satisfy the various factions within government.[81] Gradually, however, he became more critical. In 2002, he thought that his former friend had a highly inflated idea of his own position and influence. Mbeki's earlier self-deprecating attitude, which Slabbert had appreciated when they first met, seemed to have disappeared altogether. 'Now,' Slabbert said, 'I get the feeling of somebody who takes himself absolutely seriously. All the little gestures and the talking, talking.' Mbeki, he claimed, had unrealistic grandiose ideas of his own place in history. He projected himself as a 'man of history and his time in history, that kind of stuff ... You just take the number of times he uses the word "humanity", "the planet", "the world"; I don't know what those concepts mean quite frankly except in a sort of geographic sense or astrological sense. He uses them as if they are collective actors. "The world" must come to its senses.'[82] Slabbert was astounded that such a personality change was possible. 'Overnight,' he observed, Mbeki became 'politically papal, with all the handwringing and formal little coughs when he spoke and being totally inaccessible.'[83]

The differences between Slabbert and Mbeki spilled over into the public arena in 2007 following the publication of Slabbert's book *The Other Side of History*, in which he was highly critical of Mbeki. At a meeting on social cohesion organised by Stellenbosch University, Bheki Khumalo took Slabbert to task, accusing him of 'having fallen off the truck' and of being ungrateful to Mbeki as president, who was 'no longer so needy' as during their meeting in Dakar in 1987.[84] Slabbert listened impassively to Khumalo and then pointed out that the relationship between him and Mbeki was considerably more complex than what Khumalo had conveyed. Slabbert continued, saying that he respected Mbeki as president, but that he was not prepared to prostrate himself before Mbeki, telling him, 'You may kick me.'[85] There was a last attempt at reconciliation, to which Slabbert agreed in 2010, but before arrangements could be finalised he had passed away.[86]

Besides the personal falling-out between the two men, it remains in wider political terms highly dubious whether Slabbert could ever have imagined himself comfortably ensconced in the ANC fold. His disillusioning experience with the Electoral Task Team would have disabused him of any such notion, even if he had possibly harboured such ideas. This was not ameliorated by Mbeki's increasingly Africanist ideology, which Slabbert found exclusivist.[87] In the new dispensation, a different set of rules came into play, and Slabbert as a politician must have realised that with no constituency in tow, he had little to offer the ANC. As noted above, he was virtually told that he would have to start from the bottom level of the movement. Moreover, his generally critical outlook might well have compromised the organisation. If no formal position and recognition came his way, though, the possibility still existed that, given his anti-apartheid history, he might perhaps have expected some kind of personal affirmation from Mbeki.[88] But, if that was the case, it is unlikely that Mbeki would have been sensitive to those kinds of signals.

Business ventures and philanthropic initiatives

Slabbert's interest in the business world was partly kindled by a spell of lecturing at the Wits Business School, in 1990, on the political environment and business. It was also at this time that he established a political consultancy, Strategic Foresight, which, given the uncertainty of the transition period, was well placed – with someone as knowledgeable as Slabbert at the helm – to provide sound advice.[89]

Slabbert's reputation probably accounted for his being approached by a young German Namibian, Jürgen Kögl, with a view to his facilitating black involvement in corporate South Africa. At first, Slabbert got on well with Kögl, though their paths later separated. Together they set up an investment trust called Khula (Zulu for 'growth'). As a black investment vehicle, the idea was for Khula to buy up viable small- to mid-sized companies and at the same time transfer managerial skills. They found it difficult, though, to raise the necessary capital to fund the initiative. Large corporates feigned interest but did not reach for their chequebooks. Slabbert and Kögl nevertheless forged ahead with Khula after securing a number of black partners, including Zanele Mbeki (Thabo's wife) from the Women's Development Bank. Slabbert claimed that the venture was one of the first black economic empowerment companies.[90]

Slabbert was also chair of the Independent Media Diversity Trust, which had as one of its aims to assist smaller and 'alternative' newspapers like the *New Nation* and *Vrye Weekblad* after funding dried up in the post-apartheid dispensation. It proved to be an impossible task. Despite the setback, he realised that there were opportunities in the media world and committed Khula to exploring these. Khula joined forces with newspaper and printing giant Caxton/CTP and, under a new umbrella company called CTP Directories, decided to bid for the lucrative telephone directory contract.[91] Although it was not necessarily a decisive factor in the deal, it helped that Caxton, which had just imported modern presses, could offer work for black women to operate the new equipment. The bid was successful and all parties concerned made a tidy profit. Slabbert, it seems, was a fast learner.

The next move was to acquire shares in Adcorp Holdings. Adcorp was a 'soft' financial services company that specialised in the recruitment of personnel, placement, advertising training, public relations and research. Slabbert became a non-executive director in 1994, and in 1998 he took over as chair of the listed company with a market capitalisation of R560 million. With some satisfaction, he could say: 'I moved from being adviser to decision-maker.'[92] Slabbert also served on the board of FirstRand Ltd, the holding company of FirstRand Bank, in this case in a non-executive position.

In his new role, Slabbert became increasingly aware of the need for corporate responsibility. It could come in all forms and guises. On one occasion, he took *The Citizen*, part of the Caxton stable, to task for what he regarded as sensationalist reporting on Mbeki's alleged womanising. Although Slabbert, as noted, did not hold a candle for Mbeki, he thought the report unbecoming and tendentious, and proffered an apology.[93]

Just as in his early parliamentary career, when he had to be 'house trained' to find his way around in the new environment, he now had to adjust to the labyrinth of the business world. In politics, as in business, he found the dividing line between right and wrong could be gossamer-thin. It is not easy doing 'honest business', he remarked, but not impossible either. By 'honest business', he explained, 'I mean not buying political favours, paying bribes or sacrificing your independence'.[94] He was particularly opposed to cosmetic black empowerment deals that involved placing a few black appointees in strategic positions to cream off substantial amounts from contracts and tenders without any transfer of skills being effected or real business value being added to the company. Similarly, after 1990 he had serious reservations about opportunistic businessmen who were keen to meet the 'new lot' and expected him to facilitate such contacts.[95]

For all his scepticism, Slabbert also had respect for businesspeople. The business world, he said, is not for 'softies' and one had to be wide awake not to be outwitted. He was dismissive of those who spoke in derogatory terms about 'cut-throat' businessmen; these critics most likely had never tried to make money on an entrepreneurial basis. It was, according to him, extremely hard work, with permanent built-in risks.[96]

As Slabbert's health declined from 2008 to 2010, he had to give up his positions in the business world. Although he had achieved some success, he still regarded himself as 'an apprentice businessman'. His first love, as he indicated to a friend, was still politics.[97]

While he remained outside formal politics ('A wallflower cannot ask himself to dance', he once remarked),[98] he had earlier channelled his restless energies into other directions. One of these was the establishment of an institute on the island of Gorée.

The name Gorée is derived from the Dutch 'Goede Reede' (good reason) and dates back to the 16th century, when the Dutch occupied the island. It was later taken over by the British and then the French. During the Atlantic slave trade, Gorée became notorious as the terminal for slaves brought from across West Africa. They proceeded through a narrow passage, then through the 'door of no return', and were housed in harsh conditions before being dispatched by ship to the Americas.[99]

The idea of an institute took root after the 1987 Dakar conference, and Slabbert and Breyten Breytenbach played a major role in its establishment in 1991. Initially, the financial prospects looked bleak, but matters improved substantially after George Soros decided to contribute to the initiative. Other donors from the Netherlands and the Nordic countries followed, and South African companies such as Naspers, Rand Merchant Bank, Richemont and Gencor also assisted.[100] The Gorée Institute, Centre for Democracy, Development and Culture in Africa – to give it its full name – flourished, becoming a meeting place for intellectuals from all over Africa. By 1997 an extensive network of voluntary organisations had been established, and the institute offered popular courses on development and provided computer facilities.[101]

It required considerable effort, and an ex-Dakarite, André Zaaiman, initially played a prominent role in getting the institute off the ground. Slabbert and Breytenbach were proud of the way the Gorée Institute developed, and likened their affinity for the project to a mother hen jealously guarding her brood.[102] For Slabbert, the institute represented an intellectual and practical project that went beyond narrow South African concerns by seeking to connect with Africa in a meaningful way. He was, however, not starry-eyed about Africa, and in *The Other Side of History* there is a sense of disillusionment about the chicanery and sordidness of African politics that he observed in some countries. At one point, the institute's existence and viability came under threat, partly because of internal developments but also because of hostile changes in Senegalese politics.[103]

Gorée nevertheless had a personal appeal for Slabbert. It was a project that he had helped to launch with scarce resources at first, and he also might have felt that the island, with its stark history, held in equal measure a certain mystic promise and residual bleakness. His friend Breytenbach had a vivid memory of Slabbert on Gorée:

Of how he stands in the courtyard of the house on Gorée, early before sunrise, in bathing trunks and with a towel over the shoulder, whistling softly to wake me up so that we may go and swim just as the light dawns silvery over the immense sadness of our continent.[104]

Gorée also featured in the lives of Tania and Riko. Tania, fluent in French, worked on the island and in Dakar in her early twenties. She found it a challenging but life-changing experience that helped her to think beyond the cocooned South African environment. Riko once went there on a bonding trip with his father – a meaningful experience for both father and son.[105]

Apart from the Gorée project, Slabbert was also involved with George Soros in establishing the Open Society Foundation in South Africa in 1993, and in 1997 the initiative broadened out into southern Africa. Under Soros, the Open Society Foundations had a global reach in developing countries and focused on a number of key developmental issues: literacy, general education, emancipation of rural women and consolidation of crucial democratic features such as freedom of speech and independent courts. In southern Africa the organisation was well run and regarded as the best of its kind globally.[106]

Slabbert stayed with the Open Society Foundation until 2003. Most of the organisational work he did in this respect was not in the public eye. He found it an immensely satisfying experience and had a high regard for those committed to such work, who soldiered on despite obstacles. In retrospect, he said, he realised that had he stayed in Parliament, such opportunities might not have come his way. More than ever, he was grateful that he had resigned. His perspectives were broadened and his knowledge of Africa deepened.[107]

Slabbert's understanding of, and contributions to, the strengthening of civil society do not often receive the necessary recognition. His friend Mike Savage, who worked closely with him in this regard, was most impressed with the energies he poured into the promotion of key elements of civil society as a way of asserting the consolidation of a viable constitutional democracy. Slabbert accomplished this, said Savage, with his 'usual intellectual verve, clear vision and leadership'.[108]

9
'VAN': PUBLIC IMAGE AND PRIVATE LIFE

Charisma

'Van', as Slabbert was fondly called – or sometimes 'Super Van' if the press wished to emphasise his abilities and attributes – was frequently described as a charismatic politician with exceptional personal magnetism. Sometimes likened to John F Kennedy, Slabbert was deemed to possess similar qualities of youthfulness, charm and appeal to voters.

In some sections of the Afrikaans press, this was fully recognised and it was regretted that he belonged to the 'wrong' party, that he was not 'one of us', though he belonged to 'us'. His ability, it was said, to 'attract people to him on a purely human level was not to be disputed'. His background was considered perfect: 'a pure boer son of the soil' from the countryside, and, to top it all, 'with a Kennedy charisma' as he amply demonstrated during television appearances.[1]

Slabbert was not oblivious to the positive and at times fawning way in which he was viewed. In 1974, during his first election campaign, he made the point that English-speakers saw him as being charismatic and there was little he could do about it. Such fulsome praise did, however, leave him somewhat embarrassed. On one occasion he responded with a friendly but wry comment to an effusive admirer who had commented on his charismatic appeal: 'Yes, I studied Charisma 1, Charisma 2 and Charisma 3 at university.'[2] Such ready self-deprecation was typical Slabbert, though it should be borne in mind that casual dismissals of one's talents can inadvertently also further charm those who are already enthralled.

While the notion of charisma is relevant in analysing Slabbert's appeal, it can easily become tautological – merely repeating that which should be explained. What needs to be done is to unpack some of the constitutive elements of charisma to form a clearer idea of exactly what in Slabbert's make-up had such an appeal, and, equally importantly, to try and understand why he so endeared himself to the public. Writing on the general nature of charisma, the Dutch scholar Jan Stutje alerts us to the following: 'Charismatic leaders have an impressive personal presence, a strong "magnetism". In some cases this involves even physical traits, in all cases at least a convincing power of oratory … Charismatic politics is not ordinary, routine politics. It has the revivalist flavour of a movement, powered by the enthusiasm that draws normally non-political people into the political arena.'[3] To what extent is this applicable to Slabbert and can some additional dimensions be added?

Observers often commented on Slabbert's film-star looks. He was invariably described as 'tall, broad and heavily handsome … exuding intelligence, alertness, concern, caution and a sense of humour', with his 'resonant baritone voice' added for good measure.[4] Women found him particularly appealing. Even a female political opponent, Sheila Camerer, then a National Party MP, admitted that 'as a woman she has a soft spot for Slabbert' and that he was a 'smashing guy'.[5] She was certainly not alone, as other women concurred (see Chapter 2, on the 1974 campaign in Rondebosch). Novelist JM Coetzee wrote: 'One … reason Slabbert should have had a quiet sense of confidence in himself was the fact that he was much loved by women.' He admitted that he knew nothing about Slabbert's private life, but continued: 'I do know that most of the women who crossed his path were half in love with him. No matter how firmly your feet are planted on the ground, that sort of adulation does wonders for the ego.'[6] While this might well have been the case, Slabbert did not actively pursue such attention. In fact, though outwardly courteous, he found it wearisome at times. The celebrity journalist Jani Allan commented: 'Swooned over by groupies, grown women and gays, Van is always the perfect gentleman. In the face of constant admiration, he remains as amiable as a pub dog who has been patted too often – ever polite, even if there is a look in his eyes that says he is looking for closing time.'[7]

Slabbert was not the sort of person who could easily be ignored; his presence was generally tangible. 'Van had a strong sense of himself and exuded that very strongly so you could feel it in a room full of people,'[8] RW Johnson recalls. For Mark Gevisser, Thabo Mbeki's biographer, 'Slabbert always seemed constrained by his environment, needing to burst out of his clothes, his office, the world's expectations of him, the Afrikaner stereotype, the paralysis of white politics.' Especially during the 1980s, Gevisser says, Slabbert was 'always a little too bluff and oversized for the polite parlour rooms of Anglo-South African liberalism but magnetic in his appeal to white South Africans looking for a trailblazer to lead them out of apartheid's mire …'.[9]

Besides his imposing appearance, Slabbert's oratorical skills further contributed to his appeal. Fully bilingual and speaking in a measured yet animated tone, he had the ability to make politics comprehensible to ordinary people, to break policy matters into digestible units, and to build upon that logically to reach an inescapable conclusion.[10] He was anything but a rabble-rousing demagogue; on the contrary, his appeal lay in exactly the opposite direction. He respected the audience's intelligence and did not talk down to them; regardless of their political persuasion, he understood their fears and sought to assuage these by rational argument. Anyone convinced against their will, he realised, is of the same opinion still.

One of the key features of his speeches was to show the interconnectedness of various aspects of society. In Bloemfontein in 1982, for example, a fairly hostile audience took him to task over the PFP's perceived focus on racial matters to the exclusion of bread-and-butter issues such as rising prices and inadequate old-age pensions. He took the criticism seriously, but proceeded to explain the connection between racial matters and rising daily expenditure. The lack of a skilled black workforce, he said, made products more expensive, while higher government grants for elderly people were difficult to fund, as the tax base, which was mainly restricted to white people, was too narrow and could only be augmented through the growth of a black middle class. Comprehension dawned upon the audience; they still might not vote for the PFP, but they certainly walked away with greater respect for Slabbert.[11]

His speeches by and large steered clear of what could be termed 'apartheid moralism'. Though he realised that many aspects of apartheid could be viewed as morally questionable, he refrained from preaching to an audience and making them feel morally culpable.[12] By choice, his appeal was rational rather than moralistic. Slabbert himself said that he could not imagine himself in the role of a bombastic politician.[13] He was, as his parliamentary colleague Ray Swart observed, never 'one for histrionics', but 'was nonetheless a forceful speaker with a fine turn of phrase which he used effectively to devastate the policies and attitudes of his opponents ...'.[14]

Journalists generally found his approach refreshing, and this was reflected in their reportage. Some tried to capture the flavour and texture of his speechmaking, as is evident from this report in an East London newspaper:

> Incisive, sincere, never clowning for laughs but drily and spontaneously witty, courteous and, best of all, free from hackneyed platitudes ... He appeals to the intellect, reason, sense – call it what you will – rather than blind emotion, something unusual for a politician ... he presents good policy clearly, adds his own fascinating historical and sociological insight ... expresses one's own vague, ill-formed ideas, and adds to that a lot more besides – like non-evasion of tricky questions.[15]

'VAN': PUBLIC IMAGE AND PRIVATE LIFE

While Slabbert's repertoire contained considerable factual content, it was not devoid of humour, as noted above, and he realised the importance of smuggling in some levity to what could otherwise easily descend into a diatribe, haranguing listeners with dour and gloomy statistics. He laced his presentations with a number of off-the-cuff gems. Obviously these varied from occasion to occasion. He was generally opposed to personal attacks on his political enemies, even if cast in a humorous mode, but he was not above gentle ribbing of his opponents. Thus, commenting on a long-standing MP, Cas Greyling of the Conservative Party, Slabbert quipped: 'Parliament does not need Cas Greyling, but heaven knows, Cas Greyling needs Parliament.' He also professed to have some respect for Piet Koornhof, a prominent National Party cabinet member who at one stage had the unenviable task of being minister of so-called cooperation and development. Koornhof, he said, tongue firmly in cheek, deserved to be admired, as he was 'totally uncontaminated by failures'. Politicians as a species were not spared. He defined a politician as 'somebody who asks money from the rich and votes from the poor and promises to protect the one from the other'. In this vein, he was even given to mocking democracy: 'Give everyone in this country the vote and you will soon see what happens to democracy.'[16] Irony had a special appeal for him; 'To destroy the authority of the pulpit, take it to the pavement,' he would quip. He could also take the sting out of too-earnest political probing. Asked after a political meeting what he would do if he became state president 'tomorrow', he jokingly replied: 'I am shocked, this has all happened so soon ...'[17] He knew how to make humour work to his advantage and to use it effectively without being ponderous. In private, he was also known to regale his friends with precise and hilarious mimicry of public figures, the accents reproduced faultlessly.[18]

In terms of drawing audiences, Slabbert was undoubtedly the PFP's star attraction. In the early 1980s newspapers routinely wrote about the 'Slabbert factor' and how well-attended his meetings were.

In the 1981 general election campaign, 1 400 people attended a rally in Pretoria, followed by 2 000 in Durban, 1 200 in Port Elizabeth and 2 500 in Randburg.[19] These were large numbers, and although it did not necessarily mean that all those who attended were converted to the Progs, Slabbert's ability to get voters to come and listen to a different message was clear.

A part of Slabbert's public image also revolved around his sporting background. He confessed to having been a typical 'rugger bugger at Stellenbosch' and for a while 'lived for rugby'. After his student days he joined the local town club, Van der Stel. Slabbert was not oblivious to the downside of rugby, which he viewed as a kind of narcotic, sheltering one from South Africa's harsh social realities, but at the same time he admitted to enjoying the game fully and would not denigrate it.[20]

When he went to Rhodes University as a lecturer, he coached the university's first team and made a lasting impression on some of the players. Ray Carlson was one who came under Slabbert's tutelage and was encouraged to go on to Stellenbosch to advance his rugby career. Carlson ended up playing in one Test for the Springboks in 1972. He recalled Slabbert as a 'great man' and still remembered 'how easily and naturally he could come down or up to any person's level. There was nothing more stimulating than when he was just "one of the boys!"'[21] Rugby was the important catalyst here; it was more than just a game, and signified wider sentiments and mutual understanding. Top rugby players, and even some in lower tiers, were widely admired.[22] For Afrikaners in particular this meant a great deal, as one J Buys from Pretoria wrote to Slabbert; although Buys disagreed with him politically, Slabbert was nevertheless blessed with 'what the Americans called charisma' and part of that appeal was his sporting image and enthusiasm.[23]

Besides rugby, long-distance running also placed Slabbert in the spotlight. On the election trail he often set aside time for jogging, which newspapers were quick to report on.[24] Slabbert was also given

'VAN': PUBLIC IMAGE AND PRIVATE LIFE

to reflecting on the rationale of his participation in marathons. He found the 1982 Comrades Marathon – 90 kilometres between Pietermaritzburg and Durban – particularly gruelling. 'Grated glass seems to grind in the knee and hip joints and the calf and thigh muscles contract in rhythmic aches,' he wrote. He wondered why he had decided to put himself through it:

> It is not just an ego trip, although there may be something of that in it. It is not just fear of getting old and inactive, although there is some of that in it as well. Perhaps it is an awareness of having been given a healthy body that one has not even begun to do justice to as far as its abilities and potential are concerned. How will I cope emotionally and physically with stress? Well, the Comrades is a very simple way of finding out.[25]

Slabbert was clearly much more than an unthinking, robotic runner and he found some kind of inner fulfilment in meeting such a challenge. While he did it for himself, the personal and the public in his case could not be separated. He realised that running the Comrades could be a risky venture for a politician, presumably should he fail or spectators interfere with him during the race.[26] But what he did not mention was the positive example of a politician exuding supreme fitness and symbolically projecting his preparedness to accept and complete an exacting task.

When assessing Slabbert's charismatic appeal, one is struck by the extent to which his profile matches some of the conceptual definitions relating to charismatic leaders and their followers. According to Jane Howell and Boas Shamir, academic specialists in organisational behaviour and leadership, respectively, such a relationship includes

> communicating an ideological vision that is discrepant from the status quo, intellectually stimulating followers

to think in new and different directions, communicating high expectations and confidence in followers, referring to followers' worth and efficacy as individuals and as a collective, and engaging in exemplary and symbolic behaviour and role modelling.[27]

One could almost be forgiven for thinking they had Slabbert in mind. However, to take the argument further, it should be factored in that a charismatic leader does not operate in a vacuum, and in order to come to a more rounded view one should assess not only the leader but also the dynamics that animate his or her followers. While a leader may be the spark, Howell and Shamir suggest, what are also required are followers as flammable material waiting to be ignited, and the oxygen that is provided by a conducive environment.[28]

In Slabbert's case, it had much to do with the unsettled political landscape after the 1976 Soweto uprising. Although the government claimed to provide stability and a secure future for whites, reality did not seem to accord with such promises. Alienation and dissatisfaction increased as the state seemed to cast around for a solution. Particularly in the 1980s, a combustible environment existed, punctuated with the declaration of successive states of emergency in the face of unrelenting cycles of public unrest and strike action. The situation was ripe for a new leader to emerge and grasp the nettle. Slabbert was seen as such a leader. Even if many of his white followers were not sure that he had all the answers, at least he knew how to ask the right questions.

In this light, it is tempting to see Slabbert as an almost messianic figure, blessed with charisma and destined to lead 'his people' to new pastures. Max Weber, writing on charisma and politics as a vocation, observed that support for the charismatic figure 'means that the leader is personally recognised as "the innerly called" leader of men. Men do not obey him by virtue of tradition or statute, but because they believe in him … The devotion of his disciples, his followers, his ... party ... is oriented to his person and to its qualities.'²⁹ Friends and acquaintances occasionally picked up on Slabbert's tendency to indulge in what they described as 'a sense of calling' and his need to play a 'prophetic role in politics'.³⁰ An Afrikaans theologian who later interviewed him was struck by the way Slabbert communicated: 'He did not have a Bible in hand, but he spoke as if he had.'³¹

This could be traced back to his early years when he contemplated entering the ministry of the Dutch Reformed Church and then later became 'uncalled'. Politics could then easily become a second calling. The extent to which this actively informed his thinking is hazy, but it does have a credible ring to it. It should, however, not be exaggerated. While Slabbert had a good measure of idealism, an ingredient that many politicians like to claim as a driving force, he was on the whole rational and sober in his assessment of political situations and realistic about his own role. In terms of leadership, he believed neither that the individual was completely at the mercy of historical forces nor that the individual or leader could blithely ignore historical realities. He opted for an in-between position where some form of exchange or interaction could be engineered. It was in this space that individuals could confront contextual tendencies and options could emerge, ultimately determining how history was made.³²

As his parliamentary career unfolded and he became involved in the hurly-burly of party politics, his position as the leader of the PFP kept him in the spotlight. But without any enduring and significant successes, he was constantly aware of the lurking dangers of being ensnared by supporters and trading in what might turn out to be counterfeit political currency. During his first speech as leader of the PFP, at its congress in September 1979, he made it clear that he was wary of a 'personality cult and the creation of seven-day charismatic miracles'.³³ The image of Super Van, he realised, could only take him so far, and to keep on peddling the same political wares with no real prospects of meaningful breakthroughs would be misguided and ultimately counterproductive. After his resignation from Parliament in 1986 he sought in some respects to shed his earlier image and public persona. He railed in particular against what he called

> a persistent myth in white electoral politics [of] the 'Great White Hope' (GWH): an enlightened, charismatic and obviously white political figure who can mobilise non-reactionary white voters in sufficient numbers to either unseat the governing National Party or somehow decisively influence democratic reform from 'above'. Part of this myth is the often unstated assumption that all politics in South Africa is about whites deciding who gets what, when and how. Therefore, democracy, if it is ever to be, can *only* come about from white politics, and the rest of the population, or the 'masses' or the 'outside world' must curb its impatience and restrain its irrationality and wait for the GWH to lead us 'constitutionally', 'evolutionary' [*sic*] and 'peacefully' to democracy and justice.[34]

There can be little doubt that Slabbert was thinking of his own role when he penned these lines. He had clearly come to the conclusion that in a wider context, the reliance of the white electorate on a single figure of salvation actually represented an impediment to understanding the realities of South African politics. He was no longer prepared to play the charismatic role assigned to him. It was unfair to him, he argued, and furthermore conveniently absolved his followers of responsibility. It was a device they used 'to displace their own anxieties onto you and sit back and wait for you to work some sort of political magic. That's wrong.' In addition he found it 'alienating, because it makes something of me', he said, 'which I am not, and therefore it is more difficult to communicate'.[35]

What Slabbert articulated here also had something to do with the pitfalls of charismatic leadership. To return to Max Weber:

> The charismatic leader gains and maintains authority solely by proving his strength in life. If he wants to be a prophet, he must perform miracles; if he wants to be a warlord, he must perform heroic deeds. Above all, however, his divine mission must 'prove' itself in that those who faithfully surrender to him must fare well. If they do not fare well, he is obviously not the master sent by the gods.[36]

By the mid-1980s, as Slabbert fully realised, the time for white men to perform miracles on their own was rapidly running out. For miracles to happen, the whole system first had to be dismantled.

The appeal that stemmed from his physical presence, riveting speeches, analytical abilities, sporting image and common touch had come full circle. Of his own volition he now sought to limit what he regarded as the unrealistic expectations engendered by a personal brand of politics. Even though he might at times have derived some satisfaction from the impact he could generate, he was equally aware that a kind of white 'rock star' appeal was not what was required in the dire politics of the 1980s. He therefore decided to kill the symbol of the political rock star before it fizzled out.

The issue of Afrikaner identity

One of the other issues Slabbert engaged with was that of being an Afrikaner, or of being perceived to be an Afrikaner. The question of who and what is an Afrikaner is of course a perennial one that often informs much of the ethnic discourses both within the ranks of Afrikanerdom and further afield. At its core is the issue of an adequate definition. How can Slabbert's 'Afrikanerhood' be objectively determined? Breyten Breytenbach commented graphically that any time a definition is required, 'everybody stutters like a Lister engine gulping for air …'.[37]

However, in 1973 Professor WB Vosloo of the political science department at Stellenbosch was brave enough to suggest certain pertinent common factors denoting Afrikanerhood. These were: strong religious sentiments; devotion to language; a sense of common historical experience; an affinity for racial integrity; a rural background or rural connections with a penchant for *gemeinschaftliche* (community) social relationships; a tendency to act in a homogeneous fashion and to actively support Afrikaans organisations; and a will to survive as a collective.[38] If one had to subject Slabbert to such a test, it is clear that he could be slotted into most of the categories: he was religious when he first arrived at Stellenbosch, though his commitment later waned; he was keen on Afrikaans as a language; he was aware of how Afrikaners viewed their history; he came from a rural background and found satisfaction in associating with others on a community level; and he realised the importance of the will to survive, although he was implacably opposed to the idea that this should happen at all costs. The exceptions that clearly set him apart were his lack of interest in racial 'purity' and the fact that he was not a great supporter of Afrikaans organisations.

While some sense of Slabbert's Afrikanerhood can be obtained through this kind of box-ticking exercise, it is also mechanical and limiting. Slabbert himself was given to reflecting on his Afrikanerhood in a more discursive manner. He did not regard himself as a 'devout, sombre-suited' Afrikaner, nor as 'an uptight culture vulture Afrikaner', nor as a 'free-and-easy, "alternative", Woodstock one', but a 'confused and sometimes lost Afrikaner, nevertheless. The fact that this has been and remains a source of consternation for some, I have experienced at first hand. But even the consternation is an affirmation of my social identity.'[39] Slabbert, as good friends and acquaintances noted, 'never denied his Afrikaner roots'.[40] For instance, he revelled in singing traditional Afrikaans folk songs with gusto and intent.[41] He was also perceived to be 'comfortable in his skin as an Afrikaner and in speaking Afrikaans, yet he was sharply critical of Afrikaners who arrogantly extolled their identity and used colour to exclude and ostracise half of Afrikaans speakers'.[42]

His first wife, Mana, regarded him as someone who came from a *stoere boere-agtergrond* (staunch farming background).[43] Although he did have a farming background, his fractured early home life meant that he was not formally inducted into what was regarded as a 'normal' Afrikaner home. From the age of ten until his late twenties as a student and lecturer, he was a boarder. There was, as he said, 'no systematic influence on my life to make me identify subjectively with being an Afrikaner. Yet it made virtually no difference to my world. From the moment I could think, I was socially identified with being an Afrikaner'.[44]

He was fond of quoting Jean-Paul Sartre in this regard: 'You are a Jew because I look at you.' This implied that regardless of one's own self-definition, others would define one as belonging to a certain group. In South Africa, he said, the way in which one spoke English, a certain sense of humour, food preferences, professional career milieu and neighbourhood may all help to define one as an Afrikaner.[45] He, however, found it problematic to subscribe to the notion of a single 'Afrikaner' or to talk about '*the* history of the Afrikaner'. To be called an Afrikaner, he argued, is only the beginning of a conversation and not the final answer.[46]

Slabbert had a refined and multilayered understanding of the various ways in which Afrikaner identity could be expressed. His was a point of departure often absent in the views of his English-speaking Prog colleagues. For instance, while in the 1980s they were given to dismissing Eugène Terre'Blanche and his AWB summarily and imperiously, Slabbert had a different take. He was prepared to engage with Terre'Blanche, he said, though Terre'Blanche 'did not have the same table manners as me'.[47] Terre'Blanche's bombastic and racist behaviour, Slabbert explained, was the result of a 'latent sense of inferiority and lack of self-confidence'. Underneath all the bluster there lurked 'a natural warmth and simple generosity'. Slabbert thought that Terre'Blanche, without actually realising it, in fact harboured an African sense of hospitality and coexistence: 'There is no doubt about it, as a white, he is uniquely and specially African. He has missed most of what Europe has gone through culturally, philosophically and economically over the last century – and it shows … His enduring tragedy is that he is a white African who refuses to come to terms with his own continent and its people.'[48] Slabbert may well have erred somewhat on the side of generosity in his assessment of the AWB leader, and likewise in his one-dimensional assumptions of African culture, but the fact remains that he had a novel view of Terre'Blanche and Afrikaner identity that few other commentators were prepared to entertain. He was also, rather surprisingly, willing to engage Terre'Blanche in a public debate at the University of Pretoria.[49]

Moving from Terre'Blanche to academic conceptualisations of Afrikaner identity, Slabbert distinguished between what could be called primordial views of ethnicity and more historical-relativist points of departure. Primordial views imply that ethnic identity is inherently, almost genetically determined and transferred, while a historical-relativist position argues that it can be explained in terms of the social and political conditions that prevail at a specific historical juncture to underpin group identity. In this light, Slabbert regarded 'ethnicity as a variable where subjective experiences can vary according to shifting and objectively changing conditions'.[50]

He was sceptical of academics who thought of Afrikaners in essentialist metaphysical terms. One example he cited was the avuncular historian Professor Bun Booyens, for whom an Afrikaner was 'someone who, when the sun goes down, in his soul hears the tinkling of the milk cans and the cooing of the doves'.[51] This was at a time, Slabbert remarked, when Afrikaners were already largely urbanised. He later claimed to have spent most of his teaching and academic life opposing

> an ideology that treated 'the Afrikaner' as some kind of

> ahistorical organismic whole with a collective 'mind and soul' that had to be liberated from repression and persecution. History was invented to justify entitlement and retribution. Suffering became an excuse for intellectual and political tyranny. And yet, most of 'the Afrikaners' who were so eloquent about all of this lived comfortable middle-class lives and never experienced any of the hardships they became so angry about, and pretended ignorance of the hardships they were imposing on others.[52]

In some respects, this was an oversimplification of a much more complex Afrikaner history, but it stands up as a concise summary of how the dimensions of Afrikaner history had been yoked to an ideology.

Slabbert was specifically perplexed about what he regarded as the blind spots in the way Afrikaners viewed their history. To him it was astonishing that Afrikaners, with their long history of resisting British oppression, seemed unable to fathom that their policies towards black people might be seen to amount to the same. In this regard, Slabbert argued, the Afrikaners had assumed the dominant position in relation to black people that the British had earlier adopted towards the Afrikaners. It was only because of the ideological justifications for apartheid, which predisposed Afrikaners to believe that apartheid was actually in everyone's best interests, that Afrikaners failed to recognise that the self-same desire for freedom among black people in the 1980s had earlier animated Afrikaner activists and politicians.[53] It was a point he liked to underscore. During one of his first interviews with the Afrikaans press after his election to Parliament in 1974, he emphasised that as an Afrikaner, 'it is of the utmost importance to me that Afrikaners do not repeat the same mistakes as the British seventy years earlier'.[54] While Slabbert's comparison had a neat and seemingly appropriate validity, it could also be seen as somewhat instrumentalist in wanting to score political points. Moreover, what is missing is an admission that in the post-Anglo-Boer War dispensation, the British themselves accelerated the implementation of segregationist policies.

In discussing Slabbert as an Afrikaner, it should also be factored in that given the politics of the day, his identity carried weight and was an asset that stood the Progs in good stead. In Afrikaner circles, there was a tendency to dismiss Prog criticism as coming from outside the fold, but more heed was paid to someone who could claim some form of insider status. As Hermann Giliomee remarks, 'From my own experience I know that Afrikaner nationalists listened only to those critics who could genuinely speak of "we" in reasoning with them.'[55] Slabbert was in such a position, and this gave him an advantage in dealing with National Party politicians and government officials.

At the same time, his status as an Afrikaner presented a challenge to the Afrikaner establishment. Earlier Afrikaner Prog leaders such as Jan Steytler might have had the same potential, but they failed to project as strong an image as Slabbert was able to do. As a politician with a conscience, deep intent and fine analytical abilities, his pointed criticisms undermined an establishment that sought to claim respectability and moral righteousness. As an Afrikaner, he became more of a thorn in the flesh of the government than otherwise might have been the case. For the same reason he also had to endure slights that his politics constituted a form of political treachery – an accusation Afrikaners tend to use routinely against those who break ranks or are perceived to do so.[56] Despite innuendo of this kind, the mere fact that such barbs were called for can also be interpreted as proof that Slabbert's stance gave rise to a sense of introspection among some National Party members and made them feel obliged to clarify their position.[57]

Nevertheless, Slabbert's identity as an Afrikaner helped to change the public face of the Progs. In Afrikaner ranks during the early 1970s the party was often disdainfully dismissed as hardly more than

'VAN': PUBLIC IMAGE AND PRIVATE LIFE

a protest movement with little political influence, consisting primarily of rich English-speakers who needed the party to salve their consciences. Slabbert, it was reported, seemed to have broken the mould, as he became the 'only tribal Afrikaner in the Prog frontline'.[58] Slabbert's presence did not necessarily translate into votes for the PFP, but it did boost the public image of the party. Slabbert realised the dangers often hidden in such a situation. As critical as he was of Afrikanerdom, he was aware of being regarded as a mere token by the English-speaking establishment. At times he did feel that some '"Old Progs" really despised the Afrikaner, and some of their opposition to apartheid was confused with their antipathy towards Afrikaners.'[59]

As Slabbert had disassociated himself early from organised Afrikanerdom, the thought never occurred to him to try and mobilise on an ethnic basis. Afrikaner life to him was also more than just politics. Breyten Breytenbach summed up the constitutive parts: Slabbert 'was and is unabashedly an Afrikaner, with a deep love for its poetry and attachment to hospitality and humour and sports rituals'.[60]

During the post-apartheid transition, Slabbert's empathy and understanding of Afrikaner dynamics made him a popular speaker at various Afrikaner occasions. The ideological confusion and lack of direction among many members of the audience made a distinct impression on him. The comfortable and established world they were used to had in some respects collapsed. He knew the environment they originated from, he stated, as he was exposed to some of the same influences, and realised how ill-prepared they were to face the new South Africa.[61]

What impressed him, though, was the flowering of Afrikaans arts festivals during this period. In 2003 he agreed to serve as non-executive chair of the Aardklop arts festival in Potchefstroom. 'These festivals,' he argued, 'are a symptom of a new awareness that Afrikaans-speakers can flourish in a country where the state no longer looks after their culture. It says: "Come, let us show that we can do it."'[62]

His affinity for Afrikaans went back to his high-school years and the excellent teachers he had at the time. It was equally so at Stellenbosch, where he was impressed by iconic professors such as the poets DJ Opperman and WEG Louw. In 1964, soon after he was appointed as a junior lecturer in sociology, he became concerned about the future of the language and arranged a meeting at Elgin with, among others, the coloured intellectuals Adam Small and Richard van der Ross. They emphasised that apartheid was strangling the language. From early on, then, Slabbert sensed what only became apparent later on. For his troubles, however, Prime Minister John Vorster accused him of indulging in 'whoring politics with Afrikaans'.[63]

Slabbert's concern for, and enduring understanding of, the wider function of the language – Vorster's critique notwithstanding – perhaps predisposed him to take a stand on the language debates about Afrikaans as a medium of instruction at tertiary educational institutions that began at the turn of the century and continued in subsequent years. These debates took place on all the historically Afrikaans campuses but were particularly intense at Stellenbosch, Slabbert's alma mater. Stellenbosch had been established as a predominantly Afrikaans university in 1918 but had always had a sprinkling of white English-speakers. Under National Party rule they were attracted to Stellenbosch in order to improve their Afrikaans, which at the time was a dominant language in the civil service and some other sectors of professional life where bilingualism was valued. However, as the post-apartheid world ushered in changes in language usage, and English increasingly became the country's lingua franca, Afrikaans was bound to be affected. From about 2000 these changes impacted more forcibly than before on Stellenbosch. White English-speakers flocked in greater numbers than before to the campus, this time not necessarily to learn Afrikaans but rather because of systemic institutional issues at the former white English-speaking universities. Moreover, under an open-access policy, more black students with only English as an academic language were enrolling. The university's language policy was adapted and went through various permutations

'VAN': PUBLIC IMAGE AND PRIVATE LIFE

in an effort to serve the different language groupings. The risk was that Afrikaans could be completely marginalised and coloured Afrikaans-speaking students also disadvantaged.[64]

Slabbert argued that given the South African language demographics, there should be room for at least one Afrikaans-dominant university. He also warned against what he called the 'pedagogical nonsense' of trying to teach in both languages in the same class, which was one of the options under consideration. One group or the other was likely to suffer, he argued. His stand raised the ire of those in favour of the new language arrangements, and he was seen, wrongly, to be aligning himself with the white right wing.[65] Slabbert's position, though not always fully informed about the institutional language dynamics, was more sophisticated. He realised that because of apartheid, Afrikaans carried substantial political baggage, but this was not a sufficient reason to jettison the language altogether. Rather, it posed a challenge as to how a language with such charm and potency of expression, he said, could be reimagined and revitalised on a tertiary level during a time of flux and transition.[66] To diminish its higher-order status, on a campus with deep Afrikaans roots and a hinterland steeped in Afrikaans, would not be helpful in that quest, nor would white and coloured Afrikaans-speakers benefit from such a development.

Generally, Slabbert's association with, and sense of, being an Afrikaner had various qualities to it: reflective, introspective, nuanced, selective yet uninhibited participation in Afrikaans cultural life, while also being dismissive of some of the ways in which this identity played out. He never sought to reject the identity altogether in an effort to invent a new one to suit changed circumstances. In this respect, because Slabbert did not make a fetish of being an Afrikaner, it was easier for him to deal with it on his own terms, and, almost as a bonus, it allowed him to understand the dynamics of Afrikaner society with greater clarity than might otherwise have been the case. This, in part, can be traced to the fact that, right from the start, his life did not follow the usual route carved out for 'standard' Afrikaners.

Home life

The university town of Stellenbosch, populated by many young students with bubbling hormones, has a romantic aura: its oak-lined streets and white-gabled buildings, surrounded by imposing mountains with breathtaking vistas, and a rippling stream that wends its way past lush sports grounds, have been the setting for many starry-eyed liaisons. Not surprisingly, over generations, many students have found their life partners on campus.

Slabbert was one of these, and he did not have to look far to find a future spouse. Mana Jordaan, a fellow sociology student, soon crossed his path. Her father was a local Dutch Reformed Church dominee and her mother a lecturer in English. An attractive girl with flowing auburn hair, Mana was the same age as Slabbert, and also his intellectual match. She was an accomplished singer as well, and had been offered a bursary to study in Vienna, though she did not take it up. Mana spotted Slabbert on campus before he noticed her, and being in the same class helped to fan the flames. Slabbert was often invited to her house, and he felt at home with the Jordaan family, who would take him in during university holidays. Because he had spent so much of his schooldays away from home in hostels, he appreciated being part of a home life.[67]

The couple married in 1965, at the age of 25. Their two children, Tania and Riko, were born in 1967 and 1970, respectively. While the family was living in Johannesburg, Slabbert also took in his half-brother, Sean Taylor, following the death of their mother. Sean stayed with them for a while in Johannesburg and in Cape Town. He later studied drama at UCT. Slabbert became his guardian, encouraged him in his studies, stood surety for his university fees, and generally helped him to develop as an actor in his own right.[68]

Once Slabbert was elected to Parliament the couple bought a modest house at 55 Rouwkoop Road, in Rondebosch. He preferred to stay in the constituency that had elected him. They had monthly gatherings of invited guests, white as well as black. These were hospitable

'VAN': PUBLIC IMAGE AND PRIVATE LIFE

and unpretentious occasions, with plenty of wine, a pot of Mana's curry and endless cups of coffee.[69]

The children grew up in a rumbustious house. A journalist who interviewed the couple soon after they moved into their house witnessed the warm and exuberant interaction between Mana and her young brood. The reporter related that the children were in the bathroom when a small voice piped up: 'Your mother is an old witch!' Mana Slabbert slipped into the kitchen, grabbed a broom and sailed into the bathroom with eldritch wails: 'I am a witch, a witch, a witch.' Tania and Riko, stark naked, ran from their mother screaming in delighted terror. 'We have such fun together,' Mana said.[70] These high jinks, though, were countered by a sense of discipline: the children had to make sure their toys were neatly packed way before they could be told a bedtime story. Family life also featured plenty of singing. 'Mana would pick up the guitar,' the journalist reported, 'her clear soprano blending with Van Zyl's tenor in an old ballad or one of the new folk songs.' It appeared to be their favourite pastime, 'spontaneous, relaxed and unrehearsed'.[71]

Mana began her working life as an 18-year-old student nurse, moved on to study social work and sociology, and then taught at the University of the Western Cape and later UCT.[72] She had an interest in community affairs that was broadly aligned with some of her husband's sociological concerns. The immediate beneficiary of her involvement in the caring professions was her own family. Tania has very positive memories of her mother during the early days and remembers her as passionate, affectionate and concerned.[73]

The children were equally fond of their father, but it did take some time for them to digest the public and private dimensions of his life. They expressed this eloquently on the occasion of his 70th birthday:

> [A]ll the times that we would see you on billboards, on stages and public platforms, in newspapers and on TV, we would wonder at this towering presence, with his formidable

intellect and flowing speeches, which at first we understood little of. We were very proud of you, but also somewhat intimidated by this powerful man with all his adoring followers. Was this the same guy who carried us from the car to bed after nights out with friends, tickling us on the way? Then we grew up and knew that it was all you.[74]

Slabbert was not a conventional father who dutifully attended school committee meetings or took care of repair jobs around the house. In fact, he had ten thumbs when it came to fixing things. Tania still has vivid memories of a bookshelf he installed collapsing on her when the cat jumped on it.[75] When the children were very young, he allowed them the run of the house, took them camping, and even let them bodysurf in the choppy waters of Betty's Bay. As they got older, he was occasionally given to risk-taking, for example by allowing them to drive, sitting on his lap without seatbelts, careening towards a tree in the middle of the driveway. With infectious enthusiasm he would also haul the two teenagers out of their beds, even after a late night, for early-morning walks in the forest.[76] At times, the free-spirited attitude he instilled led them to test the limits of parental control, though this amounted to little more than high-spirited adventures.[77]

Slabbert's unsettled upbringing meant that he often had to fend for himself, so he was not one for mollycoddling his children. When he taught them chess, for example, he was unrelenting. He would never just give the game away, and even when he allowed them to win, they would not actually be aware of it. He recalled in 1992 that 'my relationship with my children has been mature – almost from birth. We've got a very adult relationship. I mean there is deep affection, but they've had to land on their feet. We've come through rough times together.'[78]

He was careful not to expect his children to follow in his footsteps. When Riko battled as a student at university, he encouraged him to

'VAN': PUBLIC IMAGE AND PRIVATE LIFE

follow a different career path. There was no need, he said, for Riko to become an 'egghead' like his father.[79] Although Slabbert's standing and status would always have been at the back of their minds, and at times it must have been difficult, they never felt overshadowed. On the contrary, they could truthfully tell their father: 'We have never stood in your shadow; we have always stood beside you at midday and basked in your light.'[80]

Despite their mutual respect, Mana and Van Zyl had a complex and sometimes stormy relationship. Both were highly articulate and knowledgeable and not inclined to shy away from an argument. 'Van Zyl and I often argue at night,' Mana told a journalist, 'and one of his pet phrases is "You are talking nonsense".'[81] For her part, she thought that Slabbert was inclined to a 'crisis mentality',[82] implying that he was quick to spot, and at times exaggerate, problems that needed to be addressed. Be that as it may, Mana was very much a person in her own right. A clue to this is to be found in a comment in the margins of a letter she wrote to a friend when they moved from Johannesburg to Rondebosch. 'Between you and me,' she said, 'I refuse to be an adornment for him [Van Zyl] in Rondebosch.'[83] A fellow sociologist recalled that Slabbert was 'perhaps even a bit afraid of strong women who contradicted him'.[84] However, it probably depended on the kind of relationship; he had an excellent understanding with Annie Gagiano, a close friend and lecturer in English at Stellenbosch, and also known for forthright views.[85] But, given the headstrong personalities of the Slabbert couple, and the need to cope with a highly pressured political environment, it is not surprising that verbal exchanges between the two could on occasion be volatile, or shade into resolutely combative positions.[86]

For all of this, Mana did her best to support her husband's career. During the exhausting 1981 election campaign, Slabbert's first as leader of the opposition, she told a reporter that she 'saw her task as one of not only giving full support to her husband but also of maintaining a peaceful house, to which he can come back [from] his travels and relax and unwind – and chat to and enjoy the company of our children and go and feed the pigeons at the back of the house if he wants to'. She also sensed that 'he has now reached a stage where he really needs to do this badly'.[87]

The political pressures, however, could be relentless. When he became leader of the opposition, Van Zyl felt that the 'added tension of the new position has a worsening effect on my domestic situation'.[88] Mana herself wrote to friends at this juncture: 'It is going to be a difficult time and your support will be appreciated. And may we phone deep into the dark of night if it is necessary?'[89]

The irregular lifestyle, and the stresses and strains of Slabbert's enforced absences, inexorably took their toll. Mana could not help but feel alone, and angry and frustrated at times, especially when Van Zyl became distant and withdrawn. When he focused on an issue, he was inclined to shut out everything else and become completely absorbed in the matter at hand.[90]

In 1983 the marriage was dissolved. Van Zyl later explained:

> Politics undoubtedly placed an enormous load on our relationship and she tried to be as supportive as possible in what must have been as strange a world to her as it was to me. Obviously, we hurt and misunderstood each other. In the end new mistakes compounded old ones in a cycle of increasing alienation that became too painful to endure. Now I am grateful that enough compassion remains to combat bitterness and leave the love for our children uncontaminated.[91]

He later confessed that he learnt a valuable lesson from his failed first marriage: 'It taught me to be aware of the fact that I can't let my career, or should I say involvement, which can become quite intense, cut me off from the people around me.'[92]

Van Zyl was careful not to allow his private life to become an object of public scrutiny. It was only occasionally that he let his guard

'VAN': PUBLIC IMAGE AND PRIVATE LIFE

down to talk about relationships. His handsome appearance and personable style fuelled many rumours about 'other women'. During his parliamentary days and after, he gained a reputation as something of a Don Juan. 'It is certainly not a reflection of what I am like,' he defended himself, less out of anger than embarrassment. 'My friends know that I am no Don Juan, and, honestly,' he explained to a journalist, 'I think they will laugh themselves silly if they heard that I am described as such.' He declined to talk about 'mistresses or lovers or that kind of thing'.[93] Slabbert's denials did not necessarily rule out rare dalliances on his or Mana's part.[94] Yet these did not degenerate into sordid affairs nor seemingly hasten the end of their marriage.

Van Zyl remarried on 21 April 1984. His new wife was Jane Stephens, whose father, Bob Stephens, became minister of finance of Swaziland (today eSwatini) following that country's independence in 1972. Slabbert recalled that he had 'fallen in love in the good old-fashioned way'.[95] The couple met at the christening of the daughter of Gordon Waddell (an influential figure in the PFP and for a time an MP). Jane and Van Zyl happened to be the child's godparents. It was a chance meeting, and Jane related that he had asked her how one went about acquiring Swazi citizenship. Her joking reply was: 'Marry me!'[96]

Although Jane came from a political family, her interests were more artistic. She was heavily involved in the family's renowned weaving business, established in 1949 in the picturesque Piggs Peak area. Jane was demure and quietly spoken, and had been educated at a private school in Johannesburg. She supported Slabbert fully, but was careful not to trespass on his terrain. She had her own career, which kept her occupied, and personally was given to periods of solitude in order to re-energise. She tried to create a warm and peaceful home environment, but inevitably also had to adapt to the fast-paced lifestyle of a prominent politician. Slabbert enjoyed the relative calmness of rural Swaziland.[97] He found every day with Jane 'fresh and new' and appreciated that she had successfully 'assaulted his cynicism'.[98] It could not always have been easy. Slabbert was inclined to be impatient, and everyday practical matters could easily annoy him; he detested waiting in airport queues and often drove too fast when he had to travel by road.[99]

Another important person in Slabbert's life was Jenny Nothard, his long-time secretary. She was meticulous in administrative matters and, besides her usual work, took a special interest in the family when required to do so.[100] Slabbert also appreciated the domestic workers in Swaziland and Johannesburg, respectively Bibi Msweli and Betty Dladla. They were in his employ for 20 years, including during his final days. Slabbert, who was often generous to a fault, sponsored a trip to Paris for them and a friend of Jane's, an experience that left them with enduring memories.[101]

Friends

Slabbert was a man's man in some respects, probably because in his youth he had spent so much time in male hostels and in environments where one survived by knowing certain codes and understanding the logic of certain rituals. He exuded a particular sense of robust maleness, which at times found expression in spontaneous male bonding. He regarded such friendships 'as interludes of sanity and understanding'.[102] This inevitably involved some reciprocity. It is 'in the nature of friendship', he said, that 'one cannot live as if everything is possible and nothing necessary.'[103]

He had long-standing relationships with people from his Stellenbosch days, such as the effervescent Jannie Gagiano.[104] Similarly, he maintained close ties with Ian Jones, a first-team rugby mate at Stellenbosch. Jones had a reputation as a rebel – precisely the kind of person that appealed to Slabbert. At Stellenbosch, Jones was strong enough academically to win a Rhodes scholarship to Oxford. There, his interests in manly pursuits such as rugby and boxing earned him Blues for both sporting codes, and he did well in his studies. When Slabbert visited Oxford on a travel bursary in 1964, he reconnected with Jones. The two discovered that they were born on the same day (2 March 1940), which, as Slabbert recalled, precipitated 'one of the most prolonged bouts of irrelevant celebration I can remember'. They kept up the friendship, and whenever Slabbert visited London, they would go to the same Greek restaurant 'to dance and sing and curse the Devil into the early hours'.[105]

On the whole, Slabbert preferred academics to politicians, as he thought they were more inclined to keep an open mind than politicians with overtly vested interests. At the same time, he was fully aware that academics could be woefully inept when it came to resolving practical political problems.

His academic friendships crossed geographical boundaries and disciplines. They included Heribert Adam, a German-Canadian sociologist, and Theo Hanf, a German political scientist, as well as many South African scholars: Nic Olivier, development studies expert; David Welsh, political scientist; Lawrie Schlemmer, sociologist; Mike Savage, sociologist, André du Toit, political philosopher; Johan Degenaar, philosopher; Francis Wilson, political scientist and economist; Jill Nattrass, economist; RW Johnson, political scientist; John Dugard, lawyer; and Hermann Giliomee and Charles van Onselen, historians. All differed among themselves on many issues, but generally Slabbert found in them a foil for unthinking moral outrage, and he valued their scepticism regarding grand theories of social change, as well as their grave reservations about the use of violence as a tool for change.[106]

He also had a close relationship with Breyten Breytenbach. The two first met briefly at a summer school at the University of Cape Town in 1973, when Slabbert gave a paper on literature and society.[107] They shared a critical outlook on Afrikaner political life and literary culture. Whereas Slabbert went into formal politics soon after that, Breytenbach took a different route and became involved in ANC exile politics. He hoped to establish a white resistance movement on behalf of the ANC, but was betrayed and arrested in 1975, before the organisation got off the ground. This led to a nine-year jail sentence under the Terrorism Act of 1967. He movingly described his experiences in jail in a memoir, *The True Confessions of an Albino Terrorist* (1984). Slabbert took a special interest in Breytenbach's case and sought to alleviate his jail conditions. He also worked with others to try and discuss with the authorities the possibility of early release. After a complex bureaucratic process, Breytenbach was released two years early, in 1982. In his memoir, he recalled Slabbert's role in this with fond gratitude: 'He is a discreet, efficient man, always following up the initiatives that had been started.'[108]

Despite his wariness of politicians, Slabbert did take to some individuals in the political sphere. In Harry Pitman, who won the Durban North by-election for the Progs in 1976, he found a kindred spirit who lived life to the full. Pitman was a man of parts: a controversial advocate involved in the defence of 'terrorists' during the 1970s; an unconventional farmer; a father of six children; and an erratic MP who was often absent (his speeches could either systematically demolish an argument or ramble incoherently). He was always ebullient and disdainful of pomp and ceremony. Pitman died young, and Slabbert later recalled that his premature death 'punched a hole right through me'.[109]

Slabbert was also on a good footing with Alex Boraine. They would go camping together, grill fish on the beach and converse deep into the night. Boraine related that Slabbert cherished a dream in which, in old age, he and his close friends would each have a house in Swaziland where they could socialise and reflect upon life. In general, Boraine thought that Slabbert was 'never happier than when surrounded by good, trusted friends'. They would entertain in each other's homes and the occasions were memorable for their boisterous bonhomie, yards of boerewors, dozens of lamb chops and 'of course gallons of red wine'.[110] Boraine's son Jeremy later likewise recalled how Slabbert revelled in these gatherings over weekends, often at his home in Rouwkoop Road:

'VAN': PUBLIC IMAGE AND PRIVATE LIFE

> There were braais aplenty, the wine flowed, songs were sung – especially by Mana. Van always seemed to be at the centre of conversation, his appetite for life was huge. He was physically a strong man – I remember admiring his ruined toenails from his rugby-playing days – and with braai tongs in hand he would regale the gathered company with stories and jokes. You simply wanted to listen, and his laugh was infectious. But he also had no time for stupidity, and he wouldn't hesitate to shoot down a misplaced comment before moving on as if nothing had happened.[111]

Wine and the spur it gives to conviviality were part and parcel of Slabbert's social life. He would be quite taken aback if a friend opened a bottle of wine and replaced the cork after everyone had had only one glass.[112] Heribert Adam compared him to Conor Cruise O'Brien, the Irish academic, writer and politician, of whom it was said: 'He wasn't a sip-sipper, like Churchill, but a gulp-gulper; he drank heavy red wine as if it was lemonade at a summer picnic.'[113] Although Slabbert could imbibe considerable quantities, he refrained from acting outrageously and making a spectacle of himself. He was also careful not to indulge when it could affect his daily commitments.[114] Nevertheless, the long-term effects of Slabbert's drinking patterns could not have been beneficial for his health.

A marked trait of Slabbert's personality was that he could be highly disciplined but was also given to occasional bouts of impetuous behaviour, throwing rationality and caution to the wind as his mood changed. This sometimes led him to misjudge people, to his detriment, though he could also make quick and accurate assessments. He expected friends to remain loyal and could become quite distant if he felt that he had been left in in the lurch. He had a stubborn streak once he made up his mind, but if the situation happened to change he could become more accommodating.[115] Slabbert was as flexible as he was firm.

In contrast to the warmth with which Slabbert often related to close friends, he could come across as aloof at official party functions. He was not considered a good mixer in these contexts; he avoided the usual political backslapping and was embarrassed by gushing praise from rank-and-file party members eager to talk to their leader. Ray Swart, who witnessed many such encounters, could not decide whether Slabbert's 'conduct on these occasions was a reflection of his humility or boredom'.[116] Heribert Adam, too, mentions that although Slabbert was interested in the views of others, he was easily bored by long-winded monologues. Once he lost interest, even in private conversation, he would mumble, as if barely awake, '"Is that so?", indicating that he had switched off and drifted into another realm.'[117]

Slabbert thus derived considerable satisfaction from his friendships, and was gregarious as far as his immediate circle was concerned, but wary in larger gatherings. He drew sustenance from interactions with his intellectual peers and associated readily with effervescent and jovial personalities. His own exuberance, though, masked a convoluted personal history; he had seen much, experienced much, endured much, aspired to much, and knew what was possible and what not.

Last years

Even before Slabbert turned 60, there was a sense of weariness about him and an increased awareness of his own mortality. He wrote to a friend in 1997: 'Time moves on and the old Big Bear waits for all of us till we no longer have any more small fishes to feed him. Let us make an effort to see each other again soon. After all, life is but a few good friends and a few good arguments and then everything is done and dusted.'[118]

The new decade, however, had some surprises for him. In 2005 he was roped in by his alma mater to assist in formulating a policy regarding hostel initiation rites. More importantly, in 2008 the university bestowed on him the honour of electing him as its chancellor. Those who proposed him as a candidate considered him to be the best of the generation produced by the university in the 1960s.[119] It was a kind of homecoming for him and an accolade he greatly valued. 'Stellenbosch is, and will remain, an exceptional university,' he said during his installation by the vice-chancellor, Russel Botman. 'Today is an extraordinary day to say to both you and the university: in this role, I am and will remain your humble servant.'[120] He was also careful to differentiate between his functions as political analyst and as chancellor.

As pleased as Slabbert was in his new role, as short was its duration. His health deteriorated, especially after what was described as a 'mini stroke' at the end of 2008.[121] He had had a similar stroke in the mid-1990s and had been on heart medication for an extended period.[122] After 2008 it became gradually more difficult for him to fulfil his public duties as chancellor, and university management had the difficult task of convincing him that, as a result of short-term memory loss, he was no longer in a position to carry on.[123] He was also diagnosed with cirrhosis of the liver.

The relentless decline continued as his competencies were gradually stripped away. He became increasingly forgetful and stopped reading newspapers; politics was now only a distant phantasm. Slowly he started to lose his grip on reality. To all of those close to him, it was hard to watch the disintegration of this strong and intelligent man.[124] He had to take a great deal of medication and was unable to exercise; the situation gave rise to spells of melancholy. His only solace was wine and watching sport on television.[125] Occasionally there were flickers of interest, as during his 70th birthday celebration, held at a wine farm outside Stellenbosch, when he could once again relive his youth in an environment that held pleasant memories for him.[126]

After a spell in Milpark Hospital in Johannesburg, Slabbert died peacefully, surrounded by close family, on 14 May 2010 at his home at 27 Kilkenny Road, Parktown. Traffic ground to a halt in front of the house, and, as expected, tributes poured in from far and wide. The main memorial service was held in Midrand, near the home of Jane's sister Mag.[127] Several other memorials were arranged, including one at the University of the Witwatersrand. Here, dignitaries and friends from various spheres of his career paid homage to him, including a delegation from Wilgenhof residence at Stellenbosch and their choir, Die Kraaie (The Crows).[128]

Formally, his memory lives on in commemorative occasions at his old school, Pietersburg High, and especially in the Frederik van Zyl Slabbert Institute for Student Leadership Development at Stellenbosch University and its annual Frederik van Zyl Slabbert Honorary Lecture. The university gets considerable political mileage out of Slabbert, as he is presented as an anti-apartheid symbol. All heritage projects are by definition oversimplifications of history, and the construction of Slabbert's public legacy is no different. And Slabbert was much more than an anti-apartheid activist. However, it is not as if he would have objected; he always had a positive attitude towards the university.

What Slabbert might have found more problematic was the decision of the ANC government to award him national honours in 2014. Given the government's track record and the way Slabbert was cold-shouldered during the democratic transition, Breyten Breytenbach considered the gesture to be a sanctimonious falsehood.[129]

Reflecting upon the intricacies of Slabbert's career, it is worth noting that even with the best of intentions, he was unable to separate his public and private life altogether. The effect of the pressures of politics, leading to the breakup of his first marriage, is a case in point. He was able, though, to sustain a huge circle of friends and valued their interaction. In addition, it can be emphasised that Slabbert's self-awareness and integrity helped him not to be consumed by the charismatic role assigned to him by some white supporters. Equally so, he did not subscribe to a one-dimensional perception of what it meant to be an Afrikaner, but imparted his own meaning to the concept.

CONCLUSION

In 2010, shortly after Slabbert's death, RW Johnson made some pertinent remarks about his career. Slabbert, asserted Johnson, 'represented the very best that white South Africa had to offer: intelligent, humorous, humane, liberal-minded and deeply concerned for the future of his country beyond any personal motive. So his truncated and ultimately unsuccessful political career poses the question, what went wrong?'[1]

Johnson's puzzlement articulated something that many commentators felt about Slabbert, though there is no disputing the fine qualities that Johnson saw in him. The question can be extended to consider whether Slabbert's attributes were sufficient for political success in South Africa during a period of protracted and unprecedented political upheaval. One can argue that no noted political leader came through this period with his or her reputation intact. (Mandela may be an exception, and even his period of governance has come in for criticism.) One way or the other, regardless of their mettle, political leaders were exposed to forces that at the best of times they could only hope to manage, not dominate. South Africa, given its various and deep historical fault lines, has on the whole, and perhaps more than other countries, not been kind to politicians, whatever their talents. Slabbert was no exception.

In terms of finding a formal political home, it is probably true to say not only that he was sidelined as an individual, but also that the alignments and priorities of the time were such that a thinker as independent as Slabbert was not necessarily regarded as an asset. Deep down, he may have wished for a more prominent role, but he was not prepared to compromise his independence, something that is often required in politics. He knew only too well what he did not want in terms of party politics. His friend Breyten Breytenbach summarised it well in 2010: 'Maybe he is too intellectually honest and restless for party politics. His incursions were pragmatic and, he thinks, realistic – informed by the reading of a sociologist and the optimism of a humanist. He never pushed for a dispensational alternative to the present set-up. I don't think he ever seriously supported and thought through the federal option.'[2] Whether full federalism was ever a feasible political possibility is another matter, of course.

Slabbert in 1999 explicitly described himself as 'a failed politician'.[3] As far as could be determined, this was the first and only time that he so bluntly and publicly made such an admission. One should, however, take this statement with a pinch of salt and certainly not as the last word on the topic. Slabbert was not one to broadcast his achievements. Moreover, it can be misleading to view him, despite his role in Parliament, as a politician in the conventional mode. He would often suggest that he was not 'into politics', or at least not into the kind of politics the Nationalists and even some members of his own party wanted him to play. At times, he had the habit of pronouncing the word 'politics' in a way that suggested it was malodorous.[4]

Late in his life, Colin Eglin asserted that while Slabbert did many things, 'a single theme or goal is lacking'.[5] It has indeed been a common understanding of Slabbert's career that after his controversial resignation from Parliament and the Dakar venture, he more or less faded into oblivion. While Slabbert was certainly involved in many initiatives, it is questionable to assume that there was no overarching logic. Such a conclusion is possible only if one privileges formal politics as the sole yardstick. As noted, he also had a full and rewarding career outside the limelight of institutional politics.

Moreover, to come to a fuller appreciation that probes somewhat deeper than surface events, it is useful to take a long view of his career and to search for the continuities, despite the obvious discontinuities. In this respect, we can home in on what is perhaps best described as his missionary zeal, or, more specifically, his secular missionary work without the formal trappings. This can be singled out as the wellspring of much of his endeavours, though it might not always have appeared as such.

What is the evidence for such a view? This idea, already hinted at in earlier chapters,[6] was originally rooted in his powerful and potent commitment to the Christian faith as a young and impressionable teenager, and his desire to become a Dutch Reformed Church minister. 'He felt called upon to venture out and teach the world what it should be, and this remained a strong element in his life,' Jannie Gagiano observes.[7] This, one can argue, was also the *fons et origo* of his thinking, the often hidden dynamo that in various guises provided the voltage for a variety of attempts to influence the way people thought. True, he stepped away relatively early from the formal structures of the church, but that did not mean he completely abandoned the notion of wanting to convert people to seeing the world differently. Revealingly, he remarked after the incident during his student days when he and his fellow missionaries were chased out of Langa: 'I never did missionary work again – at least of a religious kind.'[8] The earlier pathways were not that easily obliterated. This in turn linked up with his academic interest in 'big' ideas that could change the way reality was perceived. His doctoral thesis on Talcott Parsons' structural functionalism is a case in point, as is his fascination with Karl Popper's idea of the open society. Equally pertinent was his insistence, while a lecturer at Stellenbosch University, that he wished to teach ground-breaking higher-order sociology that could change students' mindsets, instead of lecturing on humdrum themes.

He then forsook the 'church' of the university for the 'cathedral' of Parliament, where the high priests of certain political persuasions gathered with the mission to influence and shape the world around them. In retrospect, it was no coincidence that he chose a grouping particularly focused on gaining converts. There was in the 1970s a tendency among some white progressives to regard themselves as political missionaries.⁹ Slabbert would have felt at home. When this endeavour proved to be less than successful in his eyes, he decided that the structures, like those of the Dutch Reformed Church he had abandoned earlier, were too inhibiting. The next step was to form his own 'church', significantly on a symbolic level with his friend the former Methodist minister Alex Boraine. New structures were put in place and the 'church' was called Idasa, the aim being to influence thinking without being hamstrung by formal parliamentary restraints. From here, the narrative continues through the Dakar venture, which in some respects incorporated missionary elements, including the establishment of a 'mission station' on Gorée Island. In a similar vein, the many newspaper columns he wrote and the forums he organised were, at least in part, attempts to influence public opinion and change thinking.

In evaluating this interpretation, however, one has to consider that, as Slabbert himself indicated, he was against the idea of the 'great white hope', a characterisation with which he was so often lumbered. He did not play into the anxieties and infatuation of white voters who saw in him a political saviour. Yet the mere fact that this discourse was cast in semi-religious terms, with Slabbert as a redeemer, is a pointer to the undertow that helped to shape it. It should also be noted that Slabbert was not a religious man in the orthodox sense of the term. He refrained from being an atheist, but regarded himself as an agnostic later in life. He had seen enough of formal religion to reject what he considered the 'rank falseness of those who spoke on behalf of GAWD'.¹⁰ This statement, though, merely confirms his distance from the church as such. The missionary element, after his youthful induction into the church and initial patterning, was potent enough to sustain a role as change agent, albeit in different formats from those originally intended and independently from the church. One has of course to bear in mind that it is the basic task of all politicians to convince others of the righteousness of their cause. Few, however, were prepared to tread the path that Slabbert chose.

CONCLUSION

None of this implies that Slabbert was some kind of mystic – a *luftmensch* (impractical dreamer) without a proper grounding in the here and now. On the contrary, he was an exceptionally rational thinker, for whom logic was the ultimate litmus test.[11] However, he was also driven by an underlying desire for South African society to be a better place, and it is the origins and continuity of that yearning that I have tried to identify and unpack in this book. The combination of rationality and idealism, not always parcelled out in equal measures, constituted the overarching dynamics of Slabbert's outlook. Because of his rational outlook, he was not given to rabble-rousing politics and had an inbuilt scepticism towards politicians who indulged in such antics.[12] Equally so, he was given to distrusting almost viscerally any system that was presented as a panacea, while he never quite lost his idealism or his faith in the country's prospects.

His initial engagement with the ANC was premised on a fusion of rationality and idealism. Despite the National Party's record of implacable rejection of the ANC, Slabbert early on realised that, logically, negotiations in South Africa would not be possible without the participation of the exiled organisation. At the same time, he idealistically hoped that the ANC, in a post-apartheid dispensation, would as far as possible honour the doctrine of non-racialism that it so fervently broadcast before it assumed power. In the process he underestimated the fatal attraction of power – 'an addiction, a pathology', Breytenbach called it. Slabbert had been 'too trusting' of the ANC, Breytenbach argued, and it took some time to realise that the movement 'is neither about building a new nation nor about reconstruction and development, but all about laying claims and "divvying" up the spoils of "victory"'.[13]

There is a narrative that views Slabbert's career as one of blunted potential, in that his early promise was not fulfilled and he failed to scale the lofty heights he was deemed capable of conquering. Such ideals often emanated from, and were formulated by, those with high hopes for him; they were not necessarily goals that he himself consistently pursued or openly articulated. Although he was certainly not without aspirations, and probably would not have turned down high office had it been offered to him under the right circumstances, it was neither a burning ambition nor an all-consuming aim. Slabbert believed that the most valuable and enduring work he could do was to 'build a bridge across the divide and engage the extra-parliamentary opposition in the quest for negotiations'.[14] This of course is what happened from 1990 onwards, as a result of De Klerk's initiatives, at which point Slabbert could justifiably feel that his earlier heartfelt pleas had been vindicated; the subsequent dynamics of how politics played out were beyond him to influence.

If one had to choose an enduring insight and contribution, even if not often recognised as such, it would be his early involvement, as a relative newcomer to Parliament, in highlighting the importance of a new constitution for a divided country and assuming a prominent role in formulating a set of proposals for the PFP along those lines.[15] Despite contemporary South Africa's many ills, the country still has a functioning constitution – a crucial dimension that Slabbert targeted early on. It took almost two decades and many upheavals to get to that point, but eventually all parties reached the position that Slabbert had identified in the 1970s. This in itself speaks volumes for his vision, at a time when such ideas were often rejected out of hand by large sections of the white population. Equally so, his proposal for a new electoral system in 2003 was vindicated in 2020 by a Constitutional Court ruling that the system has to be amended to allow for the incorporation of voting according to constituency.[16]

Breytenbach neatly summed Slabbert up as 'too hybrid a figure – politician, commentator, philosopher, civil society activist'.[17] He was indeed all of these, and was imbued with a sense of purpose in each role. Perhaps his greatest flaw was not, as often averred, that he was inclined to dissipate his energies carelessly, but rather that in his zeal he tended to overreach, and also miscalculated the professed motives of those who claimed to share his vision.

CONCLUSION

Slabbert might well have overinvested in the ANC, as he readily admitted. But the main thrust of the critique against him had its origins in his resignation from Parliament in 1986, and in the public mind that decision dogged him, particularly after his alienation from the ANC. It remains a moot point, however, whether his continued presence in Parliament would have made a significant difference to his career. Not one of the PFP politicians who stayed in Parliament reached great heights in post-apartheid South Africa. Structurally, they were frozen out of power, and despite Slabbert's exceptional talents, he found himself in the same position. In the long run, whether one stayed in the apartheid Parliament or resigned was of little consequence.

There nevertheless remains a nagging question to be addressed, namely, his so-called five-year attention span. He certainly displayed a certain restiveness throughout his career: the abandonment of his theological studies; the rapid switches as an academic from one university to another (and toying with the idea of moving to Lever Brothers in between); the literally overnight switch from the United Party to the Progressive Party in 1973; his flirtation with the idea of leaving Parliament midway through his term to perhaps become vice-chancellor of the University of Cape Town; his actual resignation in 1986; his fluctuating role in Idasa; and his diverse involvements in the post-apartheid dispensation. At the time, these were not conventional pathways for average white males. As pointed out earlier, there was a meta-logic to his career, but an additional issue is to try and explain the non-linear character of his profile that goes beyond the obvious surface manifestations.

Apart from the wider contextual factors he faced, one can go back further into his past to locate early patterning. From a very young age, he and his sister were moved from pillar to post. As far as family life was concerned, then, he knew more about discontinuities than continuities. It was a configuration that he became used to, a pattern that he had to learn to live with, and one that he probably found less unnerving than did his youthful contemporaries from more stable backgrounds. He might not have liked unexpected change, but he was certainly not daunted by it either. In a way, he was pre-programmed to deal with change in life. Apart from this, we should remember that he was an outstanding intellectual for whom the routine of political life had a stultifying effect. A combination of these two dimensions, allied with the political pressures of the time, may go some way towards explaining what at first glance may appear as unusually erratic conduct.

Whether Slabbert should be seen as a tragic figure is another thorny issue. Perhaps he can only be regarded as such because he consistently tried to rise above the extraordinary times in which he lived, and did not fully succeed in doing so. Otherwise he remained an ebullient figure for most of the time – larger than life, driven and restless, and for some an enigma. From a difficult childhood through an eventful career, his life was marked by an ability to face daunting and varied challenges uncomplainingly and creatively, not always in ways that were immediately appreciated by some of his contemporaries. His unorthodoxy probably helped to cement his enigmatic reputation; he was seeking solutions to South Africa's problems before many of his white compatriots even realised that there were real issues.

Slabbert was also more than just a politician. He is often remembered not for his political feats but for his warmth, sincerity, humour and loyalty to friends. According to Mike Savage, there were only two things he detested: blind prejudice and persistent stupidity.[18] Breytenbach described him as by far the most '"complete person" of our generation: sociologist, thinker, activist, politician, businessman, patriot, optimist, drinker, sport enthusiast, an expert in country music, benefactor, … joker, lecturer, visionary, communicator, fighter, adviser, friend, friend, brother and friend'.[19]

To this long list can be added his strong affinity for family, despite adverse circumstances and stormy patches at times. First

CONCLUSION

Mana and then Jane experienced the demands made on him and had to cope with the ramifications. Each sought to adapt in their individual ways to often challenging domestic situations, especially when Slabbert was not in a position to provide immediate succour. Moreover, Slabbert, though always respectful of women, was not necessarily a model of what today would be described as 'gender sensitivity'.[20] He had a deep appreciation for his children, Tania and Riko, and sought to care for them as best as he could in occasionally problematic times. It cannot have been easy for the children, and he had to keep that in mind in parenting them. Recollections of his own turbulent childhood might have played a role.

As Slabbert seems to have had so many endearing qualities, it is easy to fall into the trap of viewing him too favourably. Apart from his political miscalculations, he was not without some personal foibles. It was an open secret that he was fond, at times overly so, of liquor. It is a matter of conjecture whether his parents' drinking habits, especially his mother's, genetically compounded matters for him. He was furthermore occasionally too easily taken in by individuals masquerading as friends, described by Mike Savage as 'no-goodniks'.[21] Overall, though, he was generally considered a good judge of character.[22]

Slabbert's multifaceted life, which can be seen almost as a mosaic, cannot easily be reduced to one or two dimensions. This book has tried to cast some light on the man and his various initiatives. But if one were pressed to sum him up, it would be that he was indeed a man on a mission, a visionary driven by a deep sense of the need to effect change in South Africa in a fair, equitable and peaceful way.

ACKNOWLEDGEMENTS

I have been fortunate in that a number of people showed a keen interest in this topic and willingly proffered research leads, information, ideas and encouragement. They are of course not responsible for the end product.

Without elaborating on each individual's contribution, the details of which they are well aware, I would like to thank Alex Mouton, Paul Cassar, Nick Southey, Charles van Onselen, Peter Vale, Bill Nasson, Lindie Koorts, Carel van der Merwe, David Welsh, Hilary Sapire, Lauren Coetzee, Cailin Macrae, Annas Coetzee, Tania Slabbert, Jane Slabbert, Marcia Haak, Jannie Gagiano, Ken Andrew, Michael Cardo, Theuns Appelgryn, Howard Philips, Milton Shain, Peter Colenbrander, Louis Grundlingh, Louis Changuion, Heribert Adam, Kogila Moodley, Rob Kaplan, Rudolf Gouws, Arnold van Zyl, Hannah Botha, Ellen Tise, Klaus Baron von der Ropp, Mike Savage and Louis Scott.

Hermann Giliomee took a special interest in this project. He kept my nose to the grindstone and was a good sparring partner. I could also benefit from his vast knowledge of South African political history and his astute comments on some of the chapters.

I am furthermore grateful to Chris Otto and GT Ferreira, who assisted in defraying some of the research costs associated with this book.

The Stellenbosch Institute for Advanced Study kindly offered me a fellowship that allowed me to finalise the manuscript under ideal conditions.

This book is dedicated to Annamari, Mauritz, Marizanne and Mia Grundlingh, who patiently shared this journey with me.

Albert Grundlingh
Stellenbosch
2020

NOTES

Preface

1. S Loriga, 'The role of the individual in history: Biographical and historical writing in the nineteenth and twentieth century', in H Renders and B de Haan (eds), *Theoretical Discussions of Biography: Approaches from History, Microhistory and Life Writing*, Brill, Leiden, 2014, p 78.
2. P Vale, 'Unlocking social puzzles: Colony, crime and chronicle: An interview with Charles van Onselen', *Thesis Eleven*, 136(1) (2016), p 47.
3. H Renders, 'The personal in the political biography', in Renders and De Haan (eds), *Theoretical Discussions of Biography*, p 218.

Chapter 1

1. Stellenbosch University Library, Slabbert Collection, 430.Q2.1, Slabbert to M Mamdani, 14 April 1997.
2. Marcia Haak Collection, unpublished and undated reflections of Slabbert entitled, 'Es die deng wat hy es' (translated); *Insig*, March 2000, 'As jy nou dink aan al daai spermselle – en hier is ek nou sestig jaar later'.
3. *Die Burger*, 23 May 2008, 'Slabbert kom huis toe' (translated).
4. Department of Defence Archives, Personnel file, 87496, PJ Slabbert.
5. *Die Burger*, 23 May 2008, 'Slabbert kom huis toe'. Her age has been calculated from information in *The Last White Parliament*, pp 3 and 5.
6. FvZ Slabbert, *The Last White Parliament*, Jonathan Ball, Johannesburg, 1987, p 3.
7. Compare A Grundlingh, 'The King's Afrikaners? Enlistment and ethnic identity in the Union of South Africa's Defence Force during the Second World War, 1939–1945', *Journal of African History*, 40(3) (1999), p 363.
8. Department of Defence Archives, Personnel file, 87496, PJ Slabbert.
9. For example *Rapport Weekliks*, 24 May 2015, 'My pa: 'n hartseer storie'.
10. Slabbert, *Last White Parliament*, p 4.
11. Ibid, p 88.
12. Grundlingh, 'King's Afrikaners?', pp 364–365.
13. Marcia Haak Collection, 'Es die deng wat hy es'.
14. Slabbert, *Last White Parliament*, p 4.
15. Interview with Tania Slabbert, 15 July 2019.
16. Interview with Lettie Coetzee, GC du Plessis's daughter, 28 January 2019.
17. Slabbert, *Last White Parliament*, p 2.
18. Interview with Tania Slabbert, 15 July 2019.
19. Slabbert, *Last White Parliament*, pp 4–5.
20. Marcia Haak Collection, 'Es die deng wat hy es'.
21. Marcia Haak Collection, 'Es die deng wat hy es'; FvZ Slabbert, *Tough Choices: Reflections of an Afrikaner African*, Tafelberg, Cape Town, 1999, p 88.

22 *The Municipal Magazine*, October 1933.
23 Anon, *Die volledige verkiesingsuitslae van Suid-Afrika, 1910–1986*; University of South Africa Library, United Party Archives, 83, Pietersburg Minutes, 1943–1966.
24 *House of Assembly Debates*, 15 October 1974, col 5438.
25 Marcia Haak Collection, 'Es die deng wat hy es'.
26 Ibid.
27 Ibid.
28 Compare L Changuion, *Pietersburg: Die eerste eeu, 1886–1986*, Stadsraad van Pietersburg, Pietersburg, 1986, p 161.
29 L Changuion, *'n Skool soos PHS*, Pietersburg School Board, Pietersburg, 2003, p 38.
30 *Jaarblad van Pietersburg Hoërskool*, undated but probably 1970, 'FvZ Slabbert, 'Die betekenis wat Latyn vir my het'.
31 *Jaarblad van Pietersburg Hoërskool*, 1956, FvZ Slabbert, 'A tutor is taught'.
32 Slabbert, *Last White Parliament*, pp 1–2.
33 Interview with Marcia Haak, 6 August 2017.
34 Slabbert, *Last White Parliament*, p 20.
35 Telephonic interview with Attie Vermaak, 20 February 2020.
36 Ibid.
37 Slabbert, *Last White Parliament*, pp 12–13.
38 M van der Spuy, 'Van Zyl Slabbert: The reluctant progressive', unpublished memoir, dated after April 2010 (courtesy of Hermann Giliomee).
39 Slabbert, *Last White Parliament*, p 13.
40 Ibid, p 14.
41 F van Zyl Slabbert, *The Other Side of History: An Anecdotal Reflection on Political Transition in South Africa*, Jonathan Ball, Cape Town, 2006, p 2.
42 Slabbert, *Last White Parliament*, pp 22–23; see also F van Zyl Slabbert, *Afrikaner Afrikaan: Anekdotes en analises*, Tafelberg, CapeTown, 1999, pp 8–9.
43 *Insig*, March 2000, 'As jy nou dink aan al daai spermselle … en hier is ek nou sestig jaar later'; interview with Jannie Gagiano, 19 April 2019.
44 Slabbert, *Last White Parliament*, p 22.
45 J Gagiano, 'Who we were', in A LeMaitre and M Savage (eds), *The Passion for Reason: Essays in Honour of Frederik van Zyl Slabbert*, Jonathan Ball, Johannesburg, 2010, p 2.
46 Marcia Haak Collection, 'Es die deng wat hy es'.
47 Interview with Marcia Haak, 6 August 2017.
48 Stellenbosch University student records, 1961.
49 P Cassar, 'The emergence and impact of Dr F van Zyl Slabbert in South African opposition politics, 1974–1981', MA thesis, University of the Free State, 1984, p 5.
50 Slabbert, *Afrikaner Afrikaan*, p 13; on the Helpmekaar, see A Ehlers, *Die Kaapse Helpmekaar, c 1916–2014: Bemiddelaar in Afrikaner opheffing, selfrespek en respektabiliteit*, Sunmedia, Stellenbosch, 2018, p 470.
51 FvZ Slabbert, 'Some contest the assertion that I am an African', in X Mangcu (ed), *Becoming Worthy Ancestors: Archive, Public Deliberations and Identity in South Africa*, Wits University Press, Johannesburg, 2010, p 48.
52 Stellenbosch University student records, 1961.
53 *Leadership SA*, 6 March 1987, 'Total immersion'.
54 P Hugo, 'The politics of untruth: Afrikaner academics for apartheid', *Politikon: South African Journal of Political Studies*, 25(1) (1998), p 48.
55 Slabbert, *Last White Parliament*, pp 12, 19.

NOTES

56 HB Thom Collection, 191.A.1 (11), HB Thom, 'Dagbreek binne die groter geheel', 1971 (translated).
57 *Eikestadnuus*, 19 September 1980, 'Die stene en mense van Wilgenhof'.
58 *Leadership SA*, 6 March 1987, 'Total immersion'.
59 Slabbert, *Tough Choices*, p 29.
60 *Die Burger*, 23 May 2008, 'Slabbert kom huis toe'.
61 Slabbert, *Tough Choices*, p 29.
62 HB Thom, 'Dagbreek binne die groter geheel', in B Booyens and K Oosthuysen (eds), *Dagbreek 1921–1971*, Dagbreek, Kaapstad, p 25 (translated).
63 Cassar, 'Slabbert', p 6.
64 H Giliomee, 'Golden boy, golden opportunity: A note on Van Zyl Slabbert', in *The Passion for Reason*, p 88.
65 'Bliksem', *Wilgenhof Koshuisblad*, article by F van Zyl Slabbert, October 1984; interview with F Bührman, Slabbert's roommate at Wilgenhof, 14 November 2019.
66 Gagiano, 'Who we were', in *The Passion for Reason*, pp 18–19.
67 Stellenbosch University Archives, Wilgenhof Volume, 20/18j, Registrar to Slabbert, 25 June 1963, and Slabbert to Registrar, 24 October 1963.
68 Interview with F Bührman, 14 November 2019.
69 Interview with Hermann Giliomee, 5 August 2019.
70 Slabbert, *Last White Parliament*, p 20.
71 Interview with Bernard Lategan, a contemporary, 6 July 2018.
72 A Grundlingh, *Potent Pastimes: Sport and Leisure Practices in Modern Afrikaner History*, Protea, Pretoria, 2013, p 68.
73 Slabbert, *Last White Parliament*, p 20.
74 *Die Huisgenoot*, 12 July 1966, 'Ons kultuurlewe, 1916–1966' (translated); for an analysis of the 1960s, see A Grundlingh. '"Are we Afrikaners becoming too rich?" Cornucopia and change in Afrikanerdom in the 1960s', *Journal of Historical Sociology*, 21(2–3) (June/September 2008), p 148; D Welsh, 'Urbanisation and the solidarity of Afrikaner nationalism', *The Journal of Modern African Studies*, 7(2) (1969), pp 265–276.
75 F van Zyl Slabbert, 'Grense', in R van Niekerk (ed), *Ons vir jou Suid-Afrika*, Van Schaik, Pretoria, 1962, pp 80, 81, 82 (translated).
76 H Giliomee, *Die Laaste Afrikanerleiers: 'n opperste toets van mag*, Tafelberg, Cape Town, 2012, p 211.
77 Slabbert, *Afrikaner Afrikaan*, pp 11–13; see also Slabbert, 'Some contest', 48–49, Slabbert, *Last White Parliament*, pp 23–25.
78 Slabbert, *Afrikaner Afrikaan*, p 13 (translated).
79 Gagiano, 'Who we were', in *The Passion for Reason*, p 30.
80 Cassar, 'Slabbert', p 17.
81 Giliomee, *The Last Afrikaner Leaders*, pp 209–210. Simon Bekker, a former member of the sociology department, provided information on its composition in the early 1970s. Interview on 21 August 2020.
82 Slabbert, *Last White Parliament*, p 25.
83 Stellenbosch University Library, Dian Joubert Collection, FvZ Slabbert file, Copy of confidential report, 11 June 1968.
84 Stellenbosch University Library, Dian Joubert Collection, FvZ Slabbert file, Slabbert to Joubert, 15 December 1968.
85 Stellenbosch University Library, Dian Joubert Collection, FvZ Slabbert file, Slabbert to Joubert, 7 April 1969.

86 Stellenbosch University Library, SP Cilliers Collection, 289/CO (1) 479, Slabbert to Cilliers, 15 March 1969.
87 Ibid.
88 Stellenbosch University Library, Dian Joubert Collection, FvZ Slabbert file, Slabbert to Joubert, 9 May 1969.
89 Stellenbosch University Library, Slabbert Collection, 430.D7.3, Academic Freedom Lecture, University of Cape Town, 2003; on Daantjie Oosthuizen, see A du Toit, 'The legacy of Daantjie Oosthuizen: Revisiting the liberal defence of academic freedom', *African Sociological Review*, 9(1) (2005), pp 40–61.
90 Stellenbosch University Library, Dian Joubert Collection, FvZ Slabbert file, Slabbert to Joubert, 1 March 1969 (translated).
91 Stellenbosch University Library, SP Cilliers Collection, 289/CO 500, Slabbert to Cilliers, 5 June 1969.
92 Stellenbosch University Library, Dian Joubert Collection, FvZ Slabbert file, Slabbert to Joubert, 1 July 1969; SP Cilliers Collection, 289/CO/425, Joubert to Cilliers, 10 August 1989.
93 Stellenbosch University Library, Dian Joubert Collection, FvZ Slabbert file, Slabbert to Joubert, 1 July 1969 (translated).
94 Stellenbosch University Library, SP Cilliers Collection, 289/CO, 1, 500, Slabbert to Cilliers, 5 June 1969.
95 Slabbert, *Last White Parliament*, p 63; C Eglin, *Crossing the Borders of Power: The Memoirs of Colin Eglin*, Jonathan Ball, Johannesburg, 2007, p 189.
96 Stellenbosch University Library, SP Cilliers Collection, 289/CO,1, 500, Slabbert to Cilliers, 5 June 1969.
97 Stellenbosch University Library, SP Cilliers Collection, 289/CO,1, 479, Slabbert to Cilliers, 15 March 1969.
98 Stellenbosch University Library, Dian Joubert Collection, FvZ Slabbert file, Slabbert to Joubert, undated, 1969.
99 Stellenbosch University Library, SP Cilliers Collection, 289 CO 1, 425, Joubert to Cilliers, 10 August 1968.
100 Stellenbosch University Library Dian Joubert Collection, FvZ Slabbert file, Slabbert to Joubert, undated, 1969 (translated).
101 These courses are listed in the *Stellenbosch University Yearbook*, 1971, Sociology, p 371.
102 Stellenbosch University Library, Dian Joubert Collection, FvZ Slabbert file, Slabbert to Joubert, undated, 1969 (translated).
103 *Cape Argus*, 18 August 1971, 'Not a Prog, says Matie professor'.
104 Slabbert, *Last White Parliament*, p 27.
105 Dunbar Moodie, email to author, 14 September 2014.
106 Van der Spuy, unpublished memoir, 2010.
107 Giliomee, *Last Afrikaner Leaders*, p 209.
108 A Grundlingh, 'Structures for sociologists: A historical perspective on associations for sociologists in South Africa, 1967–1991, in N Romm, M Sarakinsky, D Gelderblom, V McKay and C Allais (eds), *Social Theory*, Lexicon, Johannesburg, 1994, pp 58–59.
109 Stellenbosch University Library, SP Cilliers Collection, 289, CO 1729, Loubser to Cilliers, 10 August 1971; M Savage, email to author, 16 September 2014; Dunbar Moodie, email to author, 14 September 2014.
110 K Jubber, email to author, 20 October 2014; P Le Roux, interview with author, 3 March 2019; J Evert, interview with author, 19 February 2019.
111 The relevant piece was based on his doctoral dissertation and appeared in 1976 as 'Functional methodology in the theory of action', in J Loubser, R Baum, A Effrat

NOTES

and VM Lidz (eds), *Explorations in General Theory in Social Science: Essays in Honor of Talcott Parsons*, Vol I, The Free Press, London, 1976, pp 46–50.
112 M Savage, email to author, 16 September 2014; see also S Ally, K Mooney and P Stewart, 'The state-sponsored and centralised institutionalisation of an academic discipline: Sociology in South Africa, 1920–1970', *Society in Transition*, 34(1) (2003), p 85. According to these authors, the first doctoral degree in sociology from an English-speaking South African university was only awarded in 1965.
113 Stellenbosch University Library, SP Cilliers Collection, 289/22/1, Cilliers to Registrar, University of the Witwatersrand, 6 December 1972.
114 Gagiano, 'Who we were', in *The Passion for Reason*, p 35.
115 Ibid.
116 M Savage, email to author, 16 September 2014.
117 Slabbert, *Last White Parliament*, p 5.
118 Dunbar Moodie, email to author, 12 September 2014.
119 K Jubber, email to author, 20 October 2014.
120 Telephonic conversation with Stan Kahn, 16 September 2014; see also Cassar, 'Slabbert', p 19.
121 Quoted in C Kurzman and L Owens, 'The sociology of intellectuals', *Annual Review of Sociology*, 28(202) (1999), p 69.
122 Cassar, 'Slabbert', p 19.
123 S Ally, 'Oppositional intellectualism as reflection, not rejection of power: Wits Sociology, 1975–1989', *Transformation*, 59(1) (2005), p 72.
124 Cassar, 'Slabbert', p 7.
125 Giliomee, 'Golden boy', in *The Passion for Reason*, p 88.
126 See, for instance, P Duvenhage, 'Afrikaner intellectual history: An interpretation', in P Vale, L Hamilton and EH Prinsloo (eds), *Intellectual Traditions in South Africa: Ideas, Individuals and Institutions*, University of KwaZulu-Natal Press, Pietermaritzburg, 2014, p 89.
127 Slabbert, *Last White Parliament*, p 26.
128 Compare P van den Berghe, 'Some trends in unpublished social science research in South Africa', *International Social Science Journal*, XIV(4) (1962).
129 F van Zyl Slabbert, 'Beroepskeuses van studente', MA thesis, Stellenbosch University, March 1964, pp 5–6.
130 APR Kellerman, 'Inleiding', in APR Kellerman (ed), *SP Cilliers: Selected Papers*, Department of Sociology, Stellenbosch University, Stellenbosch, 1991, pp 7–8.
131 FvZ Slabbert, 'Structural-functional analysis in theoretical sociology: A methodological enquiry', PhD thesis, Stellenbosch University, 1967, pp ii–iii.
132 Stellenbosch University Library, Dian Joubert Collection, FvZ Slabbert file, 'Kritiese opmerkinge by F van Zyl, Slabbert: "Structural-functional analysis in theoretical sociology: A methodological enquiry"', undated.
133 Slabbert, *Tough Choices*, pp 33–34.
134 Slabbert, *Last White Parliament*, p 28.
135 W James, 'Van Zyl Slabbert: Sociologist at work in advancing democratic politics', in *The Passion for Reason*, p 146.
136 Ibid, pp 146–148.
137 Gagiano, 'Who we were', in *The Passion for Reason*, pp 30–31.
138 JC Alexander, 'Commentary: Structure, value action', *American Sociological Review*, 55(3) (1990), p 342.
139 M Savage, email to author, 16 September 2014; Slabbert, 'Some contest', p 50.
140 Slabbert, 'Some contest', p 50.

141 Compare Grundlingh, 'Structures for sociologists', p 69.
142 Stellenbosch University Library, SP Cilliers Collection, 289 Co 1(214), Slabbert to Cilliers, 28 January 1965.
143 *US Kampusnuus*, July 2008, 'Nuwe kanselier'.
144 Heribert Adam, email to author, 5 April 2015.

Chapter 2

1 Author's personal collection; A du Toit, 'Johan Degenaar: ter herinnering', 1 August 2015; I Macqueen, 'Resonances of youth and tensions of race: Liberal student politics, white radicals and Black Consciousness' 1968–1973', *South African Historical Journal*, 65(3) (2013), pp 372–373.
2 Giliomee, 'Golden boy', in *The Passion for Reason*, p 88.
3 J Basson, *Politieke kaarte op die tafel: Parlementêre en ander herinneringe*, Politika, Cape Town, 2006, pp 161–164; Cassar, 'Slabbert', p 7.
4 Slabbert, *Last White Parliament*, p 18.
5 Slabbert, *Other Side of History*, p 153.
6 Quoted in Cassar, 'Slabbert', p 41.
7 Ibid, p 9.
8 Grundlingh, '"Are we Afrikaners getting too rich?"', p 148; D Welsh, 'Urbanisation and the solidarity of Afrikaner nationalism', *The Journal of Modern African Studies*, 7(2) (1969), pp 265–276.
9 *Rand Daily Mail*, 10 January 1974, 'Dilemma of Verligtheid'; the academic article published later is entitled 'Afrikaner nationalism, white politics and political change', in L Thompson and J Butler (eds), *Change in Contemporary South Africa*, University of California Press, Berkeley, 1975, pp 4–14.
10 H Giliomee, 'Van Zyl Slabbert: The golden boy and the black prince', in Giliomee, *Last Afrikaner Leaders*, p 208.
11 Cassar, 'Slabbert', pp 10–12.
12 FvZ Slabbert, *The System and the Struggle: Reform, Revolt and Reaction in South Africa*, Jonathan Ball, Johannesburg, 1989, pp 17–18.
13 Cassar, 'Slabbert', pp 10, 13–14.
14 FvZ Slabbert, 'Politics and privilege in South Africa', Summer School lectures, University of Cape Town, 1973.
15 Slabbert, *Last White Parliament*, pp 6–7; Cassar, 'Slabbert', pp 19–20.
16 Eglin, *Crossing Borders*, pp 136–137.
17 Slabbert, *Last White Parliament*, pp 5–6.
18 Quoted in Cassar, 'Slabbert', p 17.
19 Slabbert, *Last White Parliament*, p 28.
20 B Hackland, 'The economic and political context of the growth of the Progressive Federal Party in South Africa, 1959–1978', in *The Societies of Southern Africa in the 19th and 20th Centuries*, Collected Seminar Papers, Vol 11, No 27, University of London, Institute of Commonwealth Studies, 1981, pp 121–123; see also E McKenzie, 'Its master's voice? The South African "Progressive" parties and business, 1959–1983', *Journal for Contemporary History*, 21(2) (December 1996), pp 34–48.
21 Van der Spuy, unpublished memoir, 2010.
22 For example, *Rapport*, 4 May 1974, 'Van Zyl Slabbert, voel jy tuis daar?'.
23 Quoted in Cassar, 'Slabbert', p 44.
24 Cassar, 'Slabbert', pp 22, 28; E McKenzie, 'From obscurity to official opposition: The Progressive Federal Party, 1959–1977', *Historia*, 39(1) (May 1994), pp 87–89.

NOTES

25 Slabbert, *Last White Parliament*, p 6.
26 Ibid, p 10.
27 Eglin, *Crossing Borders*, p 137.
28 Cassar, 'Slabbert', p 26.
29 Cassar, 'Slabbert', pp 26, 28; Slabbert, *Last White Parliament*, p 8; Mouton asserts that Slabbert underestimated his chances of winning; see FA Mouton, *Iron in the Soul: The Leaders of the Official Parliamentary Opposition in South Africa, 1910–1993*, Protea Book House, Pretoria, 2017, p 148.
30 *Cape Times*, 17 April 1974, letter from M Wynne.
31 Quoted in Cassar, 'Slabbert', p 31.
32 Cassar, 'Slabbert', p 29.
33 Slabbert, *Last White Parliament*, p 8.
34 Ibid, p 9.
35 Cassar, 'Slabbert', p 29.
36 Slabbert, *Last White Parliament*, p 9.
37 Eglin, *Crossing Borders*, p 137.
38 Quoted in Cassar, 'Slabbert', p 28.
39 Ibid, p 34.
40 Slabbert, *Last White Parliament*, p 9.
41 Quoted in Cassar, 'Slabbert', p 36.
42 Cassar, 'Slabbert', p 36.
43 Ibid, p 32.
44 Quoted in Cassar, 'Slabbert', p 33.
45 Ibid, pp 33–34.
46 Slabbert, *Last White Parliament*, p 9.
47 Cassar, 'Slabbert', pp 38–39.
48 Ibid, p 38.
49 Slabbert, *Last White Parliament*, p 10.
50 Interview with Marcia Haak, 6 August 2017.

Chapter 3

1   Slabbert, *Last White Parliament*, p 31.
2   Eglin, *Crossing Borders*, p 141.
3   Slabbert, *Last White Parliament*, p 34.
4   Ibid, p 35; see also Eglin, *Crossing Borders*, p 141.
5   Eglin, *Crossing Borders*, p 143.
6   *Die Burger*, 1 August 1974, 'Slabbert gee sy eie antwoorde op Dawie se vrae' (translated).
7   JC Steyn, *Penvegter: Piet Cillié van Die Burger*, Tafelberg, Cape Town, 2002, p 256.
8   Cassar, 'Slabbert', p 48; Eglin, *Crossing Borders*, p 140.
9   A Boraine, 'An amalgam that worked', in *The Passion for Reason*, p 35.
10 Cassar, 'Slabbert', p 50.
11 Quoted in Cassar, 'Slabbert', p 48; see also pp 50–51.
12 D Welsh, 'English-speaking white South Africans', Summer School lectures, University of Cape Town, 1973, p 11.
13 Cassar, 'Slabbert', p 51.
14 *House of Assembly Debates*, 24 October 1974, column 6232.

15 *House of Assembly Debates*, 21 August 1974, columns 1180–1182.
16 Ibid, columns 1180–1182.
17 Cassar, 'Slabbert', p 53.
18 Compare Cassar, 'Slabbert', pp 60–61.
19 Cassar Collection, Oral interview with BJ Vorster, 4 September 1982.
20 Cassar, 'Slabbert', p 61.
21 H Giliomee Collection, H Giliomee, 'Notes on Jan Smuts, Van Zyl Slabbert and the lessons from our history to opposition parties sniffing power around the corner and re-positioning themselves', 2013, p 2.
22 Slabbert, *Last White Parliament*, p 92; see also pp 91–92.
23 *House of Assembly Debates*, 18 September 1974, column 3270.
24 Slabbert, *Last White Parliament*, pp 38–39; see also Slabbert, *Afrikaner Afrikaan*, pp 19–20.
25 Slabbert, *White Parliament*, pp 43–52; Slabbert, *Other Side of History*, pp 159–160.
26 Much has been written on apartheid sport. See, for example, D Booth, *The Race Game: Politics and Sport in South Africa*, Frank Cass, London, 1998.
27 *House of Assembly Debates*, 14 October 1974, column 5265.
28 *House of Assembly Debates*, 2 September 1974; see also Cassar, 'Slabbert', p 55.
29 Slabbert, *Afrikaner Afrikaan*, p 20.
30 *House of Assembly Debates*, 2 September 1974, columns 2014, 2015.
31 Giliomee, *Last Afrikaner Leaders*, p 214; Slabbert, *Afrikaner Afrikaan*, p 21.
32 J D'Oliveira, *Vorster: The Man*, Ernest Stanton, Johannesburg, 1977, p 247.
33 Stellenbosch University, Dian Joubert Collection, unsorted, Slabbert to Joubert, 17 January 1977; the Afrikaans term was 'goor ou pot'.
34 A Boraine, *A Life in Transition*, Oxford University Press, Johannesburg, 2008, p 94.
35 Cassar, 'Slabbert', p 55.
36 *House of Assembly Debates*, 10 October 1974, column 5026.
37 V Thakur and P Vale, '"Negotiations in South Africa": The liberal imaginary and expertise of Frederik van Zyl Slabbert', unpublished and undated paper, p 6.
38 Giliomee Collection, Giliomee, 'Notes on Jan Smuts and Van Zyl Slabbert', p 2; see also Giliomee, *Last Afrikaner Leaders*, p 219.
39 Slabbert, *Last White Parliament*, p 60.
40 Cassar, 'Slabbert', pp 91–92, 95.
41 Quoted in Cassar, 'Slabbert' p 90.
42 *Die Burger*, 2 December 1977, 'Verkiesingsuitslae'.
43 Cassar, 'Slabbert' p 107.
44 Slabbert, *Last White Parliament*, p 42.
45 Thakur and Vale, '"Negotiations in South Africa"', p 4.
46 F Slabbert, 'Incremental change or revolution?' in J Butler, R Elphick and D Welsh (eds), *Democratic Liberalism in South Africa: Its History and Prospects*, David Philip, Cape Town, 1987, pp 401–402.
47 Slabbert, *Last White Parliament*, p 72.
48 *House of Assembly Debates*, 6 February 1975, column 350.
49 Slabbert, *Last White Parliament*, p 54.
50 Ibid, pp 54–55.
51 Giliomee, *Last Afrikaner Leaders*, p 216; Cassar, 'Slabbert', pp 142–143.
52 Cassar, 'Slabbert', p 143.
53 *House of Assembly Debates*, 6 February 1975, column 351, and 25 February 1975, column 1371.

NOTES

54 Boraine, *Life in Transition*, p 91; see also FvZ Slabbert and D Welsh, *South Africa's Options: Strategies for Sharing Power*, David Philip, Cape Town, 1979, p 151.
55 M Cardo, 'The liberal tradition in South Africa: Past and present', *Focus* (July 2012), p 19.
56 Slabbert, *Last White Parliament*, pp 55–56.
57 Cassar, 'Slabbert', pp 147–148.
58 Ibid, p 146.
59 *House of Assembly Debates*, 6 February 1975, column 350.
60 Cassar, 'Slabbert', p 146.
61 Slabbert, *Last White Parliament*, p 56.
62 David Welsh, email to author, 23 December 2018.
63 A du Toit, 'On South Africa's options', *Social Dynamics*, 5(2) (July 1979), pp 59–62.
64 N Alexander, 'Examining South Africa's options', *Social Dynamics*, 5(2) (July 1979), pp 56–59.
65 Giliomee, 'Golden boy', in *The Passion or Reason*, pp 94–95.
66 H Giliomee and L Schlemmer, *From Apartheid to Nation-Building*, Oxford University Press, Oxford, p 164.
67 Slabbert and Welsh, *South Africa's Options*, pp 133–170.
68 Slabbert, *System and the Struggle*, p 181.
69 Stellenbosch University Library, Slabbert Collection, 420.Z.2 (65), 'Slabbert's blueprint for the new SA', 22 June 2010.
70 Compare S Ndlovu, 'The African National Congress and negotiations', in South African Democracy Education Trust, *The Road to Democracy in South Africa, Vol 4, Part 1 and 2, 1980–1990*, Unisa Press, Pretoria, 2010, p 71.
71 Cassar, 'Slabbert', p 113.
72 Ibid, pp 113–114, 182.
73 Boraine, 'Amalgam', in *The Passion for Reason*, p 39.
74 Slabbert, *Last White Parliament*, p 62.
75 Mouton, *Iron in the Soul*, p 133; see also p 140.
76 Cassar, 'Slabbert', p 175.
77 Slabbert, *Last White Parliament*, p 62; Cassar, 'Slabbert', pp 150–170, 192; Eglin, *Crossing Borders*, p 188; Mouton, *Iron in the Soul*, p 142.
78 Slabbert, *Last White Parliament*, p 63.
79 *Progress*, September 1979, 'Nuwe leier'.
80 Slabbert, *Last White Parliament*, p 63.
81 Eglin, *Crossing Borders*, p 91.
82 *Rand Daily Mail*, 9 August 1979, 'Can the ivory tower star take the spit and sawdust?'
83 *Weekend Argus*, 8 February 1986, 'Van Zyl Slabbert – the reluctant politician …'.
84 Giliomee, *Last Afrikaner Leaders*, p 213.

Chapter 4

1 Cassar, 'Slabbert', p 192.
2 Cassar, 'Slabbert', p 194.
3 *Die Transvaler*, 5 September 1979, 'Aan hierdie norme sal Slabbert gemeet word' (translated).
4 *Beeld*, 4 September 1979, Editorial (translated).
5 Slabbert, *Last White Parliament*, p 64.

6   R Swart, *Progressive Odyssey: Towards a Democratic South Africa*, Human & Rousseau, Cape Town, 1991, pp 156–157.
7   Stellenbosch University Library, Slabbert Collection, 430.X3.3.1, R Schrire 'White politics during the Botha era', 1988, p 52.
8   Slabbert, *Last White Parliament*, pp 64–68; Eglin, *Crossing Borders*, p 197; Cassar, 'Slabbert', p 196.
9   *Weekend Post*, 'Slabbert's tour', 29 September 1979; see also *Progress*, December 1979, 'Ovation for Slabbert'.
10 Cassar, 'Slabbert', pp 201–202.
11 *Cape Times*, 9 November 1979, 'Slabbert sees win as vote for change'.
12 *The Star*, 8 November 1979, 'Boss Ross did it'.
13 *House of Assembly Debates*, 4 February 1980, columns 21–25.
14 Cassar, 'Slabbert', p 211.
15 *Sunday Times*, 8 February 1980, 'Election 1981 – why?'.
16 Cassar, 'Slabbert', p 235; *Rand Daily Mail*, 1 March 1981, 'PFP outlines election issues'.
17 *Sunday Times*, 19 April 1981, 'The man who guides ordinary people through the maze of politics'.
18 Stellenbosch University Library, Slabbert Collection, 430.E2.33.3, 'Why I believe voters should support the PFP', 26 April 1981.
19 Cassar, 'Slabbert', p 239.
20 Ibid, pp 241 and 244; *Rand Daily Mail*, 28 April 1981, 'The Slabbert factor'.
21 Slabbert, *Last White Parliament*, p 70.
22 Ibid.
23 Cassar, 'Slabbert', p 243.
24 Slabbert, *Last White Parliament*, p 71.
25 *Natal Witness*, 2 May 1981, 'New leader'; see also *Cape Times*, 3 May 1981, 'Slabbert'.
26 *Die Burger*, 4 May 1981, Editorial (translated).
27 D Shandler, 'Structural crisis and liberalism: A history of the Progressive Federal Party, 1981–1989', MA thesis, University of Cape Town, 1991, p 54.
28 H Giliomee, *The Rise and Demise of the Afrikaners*, Tafelberg, Cape Town, 2019, p 80; for an analysis of the electoral dynamics of the 1981 election that neatly corresponds with this view, see C Charney, 'Towards rupture or stasis: An analysis of the 1981 South African General Election', *African Affairs*, 81(325) (1982), p 531.
29 *Rapport*, 16 February 1986, 'Moet jy hom kwalik neem?'.
30 See, for example, *Die Burger*, 31 October 1979, 'Die Slabbert-vyeblaar'.
31 Slabbert, *Afrikaner Afrikaan*, p 22; *Cape Times*, 20 August 1981, 'Slabbert fire still a mystery'.
32 Shandler, 'Structural crisis', pp 59–61.
33 Giliomee, *Last Afrikaner Leaders*, p 210.
34 *Deurbraak*, September 1982, 'Balance of power will result in horse-trading'.
35 Shandler, 'Structural crisis', p 62.
36 Cassar, 'Slabbert', p 251; this explanation is based upon an interview Cassar had with Slabbert on 25 September 1984.
37 T Hanf, 'Lessons which are never learnt: Minority rule in comparative perspective', *Journal of Asian and African Studies*, XVIII(1–2) (1983), pp 31–32; for Slabbert's opinion on Hanf, see *Last White Parliament*, p 90.
38 Slabbert, 'Incremental change or revolution?', p 403, n 1.
39 Shandler, 'Structural crisis', p 82, quoting an interview with Slabbert on 28 September 1990.

NOTES

40 Giliomee, *Last Afrikaner Leaders*, p 145.
41 Shandler, 'Structural crisis', p 64; Giliomee, *Last Afrikaner Leaders*, p 170.
42 P Meiring, *Waagmoed beloon: 50 menings oor die PW-plan*, Perskor, Johannesburg, 1985, p 1.
43 Shandler, 'Structural crisis', p 65; Slabbert, *System and the Struggle*, p 65.
44 *House of Assembly Debates*, 16 May 1983, columns 7065–7066.
45 Slabbert, *Last White Parliament*, p 114.
46 Giliomee, *Last Afrikaner Leaders*, p 139.
47 Author's personal recollection of the 1983 referendum.
48 Slabbert, *System and the Struggle*, p 69.
49 Slabbert, *Last White Parliament*, p 111.
50 Stellenbosch University, Dian Joubert Collection, Unsorted, Notes of a meeting held on 14 August 1983 (translated).
51 DJA Viljoen (ed), *Koerantknipsels oor die Referendum oor 'n nuwe Grondwetlike bedeling, 1983*, Institut vir Eietydse Geskiedenis, Bloemfontein, 1984.
52 Shandler, 'Structural crisis', pp 70–72.
53 Slabbert, *Last White Parliament*, pp 115–117; Shandler, 'Structural crisis', p 70.
54 *Cape Argus*, 6 September 1983, 'Slabbert warns PFP to back "no" campaign'.
55 *Cape Argus*, 12 September 1983, 'Referendum campaign warms up'.
56 *Financial Mail*, 22 July 1983, 'The "Constitution"'.
57 *The Star*, 3 September 1983, 'Three eggs miss Slabbert'.
58 Slabbert, *Last White Parliament*, p 117.
59 *Sunday Tribune*, 21 October 1983, 'Final countdown'.
60 Shandler, 'Structural crisis', p 73.
61 Slabbert, *Last White Parliament*, p 116; FvZ Slabbert, 'Threats and challenges to South Africa becoming a more open society', in M Shain (ed), *Opposing Voices: Liberalism and Opposition in South Africa Today*, Jonathan Ball, Johannesburg, 2006, p 141.
62 Swart, *Progressive Odyssey*, p 165.
63 Shandler, 'Structural crisis', p 74.
64 Ibid, p 87; *Pretoria News*, 7 October 1983, 'Yes vote a positive movement'; *The Daily News*, 18 October 1983, 'Yes from Saunders'.
65 Shandler, 'Structural crisis', p 87; see also *Die Burger*, 28 September 1983, 'Min sake-steun vir PFP se Nee'; *The Citizen*, 5 October 1983, 'Businessmen back "Yes"'.
66 Giliomee Collection, Unsorted, Tony Delius to Tony Heard, 25 November 1981, quoting Slabbert.
67 Shandler, 'Structural crisis', p 82, quoting from an interview with Slabbert on 28 September 1990.
68 J Seekings, *The UDF: A History of the United Democratic Front in South Africa, 1983–1991*, David Philip, Cape Town, 2000, pp 54, 59.
69 *Sowetan*, 23 August 1983, 'Too early to judge UDF, Slabbert'.
70 Swart, *Progressive Odyssey*, p 164.
71 *The Natal Witness*, 4 March 1985, 'Emergence of a key figure'.

Chapter 5

1 Shandler, 'Structural crisis', p 92; the quotation is from an interview with Slabbert on 28 September 1990.
2 *Rand Daily Mail*, 2 December 1981, 'The PFP and black politics'.

3   See, for example, G Maré and G Hamilton, *An Appetite for Power: Buthelezi's Inkatha and South Africa*, Ravan Press, Johannesburg, 1987.
4   *Deurbraak*, August 1986, 'Groei' (translated).
5   *Sunday Tribune*, 23 June 1985, 'PFP and UDF'.
6   Much has been written on this; see, for example, M Swilling, 'The United Democratic Front and township revolt', in W Cobbett and R Cohen (eds), *Popular Struggles in South Africa*, James Currey, London, 1988, pp 90–113; Seekings, *The UDF*, pp 91 ff.
7   Giliomee, *Last Afrikaner Leaders*, pp 194–203.
8   Shandler, 'Structural crisis', p 143, quoting from an interview with Peter Gastrow, 28 March 1990.
9   Wits University, Cullen Library, Wits Historical Papers, PFP collection, AG 883 AC 1.13, Speech by F van Zyl Slabbert at the PFP Federal Congress, 10 August 1985.
10 Ibid.
11 Shandler, 'Structural crisis', p 131, quotation from an interview with Slabbert on 28 September 1990.
12 Stellenbosch University Library, B 33215, Patti Waldmeier Interviews, interview with Slabbert, pp 38–39, 11 November 1994.
13 Shandler, 'Structural crisis', p 132.
14 Ibid, quoting from an interview with Peter Gastrow, 28 March 1990.
15 Slabbert, *Tough Choices*, p 103.
16 Peter Gastrow, email to author, 27 February 2019, recalling the detail of arranging the PFP-ANC meeting.
17 Slabbert, *Tough Choices*, p 103.
18 Stellenbosch University Library, B 33215, Patti Waldmeier Interviews, interview with Slabbert, 11 November 1994, p 40.
19 Boraine, *Life in Transition*, 147.
20 Stellenbosch University Library, B 33215, Patti Waldmeier Interviews; interview with Slabbert, 11 November 1994, pp 40–41.
21 H Macmillan, *The Lusaka Years: The ANC in Exile, 1963 to 1994*, Jacana, Auckland Park, 2013, p 204.
22 Slabbert, *Tough Choices*, p 103.
23 Ibid.
24 M Gevisser, *Thabo Mbeki: The Dream Deferred*, Jonathan Ball, Johannesburg, 2007, p 497.
25 Stellenbosch University Library, B 33215, Patti Waldmeier Interviews, interview with Slabbert, 11 November 1994, pp 40.
26 *Cape Argus*, 14 October 1985, 'ANC, PFP may talk again'.
27 Shandler, 'Structural crisis', p 145.
28 Stellenbosch University Library, B 33215, Patti Waldmeier Interviews, interview with Slabbert, p 42, 11 November 1994.
29 Compare Giliomee, *Last Afrikaner Leaders*, pp 216–218.
30 A Venter, 'Mededingende politieke paradigmas oor die Grensoorlog, 1966–1989', *Journal for Contemporary History*, 34(1) (February 2009), pp 40–42.
31 C Eglin, 'South Africa in a southern African and international foreign policy perspective', in Friedrich Naumann Stiftung, *South Africa – A Chance for Liberalism? Papers Presented During a Seminar of the Friedrich Naumann Foundation in December 1983*, Liberal Verlag, Sankt Augustin, 1985, p 268; see also Slabbert, *System and the Struggle*, p 125.
32 P Myburgh, 'Security defence issues in southern Africa', in Friedrich Naumann

NOTES

      Stiftung, *South Africa – A Chance for Liberalism?*, p 261; see also Venter, 'Mededingende politieke paradigmas', p 50.
33   *Sechaba*, March 1986, 'Our armed offensive: Military strategy in South Africa', pp 19–20.
34   *House of Assembly Debates*, 25 March 1980, column 3445.
35   *House of Assembly Debates*, 21 March 1983, column 3551.
36   Interview with Philip Myburgh, 25 April 2016.
37   Wits University, Cullen Library, Historical Papers, PFP Archives, AG 1977/H 7, Speech by B Goodall, May 1987.
38   Slabbert, *Last White Parliament*, pp 39–42; *House of Assembly Debates*, 5 February 1976, columns 671–672.
39   *House of Assembly Debates*, 25 March 1980, column 3424.
40   Ibid, columns 3446–3447.
41   KW Grundy, *Soldiers without Politics: Blacks in the South African Armed Forces*, University of California Press, Berkeley, 1983, p 124.
42   H Giliomee, *The Last Afrikaner Leaders*, p 220.
43   *House of Assembly Debates*, 25 March 1980, column 3456.
44   Quoted in Swart, *Progressive Odyssey*, p 157.
45   *House of Assembly Debates*, 29 May 1985, column 6472.
46   *Deurbraak*, March 1984, 'Cackling politics'.
47   *Deurbraak*, April 1983, 'Defence breakthroughs'.
48   P Frankel, *Pretoria's Praetorians: Civil-Military Relations in South Africa*, Cambridge University Press, Cambridge, 1984, p 91.
49   Interview with P Myburgh, 25 April 2016.
50   Wits University, Cullen Library, Historical Papers, PFP Papers, 44.11.8, Speech delivered by FvZ Slabbert to PFP Federal Congress, 10 August 1985.
51   Frankel, *Pretoria's Praetorians*, pp 128–129.
52   Boraine, *Life in Transition*, p 117.
53   Ibid, p 130; interview with K Andrew, 5 September 2019.
54   *The Citizen*, 21 September 1987, 'Schwarz will ignore what McIntosh said'.
55   *House of Assembly Debates*, 29 May 1985, column 6465.
56   *Rand Daily Mail*, 21 November 1984, 'Sword drawn in PFP defence force row'.
57   *Eastern Province Herald*, 21 November 1984, 'Neglecting the art of the possible'.
58   *Deurbraak*, December 1984, 'Conscription'.
59   *Rand Daily Mail*, 21 November 1984, 'My view'.
60   *Die Suid-Afrikaan*, Autumn 1985, 'Hermann Giliomee in gesprek met Generaal Jannie Geldenhuys'.
61   Wits University, Cullen Library, Historical Papers, PFP Papers Ac 1.13, Speech delivered by FvZ Slabbert to the PFP Federal Congress, 10 August 1985.
62   Ibid.
63   *House of Assembly Debates*, 28 May 1985, column 6571.
64   Interview with Philip Myburgh, 25 April 2016.
65   L Nathan, '"Marching to a different beat": The history of the End Conscription Campaign', in J Cock and L Nathan (eds), *War and Society: The Militarisation of South Africa*, David Philip, Cape Town, 1989, p 310.
66   G van der Westhuizen, I Liebenberg and T du Plessis, 'National service and resistance to conscription in South Africa', in I Liebenberg, J Risquet and V Shubin (eds), *A Far-Away War: Angola 1975–1989*, Sunmedia, Stellenbosch, 2015, pp 124–126; Nathan, '"Marching to a different beat"', pp 317–319.

67 *Weekly Mail*, 26 August to 1 September 1988, 'Minister gives his reasons'; *Die Matie*, 20 August 1987, 'ECC ontken bande met ANC'; *Business Day*, 30 September 2009, 'The End Conscription Campaign and the power of refusal'.
68 Compare C Saunders, 'Liberal democratic anti-apartheid activity within South Africa', in South African Democracy Education Trust, *The Road to Democracy in South Africa, Vol 4*, pp 1618–1619; Nathan, '"Marching to a different beat"', pp 305–308.
69 M Phillips, 'The End Conscription Campaign: A study of white extra-parliamentary opposition to apartheid', MA thesis, Unisa, 2002, p 224; on Stellenbosch, see H Giliomee, 'Afrikaner politics, 1977–1987: From Afrikaner nationalist rule to central state hegemony', in JD Brewer (ed), *Can South Africa Survive? Five Minutes to Midnight*. Southern, Johannesburg, 1989, p 132.
70 D Pretorius and M Sauthoff, 'Challenging apartheid: Posters from the United Democratic Front and the End Conscription Campaign, *Image and Text*, 2004(11) (January 2004), pp 23–32.
71 *Die Suid-Afrikaan*, Winter 1985, 'Herman Giliomee in gesprek met Generaal Magnus Malan'; *Die Burger*, 13 May 1988, 'ECC se geld kom van die buiteland'.
72 *The Citizen*, 14 April 1987, 'The direct enemy of the SADF'.
73 *Sunday Tribune*, 9 June 1985, 'Battle lines drawn over conscription'.
74 *Cape Argus*, 14 June 2013, 'Fake liberals of PFP supported apartheid'.
75 *The Star*, 4 March 1985, 'PFP youth pressures party leaders'; *Rand Daily Mail*, 4 March 1985, 'PFP youth call for radical policy stand'; *Cape Times*, 4 March 1985, 'End call-up, say PFP youth'.
76 Interview with Philip Myburgh, 25 April 2016; *Die Matie*, 20 August 1987, 'Dienspligvoorwaardes'; *Die Burger*, 22 March 1983, 'Beswaardes behandel met deernis'.
77 *Sunday Times*, 9 June 1985, 'Battle lines drawn over conscription'.
78 Ibid.
79 *The Star*, 15 June 1985, 'ECC drive on call-up naïve – Slabbert'.
80 Stellenbosch University, Slabbert Papers, 44.11.8, Slabbert to D Runciman, 12 June 1985.
81 Wits University, Cullen Library, Historical Papers, PFP Papers 1.13, Speech delivered by FvZ Slabbert to PFP Federal Congress, 10 August 1985.
82 *Die Matie*, August 1985, 'Pasop vir mooi morele retoriek'.
83 F Verster, *Omega, oor en uit: Die storie van 'n opstandige troep*, Tafelberg, Cape Town, 2016, p 155 (translated); see also Frankel, *Pretoria's Praetorians*, pp 138–140, for the views of white English-speakers.
84 *The Citizen*, 31 August 1985, 'Slabbert calls for end to conscription'.
85 Frankel, *Pretoria's Praetorians*, pp 134–135.
86 *House of Assembly Debates*, 7 February 1986, column 422.

Chapter 6

1 Interview with Jane Slabbert, 18 November 2018; Suzman had long-standing doubts about Slabbert's political durability; see H Suzman, *In No Uncertain Terms: A South African Memoir*, Jonathan Ball, Johannesburg, 1993, p 194.
2 *Leadership SA*, August 1986, 'Slabbert'.
3 Eglin, *Crossing Borders*, p 214.
4 Ibid.
5 Ibid.
6 Compare Giliomee, *Last Afrikaner Leaders*, pp 223–224; Slabbert, *Afrikaner*

NOTES

       Afrikaan, p 26; the full version appeared in *Die Burger*, 19 February 1986, 'Volledige teks van gespek tussen SP en Slabbert' (translated).
7   Stellenbosch University Library, Slabbert Collection, 430.X1, Unpublished memorandum by Slabbert on why he resigned as party leader, August 1986, p 12.
8   Slabbert, *Afrikaner Afrikaan*, p 26 (translated).
9   Giliomee Collection, Unsorted, H Giliomee to Helen Zille, 17 May 2013.
10 *Die Burger*, 19 February 1986, 'Volledige teks van gespek tussen SP en Slabbert'.
11 Slabbert, *Afrikaner Afrikaan*, p 26.
12 Ibid, p 27; see also *Weekend Argus*, 15 February 1986, 'Slabbert tells all'.
13 Eglin, *Crossing Borders*, p 215.
14 Ibid, p 220.
15 *Die Afrikaner*, 26 February 1986, 'PW se Bandopname'.
16 Stellenbosch University Library, Slabbert Collection, 430.X1, Unpublished memorandum by Slabbert on why he resigned as party leader, August 1986, p 12.
17 *Sunday Times*, 23 February 1986, 'I knew Van's secret, says his twin'.
18 Stellenbosch University Library, Slabbert Collection, 430.X1, Unpublished memorandum by Slabbert on why he resigned as party leader, August 1986, p 17.
19 A Boraine, *What's Gone Wrong? South Africa on the Brink of Failed Statehood*, Jonathan Ball, Johannesburg, 2014, p 35.
20 RW Johnson, 'Van Zyl Slabbert: What went wrong? www.politicsweb.co.za, 21 June 2010. Accessed 17 June 2017. See also Giliomee, *Last Afrikaner Leaders*, p 226.
21 Giliomee, *Last Afrikaner Leaders*, p 226.
22 Boraine, *What's Gone Wrong?* p 33.
23 Stellenbosch University Library, Slabbert Collection, 430.C.139.1, Mbeki to Slabbert, January 1986; a copy of the letter also appears in Boraine, *What's Gone Wrong?*, pp 36–37.
24 Eglin, *Crossing Borders*, p 216; see also M du Preez, *Pale Native: Memories of a Renegade Reporter*, Zebra Press, Cape Town, 2004, p 144.
25 Slabbert, *Other Side of History*, p 47.
26 See Boraine, *What's Gone Wrong?*, p 35; in *The Other Side of History*, p 47, Slabbert incorrectly remembers his meeting with Botha as happening before he met Mbeki in Lusaka.
27 Slabbert, *Other Side of History*, p 45.
28 David Welsh Collection, Unsorted, 'Minutes of a meeting held at Dr Van Zyl Slabbert's house', 3 February 1986.
29 Ibid.
30 K Owen, *These Times: A Decade of South African Politics*, Jonathan Ball, Johannesburg, 1992, p 67.
31 *The Times* (London), 13 February 1986, 'Why I resigned'.
32 Eglin, *Crossing Borders*, p 217.
33 *Eastern Province Herald*, 8 February 1986, 'Assembly stunned as Slabbert announces his resignation'; Eglin, *Crossing Borders*, p 21; Swart, *Progressive Odyssey*, p 189.
34 *Rapport*, 9 February 1986, 'So sal ek ou Van onthou …'.
35 *House of Assembly Debates*, 7 February 1986, columns 411–412; see also *Cape Times*, 8 February 1986, 'Drama in Parliament'.
36 *House of Assembly Debates*, 7 February 1986, columns 424–425.
37 R Venter, *'n Stukkie van die legkaart*, Malan Media, Pretoria, 2019, p 128 (translated).

38 *The Star*, 8 February 1986, 'Stunned silence as PFP leader drops "bombshell"'; Du Preez, *Pale Native*, p 145.
39 *Sunday Times*, 23 February 1986, 'I knew Van's secret, says his twin'.
40 Swart, *Progressive Odyssey*, p 181.
41 *The Citizen*, 11 February 1986, 'A snub'; see also *Die Burger*, 11 February 1986, 'Slabbert toe nie daar om te groet nie'.
42 *House of Assembly Debates*, 7 February 1986, column 428.
43 Ibid, column 425.
44 Stellenbosch University Library, Slabbert Collection, 430.D4.13.1, Address by F Slabbert to the Harvard Business School, 54th Class reunion, Mala Mala, 7 November 1986, p 9.
45 Stellenbosch University Library, Slabbert Collection, 430.E1.4.1, F Slabbert, 'Time to bury the Great White Hope'.
46 *Sunday Tribune*, 9 February 1986, 'Why I had to go'.
47 *Cape Times*, 8 February 1986, 'A macabre ballad'.
48 Stellenbosch University Library, Slabbert Collection, 430.07.3, UCT Academic Freedom Lecture, 2003.
49 Slabbert, *Last White Parliament*, p 140; see also Eglin, *Crossing Borders*, p 214.
50 *Financial Mail*, 1 November 1985, 'Slabbert Trust'.
51 Slabbert, *Last White Parliament*, p 161.
52 Adam and Moodley, 'Slabbert's opening of the apartheid mind', in *The Passion for Reason*, p 55.
53 Stellenbosch University Library, Slabbert Collection, 430.X1, Unpublished memorandum by Slabbert on why he resigned as party leader, August 1986, pp 24–27; on the Vass diaries, see also Slabbert, *Other Side of History*, pp 46–47: *House of Assembly Debates*, 3 February 1986, column 42.
54 David Welsh Collection, Unsorted, 'Minutes of a meeting held at Dr Van Zyl Slabbert's house', 3 February 1986.
55 *Die Transvaler*, 11 February 1986, 'Prog-dilemma'.
56 *Sunday Times*, 9 February 1986, 'The Sunday morning assessment'.
57 David Welsh Collection, Unsorted, 'Minutes of a meeting held at Dr Van Zyl Slabbert's house', 3 February 1986.
58 Compare TPD Hughes, 'Political liberalism in South Africa in the 1980s and the formation of the Democratic Party', MA thesis, University of Cape Town, 1994, p 133.
59 *Die Vaderland*, 13 February 1986, ''n Onsekere toekoms'; see also Giliomee Collection, Unsorted, H Zille to H Giliomee, 16 May 2013.
60 Mouton, *Iron in the Soul*, p 159; Slabbert, *Last White Parliament*, p 53.
61 Owen, *These Times*, p 68.
62 Stellenbosch University Library, Slabbert Collection, 430.X1, Unpublished memorandum by Slabbert on why he resigned as party leader, August 1986.
63 Stellenbosch University Library, Slabbert Collection, 430.E1.4.1, F Slabbert, 'Time to bury the Great White Hope'.
64 *Sunday Times*, 15 February 1986, 'Resignation'.
65 Stellenbosch University Library, Slabbert Collection, 430.E1.4.1, F Slabbert, 'Time to bury the Great White Hope'.
66 *Leadership SA*, 28 February 1986, 'Into the Wilderness?'.
67 Stellenbosch University Library, Slabbert Collection, 430.X1, Unpublished memorandum by Slabbert on why he resigned as party leader, August 1986.
68 *House of Assembly Debates*, 7 February 1986, column 426.

NOTES

69 *The Star*, 8 February 1986, 'A private man who fought for principles'.
70 *House of Assembly Debates*, 7 February 1986, column 426.
71 *Beeld*, 21 February, 1986, 'Nie politikus genoeg' (translated).
72 *Sunday Star*, 9 February 1986, 'The two men in politics' day of high drama'.
73 *Leadership SA*, 28 February 1986, 'Into the Wilderness?'.
74 Giliomee, *Last Afrikaner Leaders*, p 226.
75 Stellenbosch University Library, Slabbert Collection, 430.C.140, G McIntosh to Slabbert, 28 February 1986.
76 See, for instance, Slabbert, *Afrikaner Afrikaan*, pp 1–7.
77 *Sunday Star*, 9 February 1986, 'The two men in politics' day of high drama'.
78 M Weber, 'Politics as a profession', in HH Gerth and CW Mills (eds), *From Max Weber: Essays in Sociology*, Routledge, London, 1970, p 27.
79 Giliomee Collection, Unsorted, Zille to Giliomee, 17 May 2013.
80 Ibid.
81 Stellenbosch University Library, Slabbert Collection, 430.X1, Unpublished memorandum by Slabbert on why he resigned as party leader, August 1986.
82 *Beeld*, 21 February 1986, 'Nie politikus genoeg' (translated).
83 *Financial Mail*, 21 February 1986, 'It's incomprehensible'.
84 Quoted in Du Preez, *Pale Native*, p 144.
85 *The Citizen*, 15 February, 'Life pensions for ex-PFP MPs'; see also *The Star*, 14 February 1986, 'A profitable parting for PFP MPs'; *Die Burger*, 14 February 1986, 'Ruim pensioene vir 2 Progge'.
86 Slabbert, *Other Side of History*, p 48.
87 Boraine, *Life in Transition*, p 132; see also *The Citizen*, 12 February 1986, 'Slabbert's options'.
88 Eglin, *Crossing Borders*, pp 217–218.
89 Ibid, p 218.
90 Ibid, p 217; Suzman, *In No Uncertain Terms*, p 254.
91 Stellenbosch University Library, Slabbert Collection, 430.C.226, Suzman to Slabbert, 9 March 1986.
92 Du Preez, *Pale Native*, p 145.
93 Cassar, 'Slabbert', p 22; see also Chapter 2.
94 *Sunday Star*, 2 March 1986, 'Time to stop bashing Van'.
95 *Cape Argus*, 20 March 1986, 'Hell has no fury like a political party scorned'.
96 Boraine, *Life in Transition*, p 129; Stellenbosch University Library, Slabbert Collection, 430.C.71.1 and 2, Gibson to Slabbert, 19 February 1986; and Slabbert to Gibson, 14 March 1986.
97 *Sunday Times*, 9 February 1986, 'PFP's R10-m Slabbert Trust will keep going'; *Sunday Times*, 9 February 1986, 'The PFP, alone in a hot kitchen'.
98 Stellenbosch University Library, Slabbert Collection, 430.X1, Unpublished memorandum by Slabbert on why he resigned as party leader, August 1986.
99 David Welsh Collection, Unsorted, 'Minutes of a meeting held at Dr Van Zyl Slabbert's house', 3 February 1986.
100 Eglin, *Crossing Borders*, p 219; Wits University, Cullen Library, Historical Papers, PFP Papers, AG 883, Af.5, Council meeting, 25 February 1986.
101 Quoted from an interview with Neil Ross, 30 August 1993 in Hughes, 'Political liberalism', p 137.
102 *Frontline*, September–October 1986, 'New hope for nice guys'.
103 Hughes, 'Political liberalism', pp 138–144.

104 Ibid, p 145.
105 *Leadership SA*, May 1987, 'The 1987 election'.
106 Compare Shandler, 'Structural crisis', pp 151–152.
107 *Die Burger*, 11 February 1986, 'Kans vir SA se vyande'; *Oosterlig*, 10 February 1986, "'n Ondiens aan SA'; *Die Burger*, 18 February 1986, 'Bedankings knou hervorming'.
108 For example *City Press*, 10 February 1986, 'Follow Van out'; *Sowetan*, 10 February 1986, 'Three Hours that rocked Parliament'.
109 Quoted in Slabbert, *Other Side of History*, pp 47–48.
110 Ibid, p 48.
111 Slabbert, *System and the Struggle*, p 100.
112 *Beeld*, 15 May 2010, 'As hy in die parlement gebly het, kon hy nóg meer bereik het – FW'.
113 K Owen, 'The man who wasn't there', in *The Passion for Reason*, p 135.

Chapter 7

1 H Orbon, 'Frederik van Zyl Slabbert, the dialogue programmed on Cold Comfort and the pitfalls of ideology', unpublished paper, undated, p 10.
2 Giliomee, 'Golden boy', in *The Passion for Reason*, pp 100–101.
3 Slabbert, 'Incremental change or revolution?' in Butler, Elphick and Welsh (eds), *Democratic Liberalism*, p 402; see also *Sunday Independent*, 16 May 2010, 'All I had to fall back on was my own conviction: I went ahead'.
4 Thakur and Vale, '"Negotiations in South Africa"', p 4; see also S Friedman, 'The ambiguous legacy of liberalism', in P Vale, L Hamilton and E Prinsloo (eds), *Intellectual Traditions in South Africa: Ideas, Individuals and Institutions*, University of KwaZulu-Natal Press, Pietermaritzburg, 2014, pp 42 and 45.
5 *Business Day*, 17 June 2010, 'Debate liberalism to serve Slabbert's memory' (written by Steven Friedman).
6 Orbon, 'Slabbert', p 9.
7 Giliomee, *Last Afrikaner Leaders*, pp 236–237.
8 *Cape Times*, 9 February 1986, 'I'll pursue negotiation outside Parliament'.
9 F van Zyl Slabbert, 'The struggle for a non-racial democratic South Africa', in M Swilling (ed), *Views on the South African State*, HSRC, Pretoria, 1990, pp 80–81.
10 Slabbert, *System and the Struggle*, pp 90–91.
11 Stellenbosch University Library, Slabbert Collection, 430.E2.14.3, 'Politics and resource utilisation', 1985.
12 Wilmot James, tribute to Slabbert, blog post, idasa.wordpress.com, 14 May 2010, accessed 8 May 2019.
13 Boraine, *Life in Transition*, pp 137–138.
14 Ibid, p 139.
15 Slabbert, *Afrikaner Afrikaan*, pp 33–34.
16 A Boraine, 'A democratic alternative: A brief history of IDASA', in I Liebenberg, F Lortan, B Nel and G van der Westhuizen (eds), *The Long March: The Story of the Struggle for Liberation in South Africa*. Kagiso-HAUM, Pretoria, 1994, p 205.
17 Slabbert, *Afrikaner Afrikaan*, p 34.
18 Boraine, 'A democratic alternative', p 206; see also Boraine, *Life in Transition*, p 143.
19 *Sunday Times*, 16 November 1986, 'Slabbert: This is how our new initiative hopes to get democracy to work for all South Africans'.
20 Stellenbosch University Library, Slabbert Collection, 430.E2.24.1, 'Idasa and

NOTES

opposition politics', May 1988; Boraine, *Life in Transition*, p 145.
21 S Gupta and A Kellman, 'Democracy organizations in political transitions: IDASA and the new South Africa' in M Mutua (ed), *Human Rights NGOs in East Africa: Political and Normative Tensions*, University of Pennsylvania Press, Philadelphia, 2008, p 284.
22 Stellenbosch University, Idasa Documentation, 443.A5 (11/5A), Confidential Report Idasa Workshop, 23 April 1988.
23 Gupta and Kellman, 'IDASA', pp 185–186.
24 Quoted in G Leach, *The Afrikaners: Their Last Great Trek*, Southern Book Publishers, Johannesburg, 1989, p 149.
25 Quoted in P Hugo, 'Towards darkness and death: Racial demonology', in P Hugo (ed), *South African Perspectives: Essays in Honour of Nic Olivier*, Unisa Press, Pretoria, 1989, p 239.
26 A Fisher and A Abeldas (eds), *A Question of Survival: Conversations with Key South Africans*, Jonathan Ball, Johannesburg, 1987, p 426 (emphasis in the original).
27 Boraine, 'Amalgam', in *The Passion for Reason*, p 44.
28 Boraine, *Life in Transition*, p 140; *Sunday Times*, 16 May 2010, 'Frederik van Zyl Slabbert: Afrikaner revolutionary'.
29 Boraine, *Life in Transition*, p 144.
30 *The Star*, 9 September 1987, 'Dissatisfied Idasa man gives notice'.
31 Peter Vale, one of the first board members, mentioned in passing, during an interview in 2017 with M Oelofsen, that there was some tension between Slabbert and Boraine.
32 James, tribute to Slabbert, blog post, idasa.wordpress.com, 14 May 2010.
33 *Die Volksblad*, 20 November 1986, 'Politieke koppelaar'.
34 Quoted in Leach, *Afrikaners*, p 148.
35 Boraine, *Life in Transition*, p 140.
36 I Taylor, 'South Africa's transition to democracy and the "change" industry', in *Politikon – South African Journal of Political Studies*, 29(1) (2002), p 44; see also M Swilling, 'The dynamics of reform', in A Callinicos (ed), *Between Apartheid and Capitalism*, Bookmarks, London, 1992, pp 43–44; M Barker, 'George Soros and South Africa's elite transition', blog post, swans.com, 31 May 2010, accessed 14 May 2019; on Slabbert's relationship with Soros, see *Other Side of History*, pp 113–126.
37 Slabbert, *Afrikaner Afrikaan*, p 15.
38 Stellenbosch University, Idasa Documentation, 443.A5 (11/5A), Confidential Report Idasa Workshop, 23 April 1988.
39 Fisher and Abeldas (eds), *A Question of Survival*, p 428.
40 Stellenbosch University Library, Slabbert Collection, 430.H3.45, Exclusive interview with Tos Wentzel, July 1987.
41 Slabbert, *Afrikaner Afrikaan*, p 35 (translated).
42 *Die Suid-Afrikaan*, February 1990, 'Van Dakar tot Parys; die verskille'.
43 Stellenbosch University Library, Slabbert Collection, 430.H3.45, Exclusive interview with Tos Wentzel, July 1987; see also Leach, *The Afrikaners*, p 149.
44 Stellenbosch University Library, Slabbert Collection, 430.H3.45, Exclusive interview with Tos Wentzel, July 1987; Slabbert, *Afrikaner Afrikaan*, p 38.
45 Stellenbosch University Library, Slabbert Collection, 430.H3.45, Exclusive interview with Tos Wentzel, July 1987.
46 *Insig*, 27, 31 December 2004, 'Die Pad na Dakar' (translated); see also Boraine, *Life in Transition*, p 148.

47 Stellenbosch University Library, Slabbert Collection, 430.H3.11.1, Slabbert to Mbeki, 10 June 1987.
48 Stellenbosch University Library, Slabbert Collection, 430.H3.4, Slabbert to Breytenbach, 1 March 1987 (translated).
49 *Insig*, 27, 31 December 2004, 'Die Pad na Dakar'.
50 Ibid; Boraine, *Life in Transition*, p 149.
51 Stellenbosch University Library, Slabbert Collection, 430.H3.25.6, H Giliomee, 'The ANC, Afrikaners and a baboon', unpublished manuscript, undated, p 1; H Giliomee, 'True Confessions, End Papers and the Dakar conference: A review of political arguments', *Tydskrif vir Letterkunde*, 46(2) (2009), p 33; *Oosterlig*, 8 July 1987, 'Kyk hoe lyk dié safari'.
52 *Insig*, 27, 31 December 2004, 'Die Pad na Dakar'; see also *De Kat*, 30 September 1987, 'Dakar'.
53 Stellenbosch University Library, Slabbert Collection, 430.H3.19.3, Slabbert to Piet Muller, 10 August 1987; *Business Day*, 18 July 1987, 'That's showbiz?'.
54 Quoted in Leach, *The Afrikaners*, p 153.
55 *Rapport*, 12 July 1987, 'Stilte voor Dakar storm'; *Cape Times*, 4 July 1987, 'Govt silent on new ANC talks'; *Die Burger*, 9 July 1987, 'Fiasko volg fiasko op Dorsland-trek van Slabbert se linkses'; *Die Transvaler*, 14 July 1987, 'Stappe kom dalk ná ANC-beraad'; *The Nationalist*, 30 September 1987, 'Dakar: Action pending'; Gevisser, *Thabo Mbeki*, p 513.
56 Slabbert, *Afrikaner Afrikaan*, p 38.
57 *Frontline*, 31 July 1987, 'The human face of Dakar'.
58 *Insig*, 31 December 2004, 'Paartie met die totale aanslag' (translated).
59 *Weekend Argus*, 11 July 1987, 'Dateline Dakar'; *De Kat*, 30 September 1987, 'Dakar'; M du Preez, *Dwars: Mymeringe van 'n gebleikte Afrikaan*, Zebra Press, Cape Town, 2009, p 191.
60 *Insig*, 31 December 2004, 'Paartie met die totale aanslag' (translated).
61 Gevisser, *Thabo Mbeki*, p 511.
62 Quoted in *Die Burger*, 22 June 2017, 'Die ander kant van Dakar' (translated).
63 Stellenbosch University Library, B 33215, Patti Waldmeir Interviews, interview with Slabbert, 24 November 1994, pp 27–28; see also Du Preez, *Dwars*, pp 195–196 for a fuller description.
64 Leach, *The Afrikaners*, p 161.
65 *Mail & Guardian*, 4 October 2007, 'Sustaining the spirit of Dakar'.
66 Gevisser, *Thabo Mbeki*, p 510.
67 RW Johnson, *Foreign Native: An African Journey*, Jonathan Ball, Johannesburg, 2020, p 231. Johnson was informed of this by a close friend of Mbeki's at Sussex.
68 *Weekly Mail*, 10 July 1987, 'A long way from home: a small step closer to hope'.
69 Giliomee, *Last Afrikaner Leaders*, p 232.
70 Leach, *The Afrikaners*, p 246; Du Preez, *Dwars*, pp 196–198; Giliomee, *Last Afrikaner Leaders*, p 231; H Giliomee, *Historian: An Autobiography*, Tafelberg, Cape Town, 2016, p 166; Mayibue Archives, University of Western Cape, ANC Documentation, 1987 (1 a), Notes on Paris-Dakar Meeting.
71 Giliomee, 'True Confessions', p 33.
72 *Weekend Argus*, 11 July 1987, 'Slabbert'.
73 B Shapiro, 'Performing "middlingness": Frederik van Zyl Slabbert and the South African transition', *Quarterly Bulletin of the National Library of South Africa*, 67(4) (December 2013), p 186.
74 Giliomee, *Last Afrikaner Leaders*, p 233.

NOTES

75 Interview with Hermann Giliomee, 8 May 2019.
76 Slabbert, *Other Side of History*, p 50.
77 *Pretoria News*, 20 July 1987, 'AWB waits in vain for Idasa group'; *Cape Times*, 22 July 1987, 'Airport ruckus, Dakar group diverted by police'; J du Rand, *Protes-stem, Oomblikke van herinnering*, Bybelkor, Wellington, 2016, p 200.
78 W Esterhuyse, *Endgame: Secret Talks and the End of Apartheid*, Tafelberg, Cape Town, 2012, p 34.
79 *The Star*, 1 August 1987, 'Slabbert: Talking is useless if it was ANC'.
80 *The Citizen*, 1 August 1987, 'Pathetic'.
81 *The Citizen*, 6 August 1987, 'Height Street Diary'.
82 *Cape Times*, 14 August 1987, 'Ongoing violence doesn't make Dakar a failure'.
83 *Die Burger*, 1 August 1987, 'Weersin teen geweld gaan SA linkses nou 'n baie lang tyd tref'.
84 Slabbert, *Afrikaner Afrikaan*, pp 79–80.
85 Stellenbosch University Library, Slabbert Collection, 430.H3.47.5, Conference Statement, July 1987; see also 'South Africa and negotiating in politics: Myths and prospects', *South Africa International*, October 1987, p 98.
86 *Weekend Argus*, 11 July 1997, 'Slabbert'.
87 *Weekly Mail*, 30 July 1987, 'We started riding a donkey and ended on a tiger'.
88 *Insig*, 30 September 2001, 'Potch se bontrok-bul' (translated); see also *Beeld*, 16 October 2010, 'Kyk net hoe lei so 'n dominee'.
89 Stellenbosch University Library, Slabbert Collection, 430.H3.35.1, L du Plessis to Slabbert, 10 August 1987; 430.H3.43.1, J van der Westhuizen to Slabbert, 3 December 1987; 430.H3.18.1, A Odendaal to Slabbert, 13 July 1987; *Die Burger*, 14 July 1990, 'Flieks is spieëls vir Van Rensburg'.
90 Stellenbosch University Library, Slabbert Collection, 430.H3.18.1, Slabbert to Odendaal, 2 September 1987.
91 For example, *Beeld*, 17 May 2010, 'Slabbert: Skerp van intellek en ruim van gees'.
92 *Cape Times*, 3 July 1997, 'Dakar connection to the new politics'.
93 W van Vuuren, 'The meaning of Dakar', in *The Dakar Reports: Responses from 16 Delegates to the Dakar Conference*, Idasa Occasional Papers, 11 (1987), p 28.
94 I Liebenberg, *Dakar – reflections on a conference*, unpublished paper, ResearchGate, 17 September 2017.
95 *Die Burger*, 31 March 2007, 'Breyten Breytenbach'.
96 Stellenbosch University Library, Patti Waldmeier Interviews, 332.05 (2), interview with Niël Barnard, 25 November 1994.
97 M Savage, 'The Dakar talks and meetings between South Africans and the ANC in exile, 1983–2000', unpublished manuscript, June 2016; and M Savage, 'Trekking outward: A chronology of meetings between South Africans and the ANC in exile, 1983–2000', unpublished manuscript, 2017; see also *Die Burger*, 30 January 2010, 'Méér as "bruikbare idiote"'.
98 *Die Suid-Afrikaan*, 30 April 1995, 'Die "Insiders" se "inside" storie' (translated).
99 Stellenbosch University Library, Patti Waldmeier Interviews, 332.05, interview with Niël Barnard, 25 November 1994; M Savage, 'Trekking outward', p 13.
100 Stellenbosch University Library, Patti Waldmeier Interviews, 332.05, interview with Mike Louw, 29 May 1995.
101 Quoted in Du Preez, *Dwars*, p 214.
102 Stellenbosch University Library, Patti Waldmeier Interviews, 332.05, interview with Mike Louw, 29 May 1995; for more detail on the inner workings of the government and ANC responses, see Esterhuyse, *Endgame*, pp 34–35;

M Spaarwater, *A Spook's Progress: From Making War to Making Peace*, Zebra Press, Cape Town, 2012, pp 71–72.
103 W Esterhuyse and G van Niekerk, *Die Tronkgesprekke*, Tafelberg, Cape Town, 2018, p 203.
104 Compare D Lieberfeld, 'Evaluating the contributions of two-track diplomacy to conflict termination in South Africa, 1984–90', *Journal of Peace Research*, 39 (3 May 2002), p 370.
105 U van der Heyden, *Der Dakar-prozess: Der Anfang vom Ende der Apartheid in Südafrika*, Solivagus, Kiel, 2018, p 15 (translated).
106 *Cape Argus*, 4 August 1987, 'Slabbert slams "hysterical" reaction to Dakar'.
107 Ibid.
108 Slabbert, *Afrikaner Afrikaan*, p 38; *Cape Argus*, 13 July 1987, 'Dakar talks a great meeting of minds'.
109 Esterhuyse, *Endgame*, p 35.
110 Compare *Insig*, 31 December 2004, 'Die Pad na Dakar'.
111 *Sunday Independent*, 16 May 2010, 'All I had to fall back on was my own conviction: I went ahead'.
112 Slabbert, *Afrikaner Afrikaan*, p 38.
113 Shapiro, 'Performing "middlingness"', p 189.
114 Esterhuyse states that elements in the NIS thought that he was driven by a need for political power; see Esterhuyse, *Endgame*, p 35.
115 Adam and Moodley, 'Slabbert's opening of the apartheid mind', in *The Passion for Reason*, p 58.
116 Slabbert, *Other Side of History*, p 86; Du Preez, *Dwars*, p 219.
117 Stellenbosch University Library, Slabbert Collection, 430.2.1.2.9, 'Diary for 1988'.
118 *Sunday Independent*, 3 August 1997, 'Ten years on, new fears seize the brave Afrikaner trekkers of Dakar'.
119 *Rapport*, 3 August 1997, 'ANC skuif die fokus só weg van die parlement'.
120 Ibid; *Cape Times*, 16 June 1997, 'Together as new Voortrekkers'.
121 *Sunday Independent*, 3 August 1997, 'Ten years on, new fears seize the brave Afrikaner trekkers of Dakar'.
122 J Brits, 'Thabo Mbeki and the Afrikaners, 1986–2004', *Historia*, 53(2) (November 2008), pp 66–68.
123 *Die Burger*, 14 July 2007, 'Wat ek nog wou gesê het'.
124 *Die Burger*, 31 March 2007, 'Breytenbach' (translated).
125 *Daily Dispatch*, 30 July 2007, 'Dazed by the revolution'.
126 *Die Burger*, 26 June 2017, 'Verraaiers lei land'; see also *Die Burger*, 26 June 2017, 'Dakar-reünie: Vuurwarm debat oor Afrikaans'.
127 Author's personal observation, recorded as a guest during the discussions.
128 Giliomee, *Last Afrikaner Leaders*, p 235.
129 Stellenbosch University Library, Slabbert Collection, 430.07.3, Academic Freedom Lecture, UCT, 2003; Lawrence Schlemmer was also struck by the degree to which the ANC was wedded to the armed struggle; see L Schlemmer, in *The Dakar Reports*, p 25.

Chapter 8

1 Slabbert, *Afrikaner Afrikaan*, p 111.
2 *Die Transvaler*, 15 November 1989, 'Slabbert gee FW krediet vir stappe'.
3 FvZ Slabbert, 'Negotiating reconciliation', in K Asmal, D Chidester and WG

NOTES

     James (eds), *Nelson Mandela: From Freedom to the Future – Tributes and Speeches*, Jonathan Ball, Johannesburg, 2003, p 98.
4   Stellenbosch University, IDASA collection, AG 883/D6, Slabbert address to Five Freedoms Forum, 26 August 1990.
5   Johnson, 'Van Zyl Slabbert: What went wrong?'
6   Stellenbosch University Library, Slabbert Collection, 430.E1.6.1, Slabbert writing from All Souls College, Oxford, 15 February 1990.
7   *Insig*, June 1997, 'FW' (translated).
8   Slabbert, 'Negotiating reconciliation', p 99.
9   Stellenbosch University Library, Slabbert Collection, 430.E1.7.1, 'The causes of transition in South Africa', 19 June 1990.
10   H Adam, K Moodley and FvZ Slabbert, *Comrades in Business: Post-Liberation Politics in South Africa*, Tafelberg, Cape Town, 1997, p 52; although the chapter upon which this is based appears without an author's name, it is most likely that it was written by Slabbert or that he, at the very least, would have agreed with the exposition; see also Stellenbosch University, D Joubert Collection, unsorted, 'Notes on "Comrades in business"', note 35; and Stellenbosch University Library, Slabbert Collection, 430.E1.7.1, 'The causes of transition in South Africa', 19 June 1990.
11   Giliomee, *Last Afrikaner Leaders*, p 238.
12   Stellenbosch University Library, Slabbert Collection, 430.E5.1, 'FW de Klerk', 1998 (translated).
13   Ibid.
14   FvZ Slabbert, *The Quest for Democracy: South Africa in Transition*, Penguin, Johannesburg, 1992, p 103.
15   Compare Giliomee, 'Golden boy', in *The Passion for Reason*, pp 110–111; Hermann Giliomee, email to author, 11 June 2019; for unguided changes during the 1980s, see J Kane-Berman, *South Africa's Silent Revolution*, South African Institute of Race Relations, Johannesburg, 1990, pp 1–19 and *passim*.
16   *Sunday Tribune*, 21 April 1990, 'Van Zyl Slabbert not keen on middleman job, but he'll muck in'.
17   *Rapport*, 14 July 2007, 'Twee deftige here'; Slabbert, *Afrikaner Afrikaan*, p 83.
18   Giliomee *Last Afrikaner Leaders* p 238; see also Stellenbosch University Library, Slabbert Collection, 430.D6.3.3, 'Jan Smuts Memorial Lecture', July 1992; Stellenbosch University Library, Slabbert Collection, 430.H1.6.1, 'Democracy: A vision for the future', November 1991.
19   Stellenbosch University Library, Slabbert Collection, 430.Z.2. (48), Mark Behr, 'Anchor man or Super Van?', 1992.
20   Slabbert, *The Quest for Democracy*, p 3.
21   *Rapport*, 8 March 2020, 'Die DA en die R woord'; email from D Kotzé, 9 March 2020.
22   R Verbuyst, 'History, historians and the South African Truth and Reconciliation Commission', *New Contree*, 66 (July 2013), pp 1–26.
23   Slabbert, *Afrikaner Afrikaan*, pp 111–118.
24   *Insig*, May 1998, 'Ons stories poëties vertel' (translated).
25   Peter Vale, email to author, 17 June 2019; Vale worked with Boraine on Idasa's first board.
26   *Insig*, May 1998, 'Ons stories poëties vertel'.
27   Stellenbosch University Library, Slabbert Collection, 430.Z.2. (48), Mark Behr, 'Anchor man or Super Van?', 1992.
28   *The Star*, 28 May 2010, 'Van Zyl helped unify SA cricket'.
29   Stellenbosch University Library, Slabbert Collection, 430.Z.2. (48), Mark Behr, 'Anchor man or Super Van?', 1992.

30 Slabbert, *Other Side of History*, p 91.
31 *Die Volksblad*, 26 October 1991, 'Basiese dienste van politiek geskei'; Slabbert, *Other Side of History* p 93; Stellenbosch University Library, Slabbert Collection, 430.E4.6.5, Slabbert to E Bulbring, 6 September 1991; *Die Suid Afrikaan*, October/November 1992, 'Barskyk'.
32 Stellenbosch University Library, Slabbert Collection, 430.Z.2. (48), Mark Behr, 'Anchor man or Super Van?', 1992
33 *Business Day*, 27 May 2010, 'Xolela Mangcu: Slabbert had a true mark of a historic leader'.
34 Stellenbosch University Library, Slabbert Collection, 430.Z.2. (48), Mark Behr, 'Anchor man or Super Van?', 1992.
35 Slabbert *Tough Choices* p 110; see also Slabbert, *Other Side of History*, pp 93–96; for Slabbert's correspondence with De Klerk on the composition of the board, see Stellenbosch University Library, Slabbert Collection, 430.T3.4, Slabbert to De Klerk, 4 June 1993.
36 Slabbert, *Tough Choices*, p 111.
37 J Matisonn, *God, Spies and Lies: Finding South Africa's Future Through its Past*, Missing Ink, Cape Town, 2015, p 259.
38 *Vrye Weekblad*, 25 June 1993, 'Oor skuimbekke, kruisvaarders en lapelvreters' (translated).
39 Slabbert, *Other Side of History*, p 96.
40 *Vrye Weekblad*, 25 June 1993, 'Oor skuimbekke, kruisvaarders en lapelvreters'.
41 *Rapport*, 22 October 1995, 'Jy kyk nou na 'n man wat wat van binne bloei' (translated).
42 Stellenbosch University Library, Slabbert Collection, 430.R.2.12, Slabbert to Roelf Meyer, 3 July 1995.
43 *Rapport*, 27 July 2002, 'Leon se voorstelle vir nuwe kiesstelsel na Slabbert-span'; see also Stellenbosch University Library, Slabbert Collection, 430.E3.9.1, 'Die kiesstelsel en politieke verandering in Suid-Afrika', 2007.
44 Stellenbosch University Library, Slabbert Collection, 430.R.5.1, Slabbert to Buthelezi, 21 June 2001.
45 Slabbert, *Other Side of History*, p 106.
46 Stellenbosch University Library, Slabbert Collection, 430.E3.9.1, 'Die kiesstelsel en politieke verandering in Suid-Afrika', 2007; A Boraine, *What's Gone Wrong?*, pp 70–71.
47 K Asmal, *Politics in My Blood: A Memoir*, Jacana, 2011, pp 123–124.
48 Slabbert, *Other Side of History*, pp 105, 107.
49 Boraine, *What's Gone Wrong?*, p 69.
50 C Botha, 'Time for electoral reform and dusting off the Van Zyl Slabbert Report', politicsweb, 22 May 2019, accessed 8 May 2020.
51 *Die Burger*, 13 June 2020, 'Herbekyk van Kieswet welkom'.
52 *Rapport*, 22 October 1995, 'Jy kyk nou na 'n man wat wat van binne bloei'.
53 Slabbert, *Other Side of History*, p 57.
54 Slabbert, *Tough Choices*, pp 105–106.
55 *The Citizen*, 21 December 2002, 'Our goal should be to open up the future for all'.
56 Slabbert, *Other Side of History*, p 51.
57 I Filatova and A Davidson, *The Hidden Thread: Russia and South Africa in the Soviet Era*, Jonathan Ball, Johannesburg, 2013, p 435.
58 V Shubin, *ANC: A View from Moscow*, Jacana, Johannesburg, 2008, p 277.
59 Giliomee, *Last Afrikaner Leaders*, p 242.

NOTES

60 Adam, Moodley and Slabbert, *Comrades in Business*, p 83; see also Giliomee, *Last Afrikaner Leaders*, p 240.
61 Adam, Moodley and Slabbert, *Comrades in Business*, p 84.
62 Ibid.
63 R Renwick, *Helen Suzman: Bright Star in a Dark Chamber*, Jonathan Ball, Johannesburg, 2014, pp 90–91.
64 Interview with Max du Preez, 30 July 2019.
65 Slabbert, *Tough Choices*, p 108.
66 Stellenbosch University Library, Slabbert Collection, 430.Z.2(12/2), Transcript from Classic FM interview, 2007.
67 *The Star*, 23 May 1989, 'Slabbert asked to stand for DP'; *Eastern Province Herald*, 7 June 1989, 'Keeping out of it'.
68 T Leon, *On the Contrary: Leading the Opposition in a Democratic South Africa*. Jonathan Ball, Johannesburg, 2009, pp 302–303.
69 *Insig*, May 1999, 'Nelson Mandela' (translated).
70 Slabbert, *Afrikaner Afrikaan*, p 99.
71 Slabbert, *Other Side of History*, p 122.
72 Stellenbosch University Library, Slabbert Collection, 430.E3.11.1, 'Mandela: He who reduced the complexity of transition and made its rewards accessible to South Africans', 25 September 2007.
73 Slabbert, *Other Side of History*, p 58.
74 Adam and Moodley, 'Portrait', in *The Passion for Reason*, p 68.
75 Interview, W Esterhuyse, 21 July 2019.
76 Gevisser, *Thabo Mbeki*, for example p 499.
77 *Business Day*, 21 June 2010, 'Slabbert's political career cut short at great cost to all SA'.
78 Adam and Moodley, 'Portrait', in *The Passion for Reason*, p 71.
79 Johnson, *Foreign Native*, p 206.
80 Compare Gevisser, *Thabo Mbeki*, pp 61–63.
81 A Sparks, *Beyond the Miracle: Inside the New South Africa*, Jonathan Ball, Johannesburg, 2003, p 259.
82 Nelson Mandela Centre of Memory, Patrick O'Malley Archives, interview with Slabbert, 4 September 2002.
83 Stellenbosch University Library, Slabbert Collection, 430.E3.2.1, ''n Waardering van die bydrae van Thabo Mbeki tot die politiek in Suid-Afrika', 2 November 2008 (translated).
84 *Cape Argus*, 12 July 2007, 'Mbeki man in clash with Van Zyl Slabbert'.
85 *Beeld*, 12 July 2007, 'Oud-segsman van Mbeki looi Van Zyl Slabbert'.
86 *Beeld*, 15 May 2010, 'Hy en Mbeki sou versoen'.
87 Slabbert, *Other Side of History*, pp 11–13.
88 Adam and Moodley, 'Portrait', in *The Passion for Reason*, p 70.
89 Slabbert, *Other Side of History*, p 127.
90 Ibid, pp 127–128; interview with Tania Slabbert, 15 July 2019.
91 Slabbert, *Afrikaner Afrikaan*, p 133.
92 *Sunday Times*, 8 November 1998, 'Slabbert gets down to some real business'; see also Slabbert, *Afrikaner Afrikaan*, p 135.
93 *The Star*, 19 April 2001, 'Van Zyl condemns *The Citizen* for report on Mbeki's alleged womanising'; interview with Max du Preez, 30 July 2015.
94 Slabbert, *Other Side of History*, p 135.

95 Ibid, pp 133, 135, 137.
96 Slabbert, *Afrikaner Afrikaan*, p 135.
97 Interview with Mike Savage, 9 September 2017.
98 *Insig*, March 2000, 'As jy dink aan al daai spermselle … en hier is ek nou sestig jaar later'.
99 *Rapport*, 15 April 2001, 'Klein eiland word sentrum van denke en kultuur'.
100 Ibid; Slabbert, *Other Side of History*, p 87.
101 Slabbert, *Afrikaner Afrikaan*, pp 42–43.
102 Ibid, p 43.
103 Slabbert, *Other Side of History*, pp 88–89.
104 B Breytenbach, 'The slow quickness of life *(Thinking about my friend, the Chief)*', in *The Passion for Reason*, p 17.
105 Interview with Tania Slabbert, 15 July 2019; see also *Die Suid-Afrikaan*, February–March 1991, '15 maande in die hart van Senegal'.
106 Slabbert, *Other Side of History*, p 119; see also Slabbert, *Afrikaner Afrikaan*, p 44.
107 Slabbert, *Afrikaner Afrikaan*, p 45.
108 M Savage, 'Ice, steam and water: Non-profit organisations in South Africa', in *The Passion for Reason*, p 178.

Chapter 9

1 *Woord en Daad*, November 1979, 'Die PFP en sy nuwe leierskap' (translated).
2 Quoted in Giliomee, *Last Afrikaner Leaders*, p 213.
3 J Stutje, 'Historiographical and theoretical aspects of Weber's concept of charismatic leadership', in J Stutje (ed), *Charismatic Leadership and Social Movements*, Berghahn Books, Amsterdam, 2012, p 8.
4 *The Times* (London), 26 September 1980, 'The man facing Mr Botha'; G Evans, 'Frederik van Zyl Slabbert: Politician and activist in the vanguard of the struggle against apartheid', independent.co.uk, 19 May 2010, accessed 8 May 2020.
5 *Rand Daily Mail*, 2 March 1982, 'Sheila thinks Fredrik is nice'.
6 Private Collection, Hermann Giliomee correspondence, JM Coetzee to H Giliomee, 2010.
7 *Sunday Times*, 30 October 1983, 'Dr Slabbert looking for closing time'.
8 Private collection, Hermann Giliomee correspondence, RW Johnson to H Giliomee, 2010.
9 Gevisser, *Thabo Mbeki*, p 497.
10 *Sunday Times*, 19 April 1981, 'The man who guides ordinary people'.
11 P Cassar Collection, Tape recording of Slabbert's speech in Bloemfontein, 22 October 1982.
12 H Giliomee, 'Golden boy', in *The Passion for Reason*, p 90.
13 P Cassar Collection, Tape-recorded interview with Slabbert, 29 September 1981.
14 Swart, *Progressive Odyssey*, p 157.
15 *Daily Dispatch*, 24 July 1974, 'PFP star'.
16 *Die Volksblad*, 3 December 1982, 'Slabbert' (translated).
17 *The Star*, 18 October 1985, 'Reforms forced on government'.
18 Email from Jonathan Ball, 20 February 2020.
19 P Cassar Collection, Taped interview with Neil Ross, PFP organiser, 2 October 1981.
20 *Die Matie*, 8 August 1986, 'Die "rugger bugger" wat weggebreek het' (translated); see also Giliomee, 'Golden boy', in *The Passion for Reason*, p 90; Slabbert, *Last*

NOTES

White Parliament, pp 20–21; *Die Burger*, 23 May 2008, 'Slabbert kom huis toe'; see also Chapter 1.
21. Stellenbosch University Library, Slabbert Collection, 430.A.26, R Carlson to Ian Jones, 4 September 1990.
22. Grundlingh, *Potent Pastimes*, pp 67–68.
23. Stellenbosch University Library, Slabbert Collection, 430.A.22.1, J Buys to Slabbert, undated (translated).
24. See, for example, *Rand Daily Mail*, 28 April 1981, 'The "Slabbert factor" faces its most important test'.
25. *Sunday Tribune*, 3 June 1982, 'How to become a comrade painfully but innocently'.
26. Ibid.
27. JM Howell and B Shamir, 'The role of followers in the charismatic leadership process: Relationships and their consequences', *The Academy of Management Review*, 30(1) (2005), p 99.
28. Ibid.
29. Weber, 'Politics as a vocation', in Gerth and Mills (eds), *From Weber*, p 2.
30. Hermann Giliomee Collection, H Giliomee to C van Onselen, undated, and L Schlemmer to H Giliomee, undated.
31. *Kerkbode*, 4 June 2010, 'Van Zyl Slabbert – 'n man so na aan God se hart'.
32. Stellenbosch University Library, Slabbert Collection, 430.D4.32.1, 'Sê nou maar', Oudtshoorn, March 1999.
33. *Deurbraak*, October/November, 1979 (translated).
34. Stellenbosch University Library, Slabbert Collection, 430.E1.4.1, 'Time to Bury the Great White Hope', 27 June 1988.
35. Stellenbosch University Library, Slabbert Collection, 430.22.48.1, Mark Behr, 'Anchor man or Super Van?' 1992.
36. Quoted in NJ Rhoodie, 'Importance of the eastern European democratic movement for change in South Africa', in JL Olivier (ed), *Eastern Europe and South Africa: Implications for the Future*, HSRC, Pretoria, 1990, p 57.
37. Stellenbosch University Library, Slabbert Collection, 430.E3.17.3, Breytenbach to Slabbert, 22 March 2007 (translated).
38. WB Vosloo, 'The nature of the Afrikaner people and the challenges facing Afrikaner nationalism', 'Race and politics in South Africa: a series of lectures given at the 1973 UCT Summer School', pp 2–5.
39. Slabbert, *Tough Choices*, p 88.
40. Adam and Moodley, 'Portrait', in *The Passion for Reason*, p 58.
41. Stellenbosch University Library, Slabbert Collection, 430.E2.22.7.1, 'Barskyk'.
42. Giliomee, *Last Afrikaner Leaders*, p 214.
43. Stellenbosch University Library, Dian Joubert Collection, unsorted, Mana Slabbert to Dian Joubert, 24 January 1974.
44. Slabbert, *Tough Choices*, p 88.
45. Stellenbosch University Library, Slabbert Collection, 430.D4.22.2, 'Afrikaner – Quo Vadis: Die Afrikaner: Nou en en die Toekoms', 1999.
46. Slabbert, *Afrikaner Afrikaan*, p 6 (translated).
47. *City Press*, 2 August 1987, 'Slabbert wants to meet Eugene'.
48. Stellenbosch University Library, Slabbert Collection, 430.E1.3, 'Article for Andre Brink', 1 December 1987.
49. *The Citizen*, 22 September 1988, 'Full house for Terre'Blanche, Slabbert clash'.
50. Stellenbosch University Library, Slabbert Collection, 430.D4.22.2, 'Afrikaner – Quo Vadis: Die Afrikaner: Nou en en die Toekoms', 1999.

51 Slabbert, *Other Side of History*, p 2.
52 FvZ Slabbert, 'Is Academic Freedom Still an Issue in the New South Africa?', TB Davie Memorial Lecture, University of Cape Town, October 2003, news.uct.ac.za, accessed 1 June 2020.
53 *Die Suid-Afrikaan*, Winter 1986, 'Hermann Giliomee in gesprek met Van Zyl Slabbert'.
54 *Rapport*, 5 May 1974, 'Van Zyl Slabbert, voel jy tuis daar?' (translated).
55 Giliomee, 'Golden boy', in *The Passion for Reason*, p 90.
56 See for example, *House of Assembly Debates*, 18 April 1975, columns 4434–4435.
57 P Cassar Collection, Taped interview with Lawrie Schlemmer, 14 September 1984.
58 *Rapport*, 5 May 1974, 'Van Zyl Slabbert, voel jy tuis daar?'.
59 Boraine, 'Amalgam', in *The Passion for Reason*, p 38.
60 Breytenbach, 'The slow quickness of life', in *The Passion for Reason*, p 14.
61 Slabbert, *Afrikaner Afrikaan*, p 27; see also *Insig*, September 1997, 'Praat jou uit die verlede uit'; for a similar general perspective, see T Blaser, '"I don't know what I am": The end of Afrikaner nationalism in post-apartheid South Africa', *Transformation*, 80 (2012), pp 1–21.
62 *Rapport*, 9 March 2003, 'Sy Afrikaansheid was nooit weg nie'.
63 Stellenbosch University Library, Slabbert Collection, 430.E3.2.2, Slabbert, NP van Wyk Louw Memorial Lecture, University of Johannesburg, 11 September 2008.
64 This summary is based on A Grundlingh, 'Stellenbosch University and changing nationalist trends and language over 100 years', in A Grundlingh (ed), *Stellenbosch 100 years*, Stellenbosch University, Stellenbosch, 2018; the language debate generated considerable material; see, for example, P Kapp, *Maties en taal*, Protea Books, Pretoria, 2013.
65 Stellenbosch University Library, Slabbert Collection, 430.E3.21.1, 'Taaldebat', May 2006. (translated).
66 *Insig*, September 1997, 'Praat jou uit die verlede uit'; Stellenbosch University Library, Slabbert Collection 430.E3.20.1, 'Wie en wat is "Die Afrikaner"', June 2006.
67 Based on Stellenbosch University Library, Dian Joubert Collection, unsorted, Mana Jordaan CV, 1987; interview with Hermann Giliomee, 14 December 2018; interview with Jannie Gagiano, 4 September 2018; *Fair Lady*, October 1974, 'Oh lucky girl'.
68 *Sunday Times*, 3 November 1985, 'Me and my brother Van, by actor Sean'; Stellenbosch University Library, Dian Joubert Collection, unsorted, Mana Slabbert to Dian Joubert, 24 January 1974.
69 *Fair Lady*, October 1974, 'Oh lucky girl'.
70 Ibid.
71 Ibid.
72 Stellenbosch University Library, Dian Joubert Collection, unsorted, Mana Jordaan CV, 1987.
73 Interview with Tania Slabbert, 31 October 2018.
74 Tania and Riko Slabbert, 'Introduction', in *The Passion for Reason*, p 3.
75 Interview with Tania Slabbert, 31 October 2018; Tania and Riko Slabbert, 'Introduction', in *The Passion for Reason*, p 1.
76 Tania and Riko Slabbert, 'Introduction', in *The Passion for Reason*, p 3.
77 Interview with David Dietrich, 24 March 2018 (Dietrich knew the family); interview with Tania Slabbert, 3 May 2019.
78 Stellenbosch University Library, Slabbert Collection, 430.22.48.1, Mark Behr, 'Anchor man or Super Van?' 1992; see also interview with Tania Slabbert, 31 October 2018.
79 Stellenbosch University Library, Slabbert Collection, 430.22.48.1, Mark Behr,

NOTES

'Anchor man or Super Van?, 1992.
80 Tania and Riko Slabbert, 'Introduction', in *The Passion for Reason*, p 3.
81 *Fair Lady*, October 1974, 'Oh lucky girl'.
82 Stellenbosch University Library, Dian Joubert Collection, unsorted, Mana Slabbert to Dian Joubert, 24 January 1974.
83 Ibid.
84 Heribert Adam, email to author, 5 April 2015.
85 Tania Slabbert, email to author, 30 October 2019.
86 Interview with Tania Slabbert, 31 October 2018.
87 *Rand Daily Mail*, 28 April 1981, 'The Slabbert factor'.
88 Slabbert, *Last White Parliament*, p 64.
89 Stellenbosch University Library, Dian Joubert Collection, unsorted, Mana to All, 18 September 1979.
90 Interview with Tania Slabbert, 31 October 2018.
91 Slabbert, *Last White Parliament*, p 101.
92 Stellenbosch University Library, Slabbert Collection, 430.22.48.1, Mark Behr, 'Anchor man or Super Van?' 1992.
93 Ibid.
94 On Slabbert, interview with David Dietrich, 24 March 2019; on Mana, interview with Klaus Baron von der Ropp, 31 August 2018. Von der Ropp also moved in the family circle.
95 Slabbert, *Last White Parliament*, p 101.
96 Interview with Jane Slabbert, 30 July 2017; see also *Evening Post*, 17 April 1985, 'Marriage changed her life greatly'.
97 Interview with Jane Slabbert, 30 July 2017.
98 Slabbert, *Last White Parliament*, p 101.
99 Interview with Jane Slabbert, 30 July 2017; see also Adam and Moodley, 'Portrait', in *The Passion for Reason*, p 55.
100 Interview with Tania Slabbert, 31 October 2018.
101 Jane Slabbert, email to author, 29 October 2019.
102 Slabbert, *Last White Parliament*, p 87.
103 Stellenbosch University Library, Slabbert Collection, 430.A.25.1, Slabbert to Carlisle, 31 March 1986.
104 See Chapter 1.
105 Slabbert, *Last White Parliament*, pp 100–101.
106 Ibid, pp 55, 90, 92.
107 FvZ Slabbert, 'Letterkunde en samelewing', in J Polley (ed), *Verslag oor die symposium oor Die Sestigers*, Human & Rousseau, Cape Town, 1973, pp 168–172.
108 B Breytenbach, *The True Confessions of an Albino Terrorist*, Taurus, Johannesburg, 1984, p 274; see also Slabbert, *Last White Parliament*, pp 93–100; Breytenbach, 'The slow quickness of life', in *The Passion for Reason*, pp 5–8.
109 Slabbert, *Last White Parliament*, p 89; see also pp 87–89.
110 Boraine, 'Amalgam', in *The Passion for Reason*, pp 42–43.
111 Email from Jeremy Boraine, 19 February 2020.
112 Interview with Hermann Giliomee, 2 July 2018.
113 Adam and Moodley, 'Portrait', in *The Passion for Reason*, p 54.
114 See, for example, *Rand Daily Mail*, 28 April 1984, 'The Slabbert factor'. The journalist reported that, on the campaign trail in 1981, Slabbert only ate small meals, drank very little and took regular exercise.

115 Adam and Moodley, 'Portrait', in *The Passion for Reason*, pp 55, 52; Breytenbach, 'The slow quickness of life', in *The Passion for Reason*, p 15; Gagiano, 'Who we were', in *The Passion for Reason*, p 25.
116 Swart, *Progressive Odyssey*, p 157.
117 Adam and Moodley, 'Portrait', in *The Passion for Reason*, p 55.
118 Stellenbosch University Library, Dian Joubert Collection, unsorted, Slabbert to Joubert, 2 June 1997 (translated).
119 Interview with Hermann Giliomee, 2 July 2018.
120 *Cape Argus*, 4 August 2008, 'Van Zyl Slabbert "privileged" to serve alma mater'.
121 *Die Burger*, 12 November 2008, 'Dit gaan goed met Van Zyl Slabbert ná "kleinerige" beroerte'.
122 Tania Slabbert, email to author, 30 October 2019.
123 *Rapport*, 16 May 2010, 'Die leier van die "2de Groot Trek"'.
124 *Beeld*, 15 May 2010, 'Huldeblyke stroom in vir Frederik van Zyl Slabbert'.
125 Interview with Jane Slabbert, 30 July 2017; interview with Marcia Haak, 6 August 2017.
126 *Beeld*, 15 May 2010, 'Huldeblyke stroom in vir Frederik Van Zyl Slabbert'.
127 Tania Slabbert, email to author, 30 October 2019.
128 Slabbert Collection, 430.Z.2(58/1), programme of memorial service.
129 *Rapport*, 26 April 2014, 'Breyten aan pres Zuma: "Die eer is vals"'.

Conclusion

1 *Business Day*, 21 June 2010, 'Slabbert's political career cut short at great cost to all SA'.
2 Breytenbach, 'The slow quickness of life', in *The Passion for Reason*, p 14.
3 Slabbert, *Afrikaner Afrikaan*, p 136.
4 *Weekend Argus*, 8 February 1986, 'Van Zyl Slabbert – the reluctant politician'.
5 Quoted in Giliomee, *Last Afrikaner Leaders*, p 213.
6 For example, Chapters 1 and 7.
7 Gagiano, 'Who we were', in *The Passion for Reason*, p 18.
8 Slabbert, *Last White Parliament*, p 16.
9 Mouton, *Iron in the Soul*, p 135.
10 Breytenbach, 'The slow quickness of life', in *The Passion for Reason*, p 15.
11 Interview with Max du Preez, 30 July 2019.
12 Breytenbach, 'The slow quickness of life', in *The Passion for Reason*, p 14; interview with Max du Preez, 30 July 2019.
13 Breytenbach, 'The slow quickness of life', in *The Passion for Reason*, p 14.
14 *Cape Times*, 17 May 2010, 'A great bridge builder across the racial divide' (statement by David Welsh).
15 Compare Stellenbosch University Library, Slabbert Collection 430.Z.2 (65), Robin Carlisle, 'Slabbert's blueprint for the new South Africa', 22 June 2010.
16 *Die Burger*, 13 June 2020, 'Herbekyk van Kieswet welkom'.
17 Breytenbach, 'The slow quickness of life', in *The Passion for Reason*, p 15.
18 *Rapport*, 16 May 2010, ''n Seder het geval'.
19 *Rapport*, 16 May 2010, 'Denker, aktivis, politikus, patriot' (translated).
20 The comment on gender sensitivity is based on an interview with Max du Preez, 30 July 2019.
21 Interview with Mike Savage, 6 September 2017.
22 Gagiano, 'Who we were', in *The Passion for Reason*, p 18.

SOURCES

I Archival Collections

Stellenbosch University Library
J Basson Collection
SP Cilliers Collection
Idasa Collection (Western Cape)
D Joubert Collection
FvZ Slabbert Collection
HB Thom Collection
P Waldmeier Interviews
Wilgenhof Archives

Stellenbosch University Administration
Student records

University of the Western Cape
Mayibuye Archives

University of the Free State: Archive for Contemporary Affairs
PW Botha Collection

University of the Witwatersrand: William Cullen Library
Progressive Federal Party Collection
H Suzman Collection

University of South Africa Archives and Special Collections
United Party Collection

South African National Defence Force Documentation Centre
Personnel record of Petrus Johannes Slabbert

Nelson Mandela Centre of Memory, Johannesburg
Padraig O'Malley Archives

II Private Collections
Paul Cassar Collection
Hermann Giliomee Collection
Albert Grundlingh Collection
Marcia Haak Collection
David Welsh Collection

III Government Publications
House of Assembly Debates, 1974–1986
Volledige verkiesingsuitslae van Suid-Afrika, 1910–1986, Government Printer, Pretoria, 1986

IV Interviews and Correspondence
Adam, H, email, 5 April 2015, and interview, 11 February 2019
Andrew, K, interview, 5 September 2019
Ball, J, email, 20 February 2020
Bekker, S, interview, 22 August 2020
Boraine, J, email, 19 February 2020
Bührman, F, interview, 14 November 2019
Cardo, M, email, 7 August 2019
Cluver, P, interview, 22 August 2020
Coetzee, L, interview, 28 January 2019
Dietrich, D, interview, 24 March 2019
Du Preez, M, interview, 30 July 2019
Esterhuyse, W, interview, 21 July 2019
Evert, J, interview, 19 February 2019
Gagiano, J, interviews, 4 September 2018 and 19 April 2019
Gastrow, P, email, 27 February 2019
Giliomee, H, interviews, 2 July 2018, 14 December 2018, 8 May 2019, 11 June 2019, 5 August 2019; email, 11 June 2019.
Groenewald, J, interview, 8 September 2018; email, 10 November 2019
Haak, M, interview, 6 August 2017
Jubber, K, emails, 20 October 2014 and 26 February 2015
Kahn, S, interview, 16 September 2014
Kotzé, D, email, 9 March 2020
Lategan, B, interview, 6 July 2018
Le Roux, P, interview, 3 March 2019
Moodie, D, email, 12 September 2014
Moodley, K, interview, 11 February 2019
Myburgh, P, interview, 25 April 2016
Savage, M, interviews, 6 and 9 September 2017; email, 16 September 2014
Slabbert, J, interviews, 30 July 2017, 18 November 2018; email, 29 October 2019
Slabbert, T, interviews, 31 October 2018, 3 May 2019, 15 July 2019, 21 July 2019; email 30 October 2019

SOURCES

Van der Robb, K, interview, 31 August 2018
Vale, P, email, 17 June 2019
Vermaak, A, interview, 20 February 2020
Welsh, D, email, 23 December 2018

Paul Cassar Private Collection, Taped Interviews: 1981–1984

Bamford, B
Boraine, A
Cilliers, SP
Cronjé, P
De Beer, Z
De Villiers, F
De Villiers, R
Eglin, C
Malcomess, J
Myburgh, T
Olivier, N
Ross, N
Slabbert, FvZ
Soal, P
Suzman, H
Swart, R
Tarr, M
Van Eck, J
Van Rensburg, H
Vorster, J
Waddell, G

M Oelofsen: Videographed Interviews on Idasa, Idasa Collection, Stellenbosch University Library, 2017

Boraine, A
Cherry, J
Du Plessis, T
Du Preez, M
Du Toit. A
Gagiano, J
Gastrow, P
Graham, P
Kögl, J
Krog, A
Mbeki, M
Omotoso, K
Pakendorf, H
Savage, M

Vale, P
Zaaiman, A

V Books and Book Chapters

Adam, H and Moodley, K. 'Slabbert's opening of the apartheid mind: Portrait of an unrecognised patriot'. In A LeMaitre and M Savage (eds), *The Passion for Reason: Essays in Honour of Frederik van Zyl Slabbert*. Jonathan Ball, Johannesburg, 2010.

Adam, H, Moodley, K and van Zyl Slabbert, F. *Comrades in Business: Post-Liberation Politics in South Africa*. Tafelberg, Cape Town, 1997.

Asmal, K. *Politics in My Blood: A Memoir*. Jacana, Auckland Park, 2011.

Basson, J. *Politieke kaarte op die tafel: Parlementêre en ander herinneringe*. Politika, Cape Town, 2006.

Booth, D. *The Race Game: Politics and Sport in South Africa*. Frank Cass, London, 1998.

Boraine, A. 'A democratic alternative: A brief history of IDASA'. In I Liebenberg, F Lortan, B Nel and G van der Westhuizen (eds), *The Long March: The Story of the Struggle for Liberation in South Africa*. Kagiso-HAUM, Pretoria, 1994.

Boraine, A. *A Life in Transition*. Oxford University Press, Johannesburg, 2008.

Boraine, A. 'An amalgam that worked'. In A LeMaitre and M Savage (eds), *The Passion for Reason: Essays in Honour of Frederik van Zyl Slabbert*. Jonathan Ball, Johannesburg, 2010.

Boraine, A. *What's Gone Wrong? South Africa on the Brink of Failed Statehood*. Jonathan Ball, Johannesburg, 2014.

Breytenbach, B. 'The slow quickness of life (thinking about my friend, the Chief)'. In A LeMaitre and M Savage (eds), *The Passion for Reason: Essays in Honour of Frederik van Zyl Slabbert*. Jonathan Ball, Johannesburg, 2010.

Breytenbach, B. *The True Confessions of an Albino Terrorist*. Taurus, Johannesburg, 1984.

Cardo, M. *Opening Men's Eyes: Peter Brown and the Liberal Struggle for South Africa*. Jonathan Ball, Cape Town, 2010.

Changuion, L. *Pietersburg: Die eerste eeu, 1886–1986*, Stadsraad van Pietersburg, Pietersburg, 1986.

Changuion, L. *'n Skool soos PHS*. Pietersburg School Board, Pietersburg, 2003.

De Klerk, FW. *Die outobigrafie: Die laaste trek – 'n nuwe begin*. Human & Rousseau, Cape Town, 1999.

De Klerk, W. *FW de Klerk: Die man en sy tyd*. Jonathan Ball, Johannesburg, 1991.

D'Oliveira, J. *Vorster: The Man*. Ernest Stanton, Johannesburg, 1977.

Dubow, S. *Apartheid, 1948–1994*. Oxford University Press, Oxford, 2014.

Du Preez, M. *Dwars: Mymeringe van 'n gebleikte Afrikaan*. Zebra Press, Cape Town, 2009.

Du Preez, M. *Pale Native: Memories of a Renegade Reporter*. Zebra Press, Cape Town, 2004.

Du Rand, J. *Protes-stem, Oomblikke van herinnering*. Bybelkor, Wellington, 2016.

Duvenhage, P. 'Afrikaner intellectual history: An interpretation'. In P Vale, L Hamilton and EH Prinsloo (eds), *Intellectual Traditions in South Africa: Ideas, Individuals and Institutions*. University of KwaZulu-Natal Press, Pietermaritzburg, 2014.

Eglin, C. *Crossing the Borders of Power: The Memoirs of Colin Eglin*. Jonathan Ball, Johannesburg, 2007.

Eglin, C. 'South Africa in a southern African and international foreign policy perspective'. In Friedrich Naumann Stiftung, *South Africa – A Chance for Liberalism? Papers Presented During a Seminar of the Friedrich Naumann Foundation in December 1983*. Liberal Verlag, Sankt Augustin, 1985.

SOURCES

Ehlers, A. *Die Kaapse Helpmekaar, c 1916–2014: Bemiddelaar in Afrikaner opheffing, selfrespek en respektabiliteit.* Sunmedia, Stellenbosch, 2018.
Esterhuyse, W. *Endgame: Secret Talks and the End of Apartheid.* Tafelberg, Cape Town, 2012.
Esterhuyse, W and van Niekerk. G. *Die Tronkgesprekke.* Tafelberg, Cape Town, 2018.
Filatova, I and Davidson, A. *The Hidden Thread: Russia and South Africa in the Soviet Era.* Jonathan Ball, Johannesburg, 2013.
Fisher, A and Abeldas, M. *A Question of Survival: Conversations with Key South Africans.* Jonathan Ball, Johannesburg, 1987.
Frankel, P. *Pretoria's Praetorians: Civil-Military Relations in South Africa.* Cambridge University Press, Cambridge, 1984.
Friedman, S. 'The ambiguous legacy of liberalism'. In P Vale, L Hamilton and E Prinsloo (eds), *Intellectual Traditions in South Africa: Ideas, Individuals and Institutions.* University of KwaZulu Press, Pietermaritzburg, 2014.
Gagiano, J. 'Who we were'. In A LeMaitre and M Savage (eds), *The Passion for Reason: Essays in Honour of Frederik van Zyl Slabbert.* Jonathan Ball, Johannesburg, 2010.
Gevisser, M. *Thabo Mbeki: The Dream Deferred.* Jonathan Ball, Johannesburg, 2007.
Giliomee, H. 'Afrikaner politics, 1977–1987: From Afrikaner nationalist rule to central state hegemony'. In JD Brewer (ed), *Can South Africa Survive? Five Minutes to Midnight.* Southern, Johannesburg, 1989.
Giliomee, H. 'The leader and the citizenry'. In R Schire (ed), *Leadership and the Apartheid State: From Malan to De Klerk.* Oxford University Press, Oxford, 1994.
Giliomee, H. The Afrikaners: *Biography of a People.* Tafelberg, Cape Town, 2003.
Giliomee, H. 'Golden boy, golden opportunity: A note on Van Zyl Slabbert'. In A LeMaitre and M Savage (eds), *The Passion for Reason: Essays in Honour of Frederik van Zyl Slabbert.* Jonathan Ball, Johannesburg, 2010.
Giliomee, H. *Die Laaste Afrikanerleiers: 'n opperste toets van mag.* Tafelberg, Cape Town, 2012.
Giliomee, H. *The Last Afrikaner Leaders: A Supreme Test of Power.* Tafelberg, Cape Town, 2012.
Giliomee, H. *Historian: An Autobiography.* Tafelberg, Cape Town, 2016.
Giliomee, H. *The Rise and Demise of the Afrikaners.* Tafelberg, Cape Town, 2019.
Giliomee, H and Schlemmer, L. *From Apartheid to Nation-Building.* Oxford University Press, Oxford, 1993.
Grundlingh, A. 'Structures for sociologists: A historical perspective on associations for sociologists in South Africa, 1967–1991'. In N Romm, M Sarakinsky, D Gelderblom, V McKay, C Allais (eds), *Social Theory.* Lexicon, Johannesburg, 1994.
Grundlingh, A. *Potent Pastimes: Sport and Leisure Practices in Modern Afrikaner History.* Protea, Pretoria, 2013.
Grundlingh, A. 'Stellenbosch University and changing nationalistic trends and language over 100 years'. In A Grundlingh (ed), *Stellenbosch University 100 years.* Stellenbosch University, Stellenbosch, 2018.
Grundy, KW. *Soldiers without Politics: Blacks in the South African Armed Forces.* University of California Press, Berkeley, 1983.
Gupta, S and Kellman, A. 'Democracy organizations in political transitions: IDASA and the new South Africa'. In M Mutua (ed), *Human Rights NGOs in East Africa: Political and Normative Tensions.* University of Pennsylvania Press, Philadelphia, 2008.
Hugo, P. 'Towards darkness and death: Racial demonology'. In P Hugo (ed), *South African Perspectives: Essays in Honour of Nic Olivier.* Unisa Press, Pretoria, 1989.
James, W. 'Van Zyl Slabbert: Sociologist at work in advancing democratic politics'. In A LeMaitre and M Savage (eds), *The Passion for Reason: Essays in Honour of Frederik van Zyl Slabbert.* Jonathan Ball, Johannesburg, 2010.
Johnson, RW. *Foreign Native: An African Journey.* Jonathan Ball, Cape Town, 2020.

Kane-Berman, J. *South Africa's Silent Revolution*. South African Institute of Race Relations, Johannesburg, 1990.

Kapp, P. *Maties en taal*. Protea Books, Pretoria, 2013.

Kellerman, APR. 'Inleiding'. In APR Kellerman (ed), *SP Cilliers: Selected Papers*. Department of Sociology, Stellenbosch University, Stellenbosch, 1991.

Leach, G. *The Afrikaners: Their Last Great Trek*. Southern Book Publishers, Johannesburg, 1989.

Leon, T. *On the Contrary: Leading the Opposition in a Democratic South Africa*. Jonathan Ball, Johannesburg, 2009.

Loriga, S. 'The role of the individual in history: Biographical and historical writing in the nineteenth and twentieth century'. In H Renders and B de Haan (eds), *Theoretical Discussions of Biography: Approaches from History, Microhistory and Life Writing*. Brill, Leiden, 2014.

Macmillan, H. *The Lusaka Years: The ANC in exile, 1963 to 1994*. Jacana, Auckland Park, 2013.

Maré, G and Hamilton, G. *An Appetite for Power: Buthelezi's Inkatha and South Africa*. Ravan Press, Johannesburg, 1987.

Marx, AW. *Lessons of the Struggle: South Africa's Internal Opposition, 1960–1990*. Oxford University Press, Oxford, 1992.

Matisonn, J. *God, Spies and Lies: Finding South Africa's Future Through its Past*. Missing Ink, Cape Town, 2015.

Meiring, P. *Waagmoed beloon: 50 menings oor die PW-plan*. Perskor, Johannesburg, 1985.

Mouton, FA. *Iron in the Soul: The Leaders of the Official Parliamentary Opposition in South Africa, 1910–1993*. Protea Book House, Pretoria, 2017.

Myburgh, P. 'Security defence issues in southern Africa'. In Friedrich Naumann Stiftung, *South Africa – A Chance for Liberalism? Papers Presented During a Seminar of the Friedrich Naumann Foundation in December 1983*. Liberal Verlag, Sankt Augustin, 1985.

Nathan, L. '"Marching to a different beat": The history of the End Conscription Campaign'. In J Cock and L Nathan (eds), *War and Society: The Militarisation of South Africa*. David Philip, Cape Town, 1989.

Ndlovu, S. 'The African National Congress and negotiations'. In South African Democracy Education Trust, *The Road to Democracy in South Africa, Vol 4, Part 1 and 2, 1980–1990*. Unisa Press, Pretoria, 2010.

O'Meara, D. *Forty Lost Years: The Apartheid State and the Politics of the National Party, 1948–1994*. Ravan Press, Johannesburg, 1996.

Owen, K. *These Times: A Decade of South African Politics*. Jonathan Ball, Johannesburg, 1992.

Owen, K. 'The man who wasn't there'. In A LeMaitre and M Savage (eds), *The Passion for Reason: Essays in Honour of Frederik van Zyl Slabbert*. Jonathan Ball, Johannesburg, 2010.

Papenfus, T. *Pik Botha en sy tyd*. Litera, Pretoria, 2010.

Renders, H. 'The personal in the political biography'. In H Renders and B de Haan, *Theoretical Discussions of Biography: Approaches from History, Microhistory and Life Writing*. Brill, Leiden, 2014.

Renwick, R. *Helen Suzman: Bright Star in a Dark Chamber*. Jonathan Ball, Johannesburg, 2014.

Rhoodie, NJ. 'Importance of the eastern European democratic movement for change in South Africa'. In JL Olivier (ed), *Eastern Europe and South Africa: Implications for the Future*. HSRC, Pretoria, 1990.

Saunders, C. 'Liberal democratic anti-apartheid activity within South Africa', in

SOURCES

South African Democracy Education Trust, *The Road to Democracy in South Africa, Vol 4*. Unisa Press, Pretoria, 2010.

Savage, M. 'Ice, steam and water: Non-profit organisations in South Africa'. In A LeMaitre and M Savage (eds), *The Passion for Reason: Essays in Honour of Frederik van Zyl Slabbert*. Jonathan Ball, Johannesburg, 2010.

Seekings, J. *The UDF: A History of the United Democratic Front in South Africa, 1983–1991*. David Philip, Cape Town, 2000.

Shubin, V. *ANC: A View from Moscow*. Jacana Media, Johannesburg, 2008.

Slabbert, FvZ. 'Grense'. In R van Niekerk (ed), *Ons vir jou Suid-Afrika*. Van Schaik, Pretoria, 1962.

Slabbert, FvZ. 'Letterkunde en samelewing'. In J Polley (ed), *Verslag oor die symposium oor Die Sestigers*. Human & Rousseau, Cape Town, 1973.

Slabbert, FvZ. 'Afrikaner nationalism, white politics and political change'. In L Thompson and J Butler (eds), *Change in Contemporary South Africa*. University of California Press, Los Angeles, 1975.

Slabbert, FvZ. 'Functional methodology in the theory of action'. In J Loubser, R Baum, A Effrat and VM Lidz (eds), *Explorations in General Theory in Social Science: Essays in Honour of Talcott Parsons*, Vol I. The Free Press, London, 1976.

Slabbert, FvZ. *The Last White Parliament: The Struggle for South Africa by the Leader of the White Opposition*. Jonathan Ball, Johannesburg, 1985.

Slabbert, FvZ. *The System and the Struggle: Reform, Revolt and Reaction in South Africa*. Jonathan Ball, Johannesburg, 1989.

Slabbert, FvZ. 'Incremental change or revolution?' In J Butler, R Elphick and D Welsh (eds), *Democratic Liberalism in South Africa: Its History and Prospects*. David Philip, Cape Town, 1987.

Slabbert, FvZ. 'The struggle for a non-racial democratic South Africa'. In M Swilling (ed), *Views on the South African State*. HSRC, Pretoria, 1990.

Slabbert, FvZ. *The Quest for Democracy: South Africa in Transition*. Penguin, Johannesburg, 1992.

Slabbert, FvZ. *Afrikaner Afrikaan: Anekdotes en analises*. Tafelberg, Cape Town, 1999.

Slabbert, FvZ. *Tough Choices: Reflections of an Afrikaner African*. Tafelberg, Cape Town, 1999.

Slabbert, FvZ. 'Negotiating reconciliation'. In K Asmal, D Chidester and WG James (eds), *Nelson Mandela: From Freedom to the Future – Tributes and Speeches*. Jonathan Ball, Johannesburg, 2003.

Slabbert, FvZ. *The Other Side of History: An Anecdotal Reflection on Political Transition in South Africa*. Jonathan Ball Publishers, Johannesburg, 2006.

Slabbert, FvZ. 'Threats and challenges to South Africa becoming a more open society'. In M Shain (ed), *Opposing Voices: Liberalism and Opposition in South Africa Today*. Jonathan Ball, Johannesburg, 2006.

Slabbert, FvZ. 'Some contest the assertion that I am an African'. In X Mangcu (ed), *Becoming Worthy Ancestors: Archive, Public Deliberations and Identity in South Africa*. Wits University Press, Johannesburg, 2010.

Slabbert, FvZ and Welsh, D. *South Africa's Options: Strategies for Sharing Power*. David Philip, Cape Town, 1979.

Slabbert, T and Slabbert, R. 'Introduction'. In A LeMaitre and M Savage (eds), *The Passion for Reason: Essays in Honour of Frederik van Zyl Slabbert*. Jonathan Ball, Johannesburg, 2010.

Spaarwater, M. *A Spook's Progress: From Making War to Making Peace*. Zebra Press, Cape Town, 2012.

Sparks, A. *Beyond the Miracle: Inside the New South Africa*. Jonathan Ball, Johannesburg, 2003.

Stellenbosch University Yearbook, 1971.
Strangwayes-Booth, J. *A Cricket in the Thorn Tree: Helen Suzman and the Progressive Party*. Hutchinson, Johannesburg, 1976.
Steyn, JC. *Penvegter: Piet Cillié van Die Burger*. Tafelberg, Cape Town, 2002.
Stutje, J. 'Historiographical and theoretical aspects of Weber's concept of charismatic leadership'. In J Stutje (ed), *Charismatic Leadership and Social Movements*. Berghahn Books, Amsterdam, 2012.
Suzman, H. *In No Uncertain Terms: A South African Memoir*. Jonathan Ball, Johannesburg, 1993.
Swart, R. *Progressive Odyssey: Towards a Democratic South Africa*. Human & Rousseau, Cape Town, 1991.
Swilling, M. 'The United Democratic Front and township revolt'. In W Corbett and R Cohen (eds), *Popular Struggles in South Africa*. James Currey, London, 1988.
Swilling, M. 'The dynamics of reform'. In A Callinicos (ed), *Between Apartheid and Capitalism*. Bookmarks, London, 1992.
Thom, HB. 'Dagbreek binne die groter geheel'. In B Booyens and K Oosthuysen (eds) *Dagbreek 1921–1971*. Dagbreek, Cape Town, 1971.
Van der Heyden, U. *Der Dakar-prozess: Der Anfang vom Ende der Apartheid in Südafrika*. Solivagus, Kiel, 2018.
Van der Westhuizen, G, Liebenberg, I and Du Plessis, T. 'National service and resistance to conscription in South Africa'. In I Liebenberg, J Risquet and V Shubin (eds), *A Far-Away War: Angola 1975–1989*. Sunmedia, Stellenbosch, 2015.
Venter, R. *'n Stukkie van die legkaart*. Malan Media, Pretoria, 2019.
Verster, F. *Omega, oor en uit: Die storie van 'n opstandige troep*. Tafelberg, Cape Town, 2016.
Viljoen, DJA (ed). *Koerantknipsels oor die Referendum oor 'n nuwe Grondwetlike bedeling, 1983*. Instituut vir Eietydse Geskiedenis, Bloemfontein, 1984.
Weber, M. 'Politics as a profession'. In HH Gerth and CW Mills (eds), *From Max Weber: Essays in Sociology*. Routledge, London, 1970.
Welsh, D. *The Rise and Fall of Apartheid*. Jonathan Ball, Johannesburg, 2009.
Worrall, D. *The Independent Factor: My Personal Journey Through Politics and Diplomacy*. Reach, Cape Town, 2018.
Zille, H. *Not without a Fight: The Autobiography of Helen Zille*. Penguin Books, Cape Town, 2016.

VI Journal Articles

Alexander, JC. 'Commentary: Structure, value action'. *American Sociological Review*, 55(3) (1990), pp 339–345.
Alexander, N. 'Examining South Africa's options'. *Social Dynamics*, 5(2) (July 1979), pp 56–59.
Ally, S. 'Oppositional intellectualism as reflection, not rejection of power: Wits Sociology, 1975–1989'. *Transformation*, 59(1) (2005), pp 66–97.
Ally, S, Mooney, K and Stewart, P. 'The state-sponsored and centralised institutionalisation of an academic discipline: Sociology in South Africa, 1920–1970'. *Society in Transition*, 34(1) (2003), pp 70–103.
Blaser, T. '"I don't know what I am": The end of Afrikaner nationalism in post-apartheid South Africa'. *Transformation*, 80 (2012), pp 1–21.
Brits, J. 'Thabo Mbeki and the Afrikaners, 1986–2004'. *Historia*, 53(2) (November 2008), pp 33–69.

SOURCES

Cardo, M. 'The liberal tradition in South Africa: Past and present'. *Focus* (July 2012), pp 16–20.

Charney, C. 'Towards rupture or stasis: An analysis of the 1981 South African general election'. *African Affairs*, 81(325) (1982), pp 527°545.

Du Toit, A. 'On South Africa's options'. *Social Dynamics*, 5(2) (July 1979), pp 59–62.

Du Toit, A. 'The legacy of Daantjie Oosthuizen: Revisiting the liberal defence of academic freedom'. *African Sociological Review*, 9(1) (2005), pp 40–61.

Du Toit, P. 'Bargaining about bargaining: Inducing the self-negating prediction in deeply divided societies – the case of South Africa'. *The Journal of Conflict Resolution*, 33(2) (1989), pp 210–230.

Giliomee, H. 'True Confessions, End Papers and the Dakar conference: A review of political arguments'. *Tydskrif vir Letterkunde*, 46(2) (2009), pp 28–42.

Grundlingh, A. 'The King's Afrikaners? Enlistment and ethnic identity in the Union of South Africa's Defence Force during the Second World War, 1939–45'. *The Journal of African History*, 40(3), (1999), pp 351–365.

Grundlingh, A. '"Are we Afrikaners becoming too rich?" Cornucopia and change in Afrikanerdom in the 1960s.' *Journal of Historical Sociology*, 21(2–3) (June/September2008), pp 143–165.

Hanf, T. 'Lessons which are never learnt: Minority rule in comparative perspective'. *Journal of Asian and African Studies*, XVIII(1–2) (1983), pp 22–33.

Howell, J and Shamir, B. 'The role of followers in the charismatic leadership process: Relationships and their consequences'. *The Academy of Management Review*, 30(1) (2005), pp 96–112.

Hugo, P. 'The politics of untruth: Afrikaner academics for apartheid.' *Politikon: South African Journal of Political Studies*, 25(1) (1998), pp 1–42.

Kurzman, C and Owens, L. 'The sociology of intellectuals'. *Annual Review of Sociology*, 28(202) (1999), pp 63–90.

Lieberfeld, D. 'Evaluating the contributions of two-track diplomacy to conflict termination in South Africa, 1984–90'. *Journal of Peace Research*, 39 (3 May 2002), pp 355–372.

Macqueen, I. 'Resonances of youth and tensions of race: Liberal student politics, white radicals and Black Consciousness, 1968–1973'. *South African Historical Journal*, 65(3) (2013), pp 365–382.

McKenzie, E. 'From obscurity to official opposition: The Progressive Federal Party, 1959–1977'. *Historia*, 39(1) (1994), pp 81–91.

McKenzie, E. 'Its master's voice? The South African "Progressive" parties and business, 1959–1983'. *Journal for Contemporary History*, 21(2) (December 1996), pp 34–48.

Pretorius, D and Sauthoff, M. 'Challenging apartheid: Posters from the United Democratic Front and the End Conscription Campaign'. *Image & Text: A Journal for Design*, 2004(11) (January 2004), pp 23–32.

Schlemmer, L. *The Dakar Reports: Responses from 16 Delegates to the Dakar Conference.* Idasa Occasional Papers, 11 (1987).

Shapiro, B. 'Performing "middlingness": Frederik van Zyl Slabbert and the South African transition'. *Quarterly Bulletin of the National Library of South Africa*, 67(4) (December 2013), pp 22–35.

Slabbert, FvZ. 'Sham reform and conflict regulation in a divided society'. *Journal of Asian and African Studies*, 18(1–2) (1983), pp 17–23.

Taylor, I. 'South Africa's transition to democracy and the "change industry": A case study of IDASA'. *Politikon – South African Journal of Political Studies*, 29(1) (2002), pp 31–48.

Vale, P. 'Unlocking social puzzles: Colony, crime and chronicle: An interview with Charles van Onselen'. *Thesis Eleven*, 136(1) (2016), pp 35–48.
Van den Berghe, P. 'Some trends in unpublished social science research in South Africa'. *International Social Science Journal*, XIV(4) (1962), pp 723–732.
Van Vuuren, W. 'The meaning of Dakar'. In *The Dakar Report: Responses from 16 Delegates to the Dakar Conference*. Idasa Occasional Papers, 11 (1987).
Venter, A. 'Mededingende politieke paradigmas oor die Grensoorlog 1966– 1989'. *Journal for Contemporary History*, 34(1) (February 2009), pp 36–56.
Verbuyst, R. 'History, historians and the South African Truth and Reconciliation Commission'. *New Contree*, 66 (2013), pp 1–26.
Welsh, D. 'Urbanisation and the solidarity of Afrikaner nationalism'. *The Journal of Modern African Studies*, 7(2) (1969), pp 265–276.

VII Newspapers and Periodicals

Die Afrikaner
Beeld
Die Bliksem (Wilgenhof periodical)
Die Burger
Business Day
Cape Argus
Cape Times
The Citizen
City Press
Daily Dispatch
The Daily News
Deurbraak
Eastern Province Herald
Eikestadnuus
Evening Post
Fair Lady
Financial Mail
Frontline
Die Huisgenoot
Insig
Jaarblad van Pietersburg Hoërskool
De Kat
Kerkbode
Leadership SA
Mail & Guardian
Die Matie
The Municipal Magazine
The Natal Mercury
The Natal Witness
The Nationalist
Oggendblad
Oosterlig
Pretoria News

SOURCES

Progress
Rand Daily Mail
Rapport
Sechaba
Sowetan
Die Suid-Afrikaan
Sunday Express
Sunday Independent
Sunday Star
Sunday Times
Sunday Tribune
The Star
The Times
Die Transvaler
US Kampusnuus
Die Vaderland
Die Volksblad
Vrye Weekblad
Weekend Argus
Weekend Post
Weekly Mail
Woord en Daad

VIII Theses and Unpublished Papers

Cassar, P. 'The emergence and impact of Dr F van Zyl Slabbert in South African opposition politics, 1974–1981'. MA thesis, University of the Free State, 1984.

Hackland, B. 'The economic and political context of the growth of the Progressive Federal Party in South Africa, 1959–1978'. In *The Societies of Southern Africa in the 19th and 20th Centuries*. Collected Seminar Papers, Vol 11, No 27. University of London, Institute of Commonwealth Studies, 1981.

Hughes, TPD. 'Political liberalism in South Africa in the 1980s and the formation of the Democratic Party'. MA thesis, University of Cape Town, 1994.

Liebenberg, I. *Dakar – reflections on a conference*. Unpublished paper, ResearchGate, 17 September 2017.

Mckenzie, ER. 'The relationship between the Progressive Federal Party, the English-language press and business with special reference to the 1983 referendum'. MA thesis, Unisa, 1992.

Orbon, H. 'Frederik van Zyl Slabbert, the dialogue programmed on Cold Comfort and the pitfalls of ideology'. Unpublished paper, undated.

Phillips, M. 'The End Conscription Campaign: A study of white extra-parliamentary opposition to apartheid'. MA thesis, Unisa, 2002.

Savage, M. 'The Dakar talks and meetings between South Africans and the ANC in exile, 1983–2000'. Unpublished manuscript, June 2016.

Savage, M. 'Trekking outward: A chronology of meetings between South Africans and the ANC in exile, 1983–2000'. Unpublished manuscript, 2017.

Shandler, D. 'Structural crisis and liberalism: A history of the Progressive Federal Party, 1981–1989'. MA thesis, University of Cape Town, 1991.

Slabbert, FvZ. 'Beroepskeuses van studente'. MA thesis, Stellenbosch University, 1964.

Slabbert, FvZ. 'Structural-functional analysis in theoretical sociology: A methodological enquiry'. PhD thesis, Stellenbosch University, 1967.
Slabbert, FvZ. 'Politics and privilege in South Africa'. Summer School lectures, University of Cape Town, 1973.
Thakur, V and Vale, P. '"Negotiations in South Africa": The liberal imaginary and expertise of Frederik van Zyl Slabbert'. Unpublished and undated paper.
Van der Spuy, M. 'Van Zyl Slabbert: The reluctant progressive'. Unpublished memoir, dated after April 2010 (courtesy of Hermann Giliomee).
WB Vosloo, 'The nature of the Afrikaner people and the challenges facing Afrikaner nationalism', Summer School lectures, University of Cape Town, 1973.
Welsh, D. 'English-speaking white South Africans', Summer School lectures, University of Cape Town, 1973.

IX Online Sources

Botha, C. 'Time for electoral reform and dusting off the Van Zyl Slabbert Report'. Politicsweb, 22 May 2019. Accessed 8 May 2020.
Evans, G. 'Frederik van Zyl Slabbert: Politician and activist in the vanguard of the struggle against apartheid'. Independent.co.uk, 19 May 2010. Accessed 8 May 2018.
Barker, M. 'George Soros and South Africa's elite transition'. Blog post, swans.com, 31 May 2010. Accessed 14 May 2019.
Johnson, RW. 'Van Zyl Slabbert: What went wrong?' Politicsweb, 21 June 2010. Accessed 17 June 2019.
James, W. Tribute to Slabbert. Blog post, idasa.wordpress.com, 14 May 2010. Accessed 8 May 2019.
Slabbert, FvZ. 'Is Academic Freedom Still an Issue in the New South Africa?' TB Davie Memorial Lecture, University of Cape Town, October 2003. News.uct.ac.za. Accessed 1 June 2020.

INDEX

Adam, Heribert 182, 238, 240-241, 253
Adcorp Holdings 207
affirmative-action policies 161
African National Congress (ANC) viii, 28, 104, 107-111,113, 123-124, 130, 132-133, 140, 151-152, 157, 159, 167-169, 171-181, 183-184, 188, 190, 193, 195-196, 199-202, 205-206, 238, 243, 248, 250
Afrikaans (also debate about Afrikaans at universities) vii, 14-15, 17-18, 22-23, 50, 54, 59, 65, 79, 85, 87, 90, 92, 123, 142, 165, 167-170, 177, 181-182, 184-185, 212, 223-224, 226, 229-230
Afrikaans press 65, 79, 87, 90, 92, 142, 165, 169, 182, 185, 212, 226
Afrikaner nationalism 28
Afrikaner vote 66, 92, 162
Afrikaner Weerstandsbeweging (Afrikaner Resistance Movement, AWB) 175, 224-225
Allan, Jani 214
Andrew, Ken 253
Anglo American Corporation 54, 101
apartheid vii, 24-25, 28-30, 36-37, 43-44, 46-48, 63, 70-71, 73, 82, 90, 105-107, 109-112, 118, 124-126, 131, 134-137, 141, 143-144, 153, 156-157, 159-163, 165, 167, 173, 182, 189-193, 195, 198-199, 203, 206-207, 214-215, 226, 228-230, 243, 248, 250
Appelgryn, Theuns 253
armed struggle 110-111, 173, 176, 199-200, 279
Asmal, Kader 197
Association for Sociology in Southern Africa (ASSA) 36-37

Bacher, Ali 193
Bamford, Brian 56-57, 72
Barlow, Eddie 61
Barnard, Niël 131, 178-179
Basson, Japie 47, 52, 74, 88-89, 260
Beeld 142-143, 146
Berlin Wall, fall of 188
Bill of Rights 77-78, biographical and autobiographical writing vii-viii, 20, 189
Black Consciousness Movement 104
Black Sash 123
Blignaut, Chris 15
Boer rebellion 22
Boesak, Allan 108
Booyens, Bun 225
Boraine, Alex 65, 69, 72, 83, 109, 119, 133, 147, 149, 159-160, 163-164, 168, 192, 239, 247
Boraine, Jeremy 119, 239
Botha, Hannah 253
Botha, Pik 84, 134
Botha, PW 65, 71, 79, 90-91, 95, 97-100, 105-106, 111-112, 115-116, 126, 129-131, 134-139, 146, 151, 153, 172, 175, 178-180, 186, 188
Botman, Russel 242
Breytenbach, Breyten 167-168, 173, 178, 184, 209, 222, 228, 238-239, 243, 245, 248-249, 251
Broederbond 22, 46, 167
Buthelezi Commission 105
Buthelezi, Mangosuthu 47, 104-105, 107-108, 267
Buys, J 217

Camerer, Sheila 213
Cape Times 58-59
Cardo, Michael 253
Carlisle, Robin 82
Carlson, Ray 217
Carnation Revolution 63
Cassar, Paul 253
Changuion, Louis 253
Churchill, Winston 240
Cillié, Piet 65
Cilliers, SP 34-39, 41
Coetzee, Annas 253
Coetzee, JM 213
Coetzee, Lauren 253
Colenbrander, Peter 253

Compton, Everald 149
conscription (military service) 116-118, 120-126, 128
Conservative Party 93, 98, 140, 151, 216
consociationalism 94
Constitutional Court 77, 198, 249
Convention Alliance 106-108, 127
co-optive domination 97
Craven, Danie 28
CTP Directories 207

Dakar meeting of white South Africans with banned ANC viii, 166-185, 205, 209-210, 245, 247
Dalling, Dave 119
Degenaar, Johan 40, 238
De Klerk, FW 130, 153, 186-190, 195-196, 249
De Lange, Pieter 167
Democratic Alliance (DA) 145, 191
détente policy of National Party 55, 63
detention without trial 87
Deurbraak 50
De Villiers, Dawie 92
Die Burger 65
Dingane 23
Diouf, Abdou 171
Dladla, Betty 237
Dugard, John 238
Du Plessis, A 13
Du Plessis, Lourens 177
Du Plessis, Morné 61
Du Preez, Max 147, 170-171, 182,
Dutch Reformed Church 21, 23, 158, 164, 182, 220, 231, 246-247
Du Toit, André 40, 173, 179, 238

Edenvale by-election 89
Eglin, Colin 47, 49-50, 52-53, 55-56, 64, 66, 75, 77-78, 83-85, 113, 128-132, 134, 148-150, 153, 245
Eglin, Joyce 85
Ehlers, Ters 98
Eloff, Theuns 177
End Conscription Campaign (ECC) 122-126
Enthoven, Dick 52, 186
Esterhuyse, Willie 180

Ferreira GT 253
Financial Mail 138
Florina (black domestic worker) 18-19
France Libertés 166-167
Frederik van Zyl Slabbert Honorary Lecture 243
Frederik van Zyl Slabbert Institute for Student Leadership Development (Stellenbosch University) 243
Freedom Charter 82
Friedrich Naumann Foundation 167

Gagiano, Annie 234
Gagiano, Jannie 26, 30-31, 36, 38, 40, 43, 47-48, 237, 246, 253
Gastrow, Peter 106, 108-109, 119
Geldenhuys, Jannie 115
Gevisser, Mark 214
Gibson, Douglas 149
Giliomee, Hermann 143, 174, 176, 183, 189, 227, 238, 253
Goodall, Brain 114, 119
Gorée Institute 182, 208-209
Gouws, Rudolf 253
Government of National Unity 200
Graaff, De Villiers 56, 58, 74
Greyling, Cas 216
Grundlingh, Annamari 253
Grundlingh, Louis 253
Grundlingh, Marizanne 253
Grundlingh, Mauritz 253
Grundlingh, Mia 253

Haak, Marcia (see Slabbert, Marcia)
Haig, Scott 68
Hanf, Theodor 94, 238
Helpmekaar Vereniging 22-23
Herstigte Nasionale Party (Reformed National Party) 131
Heunis, Chris 131, 138
homeland policy 36, 47, 51, 61, 63, 69, 82, 96, 104, 189
Howell, Jane 218-219
Hulley, Roger 119

Independent Media Diversity Trust 207
influx control 24, 64, 69-70, 189
Information Scandal 84
Inkatha Freedom Party (IFP) 104-105
Institute for a Democratic Alternative for South Africa (Idasa) 160-167, 179, 181, 247, 250
Irving, James 33

James, Wilmot 42, 158, 164
Johnson, RW 132, 204, 214, 238, 244
Jones, Ian 237-238
Jordaan, Mana (see Slabbert, Mana)
Joubert, Dian 31-32, 34-35, 98
Kaplan, Rob 253

Kennedy, John F 212
Kerzner, Sol 163
Khula investment trust 206-207
Khumalo, Bheki 183, 205
Kissinger, Henry 97
Kögl, Jürgen 206
Koornhof, Piet 47-48, 216
Koorts, Lindie 253
Kriel, Jacques 170

Labour Party 47
language debate (Afrikaans) at Stellenbosch University 229-230
Lenin, Vladimir 170
Leon, Tony 197, 202
Lever Brothers 33-34
liberalism 49, 78, 95, 155, 214
Liberal Party 78
Liebenberg, Ian 178
Local Government Elections Task Group 196-198
Loubser, Jan 37
Louw, Chris 171-172, 183
Louw, Mike 179-180
Louw, WEG 229

Machel, Samora 139
Macrae, Cailin 253
Maharaj, Mac 172-173
majoritarianism (majority rule) 96, 155-156, 161, 163
Malan, Magnus 112, 116, 123
Mandela, Nelson 130, 187-188, 195-196, 202-203, 244
Marabastad Farm School 15-16
Marais, Ben 21
Marxism 40, 43, 165-166
mass-protest politics 35, 108, 117, 151, 156-157
Matsepe-Casaburri, Ivy 195
Mbeki, Govan 204
Mbeki, Thabo 109-111, 132-133, 152-153, 159, 167-169, 171-174, 183-184, 197, 199, 203-207, 214
Mbeki, Zanele 206
McHenry, Donald 84
McIntosh, Graham 119, 143-144
Meer, Fatima 195
militarisation of South Africa 63, 80, 112-114, 116-117, 119-122, 124-129, 138, 199
minority veto 77-79, 111, 154
Mitterrand, Danielle 166, 168
Mitterrand, François 166
Moerane, MT 47-48
Moodie, T Dunbar 36, 39
Moodley, Kogila 182, 253
Mouton, Alex 253
Msweli, Bibi 237
Muller, Hilgard 64
Multi-ethnic Separate Development 189
Myburgh, Philip 113, 119-120, 122, 124

Nasson, Bill 253
national convention 79, 106-108, 127, 192
national democratic revolution 184
National Intelligence Service (NIS) 131, 170, 175, 178-179, 187, 279
National Party vii, 12-13, 15, 24, 45-47, 49, 51, 54-55, 60-61, 64-65, 71, 73, 81, 84, 89-95, 97, 99, 105, 112-116, 131, 135-136, 140, 151-152, 172, 179, 186, 190, 202, 213, 216, 221, 227, 229, 248
National Union of Mineworkers 159
nation building 184
Nattrass, Jill 238
Naudé, Beyers 21
Naudé, Tom 15
Nel, Koos 16
New Nation 207
New Republic Party 74, 89, 92
Nkomati Accord 139
Nothard, Jenny 237

O'Brien, Conor Cruise 240
Odendaal, André 177, 184
Olivier, Nic 52, 91, 119, 238
Oosthuizen, Daantjie 33
Open Society Foundation 210
Operation Savannah 114-115
Oppenheimer, Harry 53-55, 101-102, 147, 150
Opperman, DJ 229
Otto, Chris 253
Owen, Ken 134, 140
Ozinsky, Max 124

Pahad, Aziz 168, 184
Pan Africanist Congress (PAC) 23, 28
Parsons, Talcott 41-43, 246
pass laws 69
Philips, Howard 253
Pitman, Harry 239
Popper, Karl 157-158, 165, 246
Population Registration Act (1950) & racial classification 70, 87, 91, 132
power-sharing 51, 53, 60, 77-78, 82, 94, 97, 154
President's Council 88, 91, 95

Progressive Federal Party (PFP) viii, 34, 39, 74-76, 82-84, 87-93, 95-107, 109-114, 116-122, 124, 126-128, 132-134, 138-141, 145, 150-152, 162, 191, 214-217, 220, 227-228, 236, 239, 249-250
Progressive Party vii, 47, 49-54, 56, 62, 66-67, 71, 83, 149, 250
proportional representation 77-78, 196

Qoboza, Percy 48
qualified franchise 51, 78, 154

Ramaphosa, Cyril 159, 193
Rand Daily Mail 145
Rationalist Thinkers Forum 23
referendum (1983) 95, 97-103, 111-112, 127, 136, 141
referendum (1992) 189
Reform Party 74
religious objections to and exemption from military service 116-117
Relly, Gavin 101
Renders, Hans viii
Retief, Piet 23
Rhodes (Makhanda) University 30-35, 77, 217
Rondebosch constituency 52-53, 56-57, 59-61, 75, 91, 213, 231, 234
Ross, Neil 89-90, 150
Roux, Eddie 23
Rubicon speech 106
Ruiterwag 22

Sapire, Hilary 253
Sartre, Jean-Paul 224
Saunders, Chris 101

Savage, Mike 210-211
Schlemmer, Lawrie 202, 238
Schoeman, Hendrik 136
Schwarz, Harry 74, 88, 99, 113, 119
Shain, Milton 253
Shamir, Boas 218-219
Shaw, Gerald 58
Simonsberg residence 27
Sive, Reuben 119
Slabbert, Barbara (Thyssen, mother) 11, 13-15, 18-19, 21, 24, 231, 252
Slabbert, Engela (grandmother) 13, 17-18, 21
Slabbert, Frederik Van Zyl
  accusations by NP of being unpatriotic 71-72;
  also on patriotism and PFP being unpatriotic by the NP 65, 71-72, 84, 118, 126, 196, 201;
  and Afrikaans arts festivals 228;
  Afrikaans background and affinity vii, 15, 17; 222-230;
  on Afrikaans language debate at Stellenbosch University 229-230;
  on Afrikaner identity 222-230;
  anger of Helen Suzman at Slabbert's resignation 86, 134, 148-150, 165, 201;
  and "apartheid moralism" 215;
  appointment as chair of the SABC Board 195-196;
  arrest in Crossroads 70;

author and political commentator vii, viii, 34, 39, 76, 87-93, 95-107, 109-114, 116-122, 124, 126-128, 132-134, 139-141, 145, 150-152, 214-216, 220, 228;
BJ Vorster's view of Slabbert 72;
breaking the logjam in white party politics 73, 75;
business ventures & Strategic Foresight, Adcorp Holdings & directorships of companies 206-208;
campaigning against Population Registration Act (1950) 70, 132;
chair of Electoral Task Team 196-198, 205;
chair of Independent Media Diversity Trust 207;
chair of Central Witwatersrand Metropolitan Chamber 193-196;
co-chair of Local Government Elections Task Group 196-198;
chancellor of Stellenbosch University 34, 242-243;
charisma among voters viii, 59-60, 84, 212 -222, 243;
childhood 11-18, 21-22, 204, 252;
compared to John F Kennedy 212;
criticism of government's sports policy 70-71;
criticism of Thabo Mbeki 205;

Dakar meeting and relationship with ANC viii, 166-185, 199-205, 209-210, 245, 247;
debate with Eugène Terre'Blanche 225;
disillusionment with big business 102;
on disinvestment from South Africa 166;
as Don Juan 236;
as drawcard for audiences 216-220;
dubbed 'Mohammed Ali of the PFP' 76;
education at: Pretoria East Primary School 14; Jan Celliers Laerskool, Linden 15; Marabastad Farm School 15-17; schools in Pietersburg (Polokwane) 17-18, 21; 243;
and extra-parliamentary politics 154-255;
fellowship at All Souls College, Oxford 186-187;
his so-called five-year attention span 250-251;
founder-member of and role in Institute for a Democratic Alternative for South Africa (Idasa) 160-167, 179, 181, 247, 250;
friendships 16, 18-20, 27, 36, 45, 52, 54, 72, 91, 164-165, 167, 182, 186, 192, 201, 204, 208-210, 216, 220, 223, 233-234, 236-241, 243, 245, 247, 251-252;
on 'Great White Hope' myth 221-222;
humour in speeches 216;
idealist and visionary 76-82, 132, 143, 146, 198, 211, 248-249, 251-252;
illness and death 242-244;
interest in UCT vice-chancellorship 84-85;
Lever Brothers offer 33-34;
maiden speech in Parliament 67-68;
marriage to Mana Jordaan 231-236, 243;
marriage to Jane Stephens 236-237, 243;
mediator and facilitator in constitutional and other negotiations 190-191, 193;
meeting with the ANC in Zambia, 1985 109-110;
member & leader of the Progressive Federal Party (PFP) viii, 34, 39, 52-62, 76, 83-93, 95-107, 109-114, 116-122, 124, 126-128, 132-134, 139-141, 145, 150-152, 214-216, 220, 228;
member of PFP's constitutional committee 77-78; 81-82;
misgivings about Parliament 72-73, 76-77, 101;
on his mortality 241;
national honours from government 243;
nickname Super Van 212, 220;
and Open Society Foundation 210;
on power-sharing 51, 53, 60, 77-78, 82, 94, 97, 154;
rational thinker 44, 68, 90, 129, 138, 214-215, 220-221, 240, 248;
and referendum (1983) 95-97;
relationship with Afrikaans press 65, 79, 87, 90, 92, 142-144, 146, 165, 169-170, 185, 212, 226;
relationship with: FW de Klerk 186, 188-189, 195; Japie Basson 88-89; PW Botha 116, 129-131, 136-139, 146; Magnus Malan 116; Nelson Mandela 202-203; Thabo Mbeki 109-110, 166, 203-206;
religion (also theological studies) & missionary zeal 20-23, 29-30, 42, 44, 158, 164, 182, 220, 231, 246-247;
resident of Wilgenhof 25-27, 82, 243;
resignation as leader of PFP and disillusionment with Parliament viii, 128-153, 156, 159, 210, 221, 245, 250;
Rondebosch candidacy & victory 52-62, 65, 75-76;
rugby player and sportsman 17-18, 27-28, 32, 217-218, 237, 240;
scepticism of Marxism 43-44;

shadow minister of defence & militarisation of South Africa 63, 80, 112-114, 116-122, 124-129, 138, 199;
sociologist and studies in sociology 23, 30-42, 68-69, 82, 144, 229, 231-232, 246;
soft spot for the underdog and outsider 14, 16;
spokesperson of Parliamentary portfolios 72;
student and lecturer at: University of the Witwatersrand 22-23, 27, 38-40, 54-55, 57, 82, 206;
Stellenbosch University vii,22-28, 35-37, 44, 59, 98, 220, 246;
Rhodes (Makhanda) University 30-35;
University of Cape Town 37;
Synthesis group 47;
Talcott Parsons' influence on Slabbert 41-43, 246;
as tragic figure 251;
on tricameral parliament 95, 97-103, 111-112, 127, 136, 141;
on trusting the ANC too much 249-250;
and the Truth and Reconciliation Commission 191-192;
United Party offer to stand in election 52;
as visionary thinker 76-77, 251-252;
visit to Zambia, Kenya & Nigeria 64-65;

and possible Western Cape premiership 202
Slabbert, Frederik Van Zyl (grandfather) 11-16, 18-19, 21-22
Slabbert, Jane (second wife: see Stephens, Jane
Slabbert, Mana (Jordaan; first wife) 32, 62, 224, 231-232, 234-236, 240, 252
Slabbert, Marcia (Haak, sister) 11, 13, 15,-17, 19, 21-22, 47, 62, 131, 135-136, 250, 253
Slabbert Papers (University of Stellenbosch) ix
Slabbert, Petrus Johannes (father) 11-13, 22, 24
Slabbert, Riko (son) 13, 93, 129, 210, 231-234, 252
Slabbert, Tania (daughter) 13-14, 32, 93, 210, 231-233, 252-253
Slovo, Joe 184
Small, Adam 229
Smelser, Neil 35
Smuts, Jan 12, 59, 61, 170
Sobukwe, Robert 23
social engineering 157
Soros, George 165, 167, 202-203, 209-210
South African Communist Party (SACP) 174, 184, 187
South African Defence Force (SADF) 113-116, 120-125, 175
South African Sociology Association (SASOV) 36
South Africa's Options: Strategies for Sharing Power 80-81
Southey, Nic 253
South West Africa People's Organisation (Swapo) 112

Soweto People's Delegation 193
Soweto uprising, 1976 76, 219
Stage and Cinema 60
Stakes, Fred 15, 22
Stakes, Martha 15, 22
Stellenbosch Institute for Advanced Study 253
Stephens, Bob 236
Stephens, Jane (Slabbert's second wife) 236-237, 243, 252-253
Stephens, Mag 243
Steytler, Jan 227
structural functionalism in sociology 41-43, 246
Stutje, Jan 213
Sunday Times 115
Suzman, Helen 55, 75, 86, 119, 128, 134, 148, 150-151, 165, 201
Swart, Ray 103, 105, 215, 241
Synthesis group 47

Tambo, Oliver 168-170, 176
Taylor, Sean 114, 231
Terre'Blanche, Eugène 224-225
The Citizen 175, 207
The Last White Parliament 138
The Open Society and its Enemies 157
The Other Side of History 205, 209
The Poverty of Historicism 157
The Quest for Democracy 191
The True Confessions of an Albino Terrorist 239
The World 47-48
Thom, HB 25-26, 28
Tise, Ellen 253
Total Onslaught slogan of SA government 112-113, 115, 122, 126, 171

301

Treurnicht, Andries 93
tricameral parliament 95-97, 103, 111, 136, 138, 141
Truth and Reconciliation Commission 191-192
Tshwete, Steve 193
Tutu, Desmond 108, 192

uMkhonto we Sizwe 124, 199
United Democratic Front (UDF) 102-108, 140, 157
United Party 12, 15, 47, 51-56, 60-62, 65, 74, 83, 91-92, 133, 250
universal franchise (suffrage; also see majoritarianism) 77-78, 81, 96, 155
University of Cape Town 19, 34, 37, 51, 66, 80, 84-85, 147, 173-174, 231-232, 238, 250
University of Stellenbosch vii, ix, 23-24, 25, 28, 30-37, 39-40, 42, 44-48, 51-52, 59, 61, 65, 98, 100, 123, 125, 180, 182, 205, 217, 220, 223, 229, 231, 234, 237, 242-243, 246, 253
Uys, Stanley 146

Vale, Peter 253
Van den Bergh, Hendrik 37
Van der Heyden, Ulrich 180-181
Van der Merwe, Carel 253
Van der Ross, Richard 47, 229
Van der Spuy, Manie 19, 36
Van der Westhuizen, Johann 177
Van Onselen, Charles vii, 238, 253
Van Oudenhove, Louis 47
Van Rensburg, Horace 52
Van Rensburg, Manie 177
Van Riebeeck, Jan 20
Van Zyl, Arnold 253
Vass, Colonel 139
Venter, Rina 135
verligte/verkrampte division among Afrikaners 39, 49-50, 55, 66

Verwoerd, Hendrik 29-31
Voltaire vii
Von der Ropp, Klaus Baron 253
Vorster, John 47, 55, 63-65, 68, 72-73, 79, 229
Vosloo, WB 223
Vrye Weekblad 192, 207

Waddell, Gordon 236
Weber, Max 144, 219, 221-222
Welsh, David 66, 80-81, 238, 253
Widman, Alf 119
Wiehahn Report 93
Wilgenhof residence 25-27, 82, 243
Wilson, Francis 238
Witwatersrand Command headquarters bomb 175-176
Women's Development Bank 206

Zaaiman, André 209
Zille, Helen 145
Zuma, Jacob 184

ABOUT THE AUTHOR

Professor ALBERT GRUNDLINGH holds a doctorate from the University of South Africa and was the Head of the History Department at the University of Stellenbosch. He is the author, co-author and editor of a number of books, and has published numerous articles in international academic journals. He specialises in social and cultural history with a particular interest in war and society. His major works deal with the so-called 'Handsuppers' and 'Joiners' during the Anglo-Boer War of 1899–1902, and black South African troops during the First World War. He is also the co-author of a book on the history of rugby in South African society. He retired in 2018.

www.ingramcontent.com/pod-product-compliance
Lightning Source LLC
Chambersburg PA
CBHW071659170426
43195CB00039B/2239